THE KING JAMES CODE

ISBN 987-0-9794117-1-7 (previously 1-57558-124-8 Hearthstone)

Printed in the United States of America

Contact the publisher for the following:

- **A free catalogue of King James Bibles** and books, DVDs, CDs, CD-ROMs, and tracts supporting it.

- **Additional copies** of Michael Hoggard's books:

  - *The King James Code*
  - *By Divine Order*

- **Other books supporting the King James Bible, such as Riplinger's** *New Age Bible Versions, In Awe of Thy Word, The Language of the King James Bible, Blind Guides,* and *The Only Authorized Picture of Christ.*

A.V. Publications Corp.
P.O. Box 280
Ararat, VA 24053 USA

To see our online catalogue, research updates,
& to sign-up for Riplinger's newsletter go to:

http://www.avpublications.com

Orders: 1-800-435-4535
Inquiries & Fax: 276-251-1734

Table of Contents

Introduction

"Christ is all, and in all" (Colossians 3:11). Jesus Christ is the **one** true God, the **twice**-spoken Word of God, the **three**-in-one of the Godhead, the **fourth** in the fiery furnace, the **fifth** smooth stone in David's hand, the **six**-day Creator of the universe, the one who holds the **seven** stars in His hand, circumcised on the **eighth** day, the giver of the **nine** fruits of the Spirit, the **Ten** Commandments, the one worshipped by **eleven** stars, the **twelve** gates and foundations of New Jerusalem, being "numbered with the transgressors" He is the **thirteenth** who walks among twelve disciples. He bore the ark of Noah to safety on the **seventeenth** day of the month. He is revealed in the **22** letters of the Hebrew alephbet, took on the sacrificial form of human flesh with its **23** chromosomes, fulfilled the wisdom of God by living **33** years, spoken of and manifest in **66** books of the Bible, and is the **70 x 7** forgiver of the sins of mankind!

The Holy Book is none other than the complete and perfect testimony of Jesus Christ. The Bible is a simple book, being understood by small children, yet its depths will be known only in the world to come. As the believer journeys through its pages, he begins to become familiar with the symbols, types, poetry, prose, songs, hymns, prophecies, blessings, and curses that are contained therein.

The Bible is an ordered book, written by the Author of order, and is therefore a mathematical book. Although it is timeless, and its thoughts endless, it contains a mathematical precision that is found in no other book. Over the course of the thousands of years that the Word of God has been in the hands of men, its students have recognized this mathematical structure, whether they were ancient Hebrew scholars or the early Greek-speaking disciples

As Jesus promised to preserve His written Word on this earth, so has the unique mathematical qualities of this Word been preserved as well. As *koine* Greek of the days of the early church was the universal language, so common English is today's dialect of choice, spoken by people in every nation on earth. While some will attempt to discredit it, the 1611 translation of the Holy Scriptures, *authorized* by King James of England, is not merely a Bible in English, but *the* Bible in English. In no other English translation will one find the mathematical uniqueness that is found in the King James translation.

Proof of this was given in my first book on this subject, *By Divine Order*. It was in this book that we were first introduced to the *King James Code*. Some have criticized the use of the word "code," falsely accusing this author of trying to advance some new and esoteric doctrine, only meant for an elite few. This is not even close to being true. Anyone can take a King James Bible and a calculator and replicate what was shown in the first book. The word "code" is merely meant to show the uniqueness of the Bible, the order of the Bible, and to show that Scripture numerics is an important key to understanding God's eternal Word. As with the first book, we deal specifically with how these numbers can be used to understand things of the last days of planet earth.

This book differs from the first in that it does not simply lay out various mathematical patterns in the Bible, but attempts to help the reader in understanding just how these mathematical patterns give us an understanding of Bible prophecy. This book is not a replacement for the teaching of the Holy Ghost, but is intended to be a help. The Holy Ghost of God will help you discard what may be in error, and keep that which is good.

"Call unto me, and I will answer thee, and shew thee great and mighty things, which thou knowest not" (Jeremiah 33:3).

The Number One

Though often overlooked, a careful study of the Scriptures will reveal that the number one is one of the most important numbers in the Bible. This number indicates several ideas, but all of them are connected by a single theme; things associated with the number one belong solely to God.

The number one as God's providence

From the pages of our Holy Bible we clearly see how the *first* things belong to God. Even throughout history, in the thinking and rationale of man, the number one has always represented that which was of *primary* importance, the word *primary* coming from the Latin root *prima* which simply means "first." Thus, in the universe that God has created, there is an understanding that things stamped with the number one are things that belong to the One who is preeminent, God the Father.

The Bible reveals to us this theme of God exacting His Divine rights over His creation by receiving that which is first. Here are a few examples.

In Exodus 12, God instituted the *Passover*. This holy feast had an extremely high significance to God's people, for it typified the Passover Lamb Himself, Jesus Christ. Notice God's use of the number one in relation to the Passover.

In the first month, on the fourteenth day of the month at even, ye
shall eat unleavened bread, until the one and twentieth day of the
month at even.

—Exodus 12:18

Your lamb shall be without blemish, a male of the first year: ye
shall take it out from the sheep, or from the goats.

—Exodus 12:5

And in the first day there shall be an holy convocation, and in the
seventh day there shall be an holy convocation to you; no manner of
work shall be done in them, save that which every man must eat,
that only may be done of you.

—Exodus 12:16

The lamb of the *first* year can be seen as a symbol of the Lamb of God,
Jesus, who is the *firstborn* and *only* begotten Son of God.

In the levitical law, we continue to see the theme of God exercis-
ing His ownership of the *first* things.

Sanctify unto me all the **firstborn**, whatsoever openeth the womb
among the children of Israel, both of man and of beast: it is mine.

—Exodus 13:2

Thou shalt not delay to offer the **first** of thy ripe fruits, and of thy
liquors: the **firstborn** of thy sons shalt thou give unto me.

—Exodus 22:29

And whatsoever is **first** ripe in the land, which they shall bring
unto the LORD, shall be thine; every one that is clean in thine house
shall eat of it.

—Numbers 18:13

Ye shall offer up a cake of the **first** of your dough for an heave offering: as ye do the heave offering of the threshingfloor, so shall ye

heave it. Of the first of your dough ye shall give unto the LORD an heave offering in your generations.

—Numbers 15:20–21

The *first* of the *firstfruits* of thy land thou shalt bring into the house of the LORD thy God. Thou shalt not seethe a kid in his mother's milk.

—Exodus 23:19

In the transition from the Old Testament to the New Testament, we understand that the law itself always pointed to the person of Christ in some way. It was Christ who came to fulfill the law, and Jesus himself said that the law spoke of Him (Luke 24:44). When we see in the Old Testament law how God placed a signification upon the *firstfruits*, the *firstborn*, or the *first* things of any offering, we can clearly understand that these all point to the *only* begotten Son of God.

And knew her not till she had brought forth her *firstborn* son: and he called his name JESUS.

—Matthew 1:25

Who is the image of the invisible God, the *firstborn* of every creature. . . . And he is the head of the body, the church: who is the beginning, the *firstborn* from the dead; that in all things he might have the preeminence.

—Colossians 1:15,18

But now is Christ risen from the dead, and become the *firstfruits* of them that slept.

—1 Corinthians 15:20

The number one as a symbol of unity

There are those who claim Christianity who do not believe the biblical doctrine of the triune Godhead—God being three persons, Father, Son, and Holy Ghost. Even many of those who profess a belief in the

Godhead find it difficult to explain the concept. This difficulty does not, however, negate its reality. A Christian's foundational belief in God must contain this understanding. In the *first* chapter of Genesis, we find the following, revealing passage.

> And God said, Let *us* make man in *our* image, after *our* likeness: and let them have dominion over the fish of the sea, and over the fowl of the air, and over the cattle, and over all the earth, and over every creeping thing that creepeth upon the earth.
>
> —Genesis 1:26

First we notice that God is specifically referring to Himself in the plural tense. Then we notice that three times this plural tense is used to indicate the creative process. In this we clearly see the three-person Godhead. Notice how the following verses back up this same theme.

> Hear, O Israel: The LORD our God is **one** LORD.
>
> —Deuteronomy 6:4

> I and my Father are **one**.
>
> —John 10:30

> For there are three that bear record in heaven, the Father, the Word, and the Holy Ghost: and these **three are one**.
>
> —1 John 5:7

The idea of unity is very important to God. It has always been His desire for His people to be united and have things in common rather than in discord. As you will see, whenever God is present among His people, working in their midst, He brings them together in perfect unity.

> And all the people gathered themselves together as **one man** into the street that was before the water gate; and they spake unto Ezra

the scribe to bring the book of the law of Moses, which the LORD
had commanded to Israel.

—Nehemiah 8:1

And now I am no more in the world, but these are in the world, and
I come to thee. Holy Father, keep through thine own name those
whom thou hast given me, that they may be **one, as we are.**

—John 17:11

These all continued with **one accord** in prayer and supplication,
with the women, and Mary the mother of Jesus, and with his brethren.

—Acts 1:14

And they, continuing daily with **one accord** in the temple, and breaking bread from house to house, did eat their meat with gladness
and **singleness** of heart.

—Acts 2:46

Fulfil ye my joy, that ye be likeminded, having the same love, being
of **one accord, of one mind.**

—Philippians 2:2

Endeavouring to keep the **unity** of the Spirit in the bond of peace.
There is **one body,** and **one Spirit,** even as ye are called in **one**
hope of your calling; **One Lord, one faith, one baptism, One God**
and Father of all, who is above all, and through all, and in you all.

—Ephesians 4:3–6

In the mystery of the Church, the theme of a future unity with Christ
is typified in the marriage of the first humans, Adam and Eve.

Therefore shall a man leave his father and his mother, and shall
cleave unto his wife: and they shall be **one** flesh.

—Genesis 2:24

For this cause shall a man leave his father and mother, and shall be joined unto his wife, and they two shall be **one flesh**. This is a great mystery: but I speak concerning Christ and the church.

—Ephesians 5:31–32

The number one representing order versus chaos
Seeing the imperative that God places on the theme of unity, there is a consistent theme throughout the Scriptures of order versus chaos. Simply put, God's ways are always ways of order and perfection; nothing out of place, nothing out of line, everything in order. We can clearly see this order and perfection in the creation. It should also become apparent that God has also *ordered* His Word in a similar fashion. Every word, chapter, verse, and book is in a very perfect place. It should be the goal of every man to attempt to understand this order and model his life by it.

In the first book of the Bible, we find a very revealing story that deals with the theme of chaos and disorder.

And the whole earth was of **one** language, and of **one** speech.

—Genesis 11:1

Up to that point in history, all men spoke the same language. It was God who put the ability of language into the mind of mankind, and since the creation there was only one language spoken by mankind. This shows the divine order of God. All things were common, all the men were together, and they all spoke the same thing. It wasn't until their rebellion, by way of the tower they were building, that God Himself sent them chaos, disorder, and confusion by way of confusing their tongues, and allowing the *spirit* of confusion to disorder what they were attempting to do. They had no choice but to abandon their task and separate from one another. This idea of chaos is the central theme behind the number eleven, which will be discussed later.

Most Christians understand that the original manuscripts of the Bible were not written in English. In fact, they were originally penned in *three* different languages: Hebrew, Aramaic, and Greek. Modern scholarship places heavy, if not total reliance upon comprehension of these original languages in order to understand anything that the Bible has to say. However, can we not reasonably assume, with the biblical basis that one language represents order and multiple languages represent confusion, that God, over the process of several thousand years, has compiled these *three* languages into a common language, hence giving the Holy Scriptures the consistent flow and order that is obviously present in the greatest of all Bible translations, the King James Version? Surely, a God who can be *three* in *one*, has the ability to take His Word, written in *three* languages, and make it into *one* word. This idea is expressed in the title given to Jesus Christ in Revelation 19. Notice that this title is *singular* and not plural.

> And he was clothed with a vesture dipped in blood: and his name is called **The Word of God**.
>
> —Revelation 19:13

In the book of Jeremiah, we see the idea of order and chaos expressed through the use of the word *whole*, which is simply a form of the number one.

> And shalt say unto them, Thus saith the LORD of hosts; Even so will I break this people and this city, as one breaketh a potter's vessel, that cannot be made **whole** again: and they shall bury them in Tophet, till there be no place to bury.
>
> —Jeremiah 19:11

Notice that God promises to judge Jerusalem by taking the *whole* city and breaking them into pieces, a form of chaos and disorder. This is very identical to what God did at Babel. Even when Moses came down from Mount Sinai with the tablets of stone in his hands, this theme was also present. Moses descended from the mountain top with the written Word of God in his hands. When he saw the children of Israel, literally in the process of breaking all ten of those commandments, the Bible tells us that Moses took the law in his hands and cast it down to the ground, breaking it in pieces. It was God's way of saying to His people, "If chaos and disorder is what you want, it is what I will give you."

There are many more examples of the use of the number one and the various themes that are associated with it. There are many places, for example, in the Scriptures that the number one is used to indicate a *prototype*. Here are but a few Scriptures that illustrate this point.

> And he hewed two tables of stone like unto the first; and Moses rose up early in the morning, and went up unto mount Sinai, as the LORD had commanded him, and took in his hand the two tables of stone.
>
> —Exodus 34:4

> And the LORD was with Jehoshaphat, because he walked in the first ways of his father David, and sought not unto Baalim.
>
> —2 Chronicles 17:3

> That Christ should suffer, and that he should be the first that should rise from the dead, and should shew light unto the people, and to the Gentiles.
>
> —Acts 26:23

The number one is also used to indicate *preeminence*, or, the importance of God and His ways over anything else.

> But seek ye first the kingdom of God, and his righteousness; and all these things shall be added unto you.
>
> —Matthew 6:33

> Jesus said unto him, Thou shalt love the Lord thy God with all thy heart, and with all thy soul, and with all thy mind. This is the first and great commandment.
>
> —Matthew 22:37–38

And Jesus answered him, The first of all the commandments is, Hear, O Israel; The Lord our God is one Lord: And thou shalt love the Lord thy God with all thy heart, and with all thy soul, and with all thy mind, and with all thy strength: this is the first commandment.

—Mark 12:29–30

The number one as God's name and character

As we have so clearly seen thus far, the number one stands as one of the most important numbers in the Scriptures. It is a number that is closely associated with the nature and character of God Himself. God is clearly a God of supreme order and not the author of confusion. We can clearly see upon examination of the Scriptures that this order is present in His Holy Word. One of the things that sets the Authorized version apart from other translations is its use of the number one in relation to this number being a title of God. Notice the following verse from the book of Revelation.

And immediately I was in the spirit; and, behold, a throne was set in heaven, and one sat on the throne.

—Revelation 4:2

According to the context of this particular verse, we clearly see that it is God Almighty on this throne, and that John, by divine inspiration, describes Him as the number one. Is this idea too farfetched or based upon an imagined assumption? Let us look at a few more passages for further proof.

And when Moses was gone into the tabernacle of the congregation to speak with him, then he heard the voice of one speaking unto him from off the mercy seat that was upon the ark of testimony, from between the two cherubims: and he spake unto him.

—Numbers 7:89

Hear, O Israel: The LORD our God is one LORD.

—Deuteronomy 6:4

Whom hast thou reproached and blasphemed? and against whom
hast thou exalted thy voice, and lifted up thine eyes on high? even
against the Holy **One** of Israel.

—2 Kings 19:22

And the LORD shall be king over all the earth: in that day shall there
be one LORD, and **his name one**.

—Zechariah 14:9

I and my Father are **one**.

—John 10:30

For there are three that bear record in heaven, the Father, the Word,
and the Holy Ghost: and these three are **one**.

—1 John 5:7

These being only a few of the many examples, it does seem clear that
the number one can adequately describe God, and we can see its use
as a rightful title of the One and true God. In comparison to this, let
us examine the same verse from the book of Revelation from the
New International Version.

Authorized Version (KJV)
Revelation 4:2
"And immediately I was in
the spirit; and, behold, a
throne was set in heaven,
and **one** sat on the throne."

New Internat'l Version (NIV)
Revelation 4:2
"At once I was in the Spirit, and
there before me was a throne
in heaven with **someone** sitting
on it."

It should be readily apparent to the reader of the obvious order found
in the King James passage, and the disorder or confusion found in the
New International passage. One who sits on the throne is easily discernable as God. *Someone* who sits on the throne is not discernable.
Must we then assume by the language of the NIV that John did not
know who was sitting on throne? This notion is utterly preposterous.

Upon viewing the throne of God Himself, there will be no doubt whatsoever as to who is sitting upon it. Could it be possible that the false rendering of Revelation 4:2 is by the design of *someone* else who wishes to sit on the throne of God?

> For thou hast said in thine heart, I will ascend into heaven, I will exalt my throne above the stars of God: I will sit also upon the mount of the congregation, in the sides of the north: I will ascend above the heights of the clouds; I will be like the most High.
>
> —Isaiah 14:13–14

> Son of man, say unto the prince of Tyrus, Thus saith the Lord GOD; Because thine heart is lifted up, and thou hast said, I am a God, I sit in the seat of God, in the midst of the seas; yet thou art a man, and not God, though thou set thine heart as the heart of God.
>
> —Ezekiel 28:2

> Who opposeth and exalteth himself above all that is called God, or that is worshipped; so that he as God sitteth in the temple of God, shewing himself that he is God.
>
> —2 Thessalonians 2:4

The Number Two

As we have seen in our study of the number one, many of the numbers used in the Scriptures take on more that just one symbolic meaning, especially the base numbers of one through thirteen, and yet these various meanings are woven together by one common theme. The meanings of each number are not randomly selected, nor are they the mere imagination of man. They are always subject to, not only the context in which they are used, but also the overall context of the Bible. Any attached meaning of a number must hold consistent throughout all Scriptures. As we will continue to see, these numbers seem to hold a general meaning, and a prophetic meaning, yet these separate ideas are part of the central theme.

In the number two, we find the themes of *union, witnessing,* and *division.* As we will see in this chapter, all of these themes are tied together and all of them speak prophetically in various ways.

The number two as a symbol of unity

In the book of Amos, we find the number two used as a symbol of unity.

Can **two** walk together, except they be agreed?

—Amos 3:3

This idea is also to be found in the *second* letter to the Corinthians. In chapter six, Paul shows by the use of the number two that there are things that we are not to be unified with.

> Be ye not unequally yoked together with unbelievers: for what fellowship hath righteousness with unrighteousness? and what communion hath light with darkness? And what concord hath Christ with Belial? or what part hath he that believeth with an infidel? And what agreement hath the temple of God with idols? for ye are the temple of the living God; as God hath said, I will dwell in them, and walk in them; and I will be their God, and they shall be my people.
>
> —2 Corinthians 6:14–16

Notice, as we carefully examine this passage we can see the *two* opposing views, and God's *twofold* answer to these oppositions. He contrasts believers with unbelievers, righteousness with unrighteousness, light with darkness, Christ with Belial, believers with infidels, and the temple of God with idols. God's response to these opposing views is for His people to be unified with Him, ". . . (1) I will dwell in them, and (2) walk in them . . . " and ". . . (1) I will be their God, and (2) they shall be my people." Jesus taught His disciples the very same idea, that He would be the unifying force behind His Church.

> For where two or three are gathered together in my name, there am I in the midst of them.
>
> —Matthew 18:20

It is no accident that, through the providential care of God over His Word, in Genesis chapter two we find the story of how God created man, took from him a rib, fashioned the woman, and united them in marriage.

> And the LORD God caused a deep sleep to fall upon Adam, and he slept: and he took one of his ribs, and closed up the flesh instead thereof; And the rib, which the LORD God had taken from man,

made he a woman, adn brought her unto the man. And Adam said, This is now bone of my bones, and flesh of my flesh: she shall be called Woman, because she was taken out of Man. Therefore shall a man leave his father and his mother, and shall cleave unto his wife: and they shall be one flesh.

—Genesis 2:21–24

Thus in this second chapter, we find the theme of *union* clearly spelled out. Eve was to be Adam's *helpmeet*, a blessing to him in all things. This story is a beautiful *type* of our Savior and His Church. The deep sleep that Adam was in represents the death of Christ at Calvary (sleep is often associated with death in the Scriptures). As God made a wound in Adam's side to extract the rib, so a wound in Christ's side from which the blood and water flowed is what provides the atonement for the sins of man. It was God who brought Eve to Adam, so God will present the Church to His only begotten Son. In Ephesians, Paul revealed this great mystery to us by quoting from Genesis 2.

For this cause shall a man leave his father and mother, and shall be joined unto his wife, and they two shall be one flesh. This is a great mystery: but I speak concerning Christ and the church.

—Ephesians 5:31–32

For God speaketh once, yea twice . . .

I have also spoken by the prophets. . . .

—Hosea 12:10

There appears to be a very important teaching in the Scriptures that gives us biblical understanding of what God will do in the last days, and how He will do it. This concept is heavily based upon the number two. In the following pages I will attempt to explain.

The prophets have always been the human mouthpiece of God. They have had to deliver both the good tidings and the bad tidings that God has given them, no matter what the earthly consequences may have been. Jesus tells us that many of the prophets were slain because of the message they carried. Those who sought to take their life did not realize that the prophets were not the source of the prophesy, God was. Killing the prophet would only further increase the wrath of God.

The Scriptures tell us that one of the ways God speaks through His Holy Word is through the office of the prophets. There is not anything that God will do in this world that He keeps secret from mankind. Consider these verses as proof of this principle.

> Surely the Lord GOD will do nothing, but he revealeth his secret unto his servants the prophets.
>
> —Amos 3:7

> But in the days of the voice of the seventh angel, when he shall begin to sound, the mystery of God should be finished, as he hath declared to his servants the prophets.
>
> —Revelation 10:7

> God, who at sundry times and in divers manners spake in time past unto the fathers by the prophets, Hath in these last days spoken unto us by his Son, whom he hath appointed heir of all things, by whom also he made the worlds.
>
> —Hebrews 1:1–2

> But now is made manifest, and by the scriptures of the prophets, according to the commandment of the everlasting God, made known to all nations for the obedience of faith.
>
> —Romans 16:26

From these verses (there are many more that could have been included), we gain these insights. First, all the actions of God have been declared to the prophets. Second, all the mysteries and secrets of the last days have already been given to the prophets. Third, Jesus Himself was one of these prophets, the greatest of them, and His words are in fact prophetic utterances. And finally, all of the prophecies concerning the last days are recorded in the Holy Scriptures and preserved for us in the Authorized Version. Beware of anyone who comes bringing a "new revelation" from God, or teaching doctrine that is not scriptural. There are many who say they hear from God and speak for God, but this is not always the case.

There are seventeen books in the Bible (five major prophets—Isaiah through Daniel—and twelve minor—Hosea through Malachi) written by the prophets that contain chapter after chapter of direct prophecies. Some of these prophecies, along with their historical background are to be found in the history books of the Old Testament (Joshua through Esther). Jesus pointed out to us that there are also prophecies in the Psalms, and the writings of Moses (Genesis through Deuteronomy). The books of Job, Proverbs, Ecclesiastes, and Song of Solomon all contain either direct prophecies, or prophetic principles and statements.

The New Testament as well contains direct prophecies in practically every book. Our Bible is indeed a sure Word of prophecy. Allow me to give some examples of direct prophecies in the Bible.

> And, being assembled together with them, commanded them that they should not depart from Jerusalem, but wait for the promise of the Father, which, saith he, ye have heard of me. For John truly baptized with water; but ye shall be baptized with the Holy Ghost not many days hence.
>
> —Acts 1:4–5

Christ spoke of this event beforehand, promised that it would come to pass, and later it was fulfilled exactly as He said it would be. In the same chapter, we are given the most famous of prophecies.

> And while they looked stedfastly toward heaven as he went up, behold, two men stood by them in white apparel; Which also said, Ye men of Galilee, why stand ye gazing up into heaven? this same Jesus, which is taken up from you into heaven, shall so come in like manner as ye have seen him go into heaven.
>
> —Acts 1:10–11

Here again, this is not hard to understand. It is plainly given as a prophecy of the return of our Lord and Savior to this earth in the exact same manner as He left.

It can be pointed out that nearly all of the prophecies in the Old Testament have had some sort of fulfillment already. The prophets warned that the tribe of Judah would be taken captive by the Babylonians for seventy years, after which God would bring them back to their land and punish Babylon for taking God's people. We can clearly see in the context of the rest of the scriptures that even the primary fulfillment of what Jeremiah prophesied concerning this event is a *type* of a future regathering and restoration of Israel as God's people in the last days.

There is a very important principle to understand about direct prophecies. They, almost without fail, have a partial fulfillment, and a last days perfect fulfillment, giving each prophecy a *twofold* fulfillment. Since prophecies are the spoken words of God placed in the mouths of the prophets, let us examine what the Scriptures say about God's spoken Word.

> For God **speaketh once, yea twice**, yet man perceiveth it not. In a dream, in a vision of the night, when deep sleep falleth upon men, in slumberings upon the bed; Then he openeth the ears of men, and sealeth their instruction, That he may withdraw man from his purpose, and hide pride from man. . . . Lo, all these things worketh God **oftentimes** with man, To bring back his soul from the pit, to be enlightened with the light of the living.
>
> —Job 33:14–17,29–30

> And that he would shew thee the secrets of wisdom, that **they are double** to that which is! Know therefore that God exacteth of thee less than thine iniquity deserveth.
>
> —Job 11:6

> And for that the dream was **doubled** unto Pharaoh **twice**; it is because the thing is established by God, and God will shortly bring it to pass.
>
> —Genesis 41:32

God hath **spoken once**; **twice** have I heard this; that power belongeth unto God.

—Psalm 62:11

Speak ye comfortably to Jerusalem, and cry unto her, that her warfare is accomplished, that her iniquity is pardoned: for she hath received of the Lord's hand **double** for all her sins.

—Isaiah 40:2

I have also spoken by the prophets, and I have **multiplied** visions, and used similitudes, by the ministry of the prophets.

—Hosea 12:10

Reward her even as she rewarded you, and **double** unto her **double** according to her works: in the cup which she hath filled fill to her **double**.

—Revelation 18:6

Each of these verses, when viewed separately, may not reveal much in the way of prophetic principles to the reader, but when grouped together by a common phrase such as "twice" or "double," you begin to see a clear doctrinal pattern emerge. There is almost always a double fulfillment of a single prophecy. Notice in Hosea 12:10, God clarifies this principle for us by saying that He reveals His plans by multiplying visions. One single prophetic dream or vision will be multiplied in order to accomplish exactly what God wants to accomplish with His Word.

The prime example of this principal is the concept behind the New Heaven and the New Earth. When God spoke the heavens and earth into existence in Genesis 1, we are told, and it is quite obvious, that it was an incomplete, imperfect fulfillment of His spoken Word.

And I saw a new heaven and a new earth: for the first heaven and the first earth were passed away; and there was no more sea.

—Revelation 21:1

Notice from this passage that this New Heaven and Earth just simply appear. God spoke all creation into being once, and what came about was the imperfect fulfillment of His final intention. Only when this present world has passed away will the new world come into being.

It has been said that God is the God of new beginnings. To all who have tasted of the heavenly gift of salvation, this is a wonderful truth. As we examine a few scriptures, we will see that this is not only God's favor to us, that we may have life anew, but it is actually at the core of His nature.

> And he said, Blessed be thou of the LORD, my daughter: for thou hast shewed more kindness in the latter end than at the beginning, inasmuch as thou followedst not young men, whether poor or rich.
>
> —Ruth 3:10

This is the beginning of the verses that lay out for us the principle, that when things are done God's way, the end of it is always better than the beginning of it. In Ruth's case, she is commended by Boaz (type of Christ), for her following of this principle. Let's look at a few more examples of how this principle is displayed in the Scriptures.

> Though thy beginning was small, yet thy latter end should greatly increase.
>
> —Job 8:7

> So the LORD blessed the latter end of Job more than his beginning: for he had fourteen thousand sheep, and six thousand camels, and a thousand yoke of oxen, and a thousand she asses.
>
> —Job 42:12

> The glory of this latter house shall be greater than of the former, saith the LORD of hosts: and in this place will I give peace, saith the LORD of hosts.
>
> —Haggai 2:9

Say not thou, What is the cause that the former days were better than these? for thou dost not enquire wisely concerning this.

—Ecclesiastes 7:10

For, behold, I create **new heavens and a new earth**: and the former shall not be remembered, nor come into mind.

—Isaiah 65:17

The understanding of these verses is clear and simple. All things that are wrought by God's hand have a *dual* nature and follow a clear pattern of going from temporary to eternal, mortal to immortal, imperfect to perfect, and so on. In order for there to be a New Heaven and New Earth, there must be the old world, with all its imperfections. This is the signature of God in His work in our lives. Our second birth, salvation, is far greater than our first birth in this world. Our old life on this earth is nothing in comparison to the new life that awaits all the saints in heaven. It is how God does things.

Jesus perfectly portrayed this important biblical concept at the marriage feast of Cana. This principal is of such importance that our Lord felt it necessary to begin his earthly ministry by teaching us the doctrine of new beginnings.

When the ruler of the feast had tasted the water that was made wine, and knew not whence it was: (but the servants which drew the water knew;) the governor of the feast called the bridegroom, And saith unto him, Every man at **the beginning** doth set forth good wine; and when men have well drunk, **then that which is worse**: but thou hast kept the good wine until now.

—John 2:9–10

As the ruler of the feast found out by tasting the water turned to wine, we also, by inviting Jesus to do a work in our lives realize that His ways are far superior to any we have seen or experienced. Also given for us in this verse is a hint of the opposite of God's way of new beginnings. Notice that the governor commented that it is the way of man to have that which is best first, and the worst always shows up later. This is the decadent nature of man: to take what is good first, then settle for decay. The devil uses this idea by offering the pleasures of sin for a season. Sin always brings on pleasure. But it is a pleasure that is short-lived. Once the initial experience is over—the "high" being achieved—there is nothing left but empty promises, broken dreams and hearts, and eventually, total ruin.

In accordance with this teaching, Peter warned us that those who practice man's form of "Christianity" by not following after the mind of Christ, their latter end is worse than their beginning.

> For if after they have escaped the pollutions of the world through the knowledge of the Lord and Saviour Jesus Christ, they are again entangled therein, and overcome, the latter end is worse with them than the beginning.
> —2 Peter 2:20

We are therefore encouraged to let God perform a work in our lives that will be both perfect and everlasting.

> That ye put off concerning the former conversation the old man, which is corrupt according to the deceitful lusts; And be renewed in the spirit of your mind; And that ye put on the new man, which after God is created in righteousness and true holiness.
> —Ephesians 4:22–24

> As obedient children, not fashioning yourselves according to the former lusts in your ignorance: But as he which hath called you is holy, so be ye holy in all manner of conversation.
> —1 Peter 1:14–15

This is the handiwork of God; it is His *modus operandi*. Paul made several references to this principal in these verses.

> For we know in part, and we prophesy in part. But when that which is perfect is come, then that which is in part shall be done away.

When I was a child, I spake as a child, I understood as a child, I thought as a child: but when I became a man, I put away childish things. For now we see through a glass, darkly; but then face to face: now I know in part; but then shall I know even as also I am known.

—1 Corinthians 13:9–12

Then said he, Lo, I come to do thy will, O God. He taketh away the first, that he may establish the **second**.

—Hebrews 10:9

Notice that the incomplete, imperfect fulfillment has to be done away with in order for the perfect and complete to come in. This is God's way. Your old self has to be completely gone before God could make a new creature out of you. Such is the way with Bible prophecy. While they may have had a partial fulfillment, most likely during Bible times, their perfect fulfillment will not come until the end of the age. Even the prophecies that relate to the coming of our Lord always have a double fulfillment. They speak partially of His first advent, and perfectly of His second advent. In Luke chapter four, this was not only illustrated, but demonstrated.

And he came to Nazareth, where he had been brought up: and, as his custom was, he went into the synagogue on the sabbath day, and stood up for to read. And there was delivered unto him the book of the prophet Esaias. And when he had opened the book, he found the place where it was written, The Spirit of the Lord is upon me, because he hath anointed me to preach the gospel to the poor; he hath sent me to heal the brokenhearted, to preach deliverance to the captives, and recovering of sight to the blind, to set at liberty them that are bruised, To preach the acceptable year of the Lord. And he closed the book, and he gave it again to the minister, and sat down. And the eyes of all them that were in the synagogue were fastened on him.

—Luke 4:16–20

Now, before we go any further, let's compare what Jesus read from Isaiah to what is actually written in the book of Isaiah.

> The spirit of the Lord GOD is upon me; because the LORD hath anointed me to preach good tidings unto the meek; he hath sent me to bind up the brokenhearted, to proclaim liberty to the captives, and the opening of the prison to them that are bound; To proclaim the acceptable year of the LORD, **and the day of vengeance of our God**; to comfort all that mourn.
>
> —Isaiah 61:1–2

If you will notice, when Christ read from Isaiah, he abruptly ends His reading in the middle of a sentence, closed the book, returns it to the minister, and sits down. This shows the *duality* of Christ's work on this earth. At His first coming, He truly preaches the gospel to the poor and proclaims the acceptable year of the Lord. Jesus was the minister of salvation to the entire world. However, at His *second* coming, it is the day of vengeance of a Holy God upon those who have rejected this great salvation. There are many other things in Isaiah 61, specifically the restoration of Israel, that have yet to be accomplished, but will be at Christ's second coming. An interesting point is the similarity between the book of Isaiah having sixty-six chapters, and the Holy Bible, containing sixty-six books. As Jesus begins His ministry at His first coming by opening *the book* (Luke 4:17), so Jesus initiates the events of His second coming by opening *the book* that is in God's right hand (Revelation 5–7.)

Another interesting direct prophecy to examine is the prophecy of Joel 2. Let's compare the prophecy with its first fulfillment in Acts 2.

> And it shall come to pass afterward, that I will pour out my spirit upon all flesh; and your sons and your daughters shall prophesy, your old men shall dream dreams, your young men shall see visions: And also upon the servants and upon the handmaids in those days will I pour out my spirit. And I will shew wonders in the heav-

ens and in the earth, blood, and fire, and pillars of smoke. The sun shall be turned into darkness, and the moon into blood, before the great and the terrible day of the LORD come. And it shall come to pass, that whosoever shall call on the name of the LORD shall be delivered: for in mount Zion and in Jerusalem shall be deliverance, as the LORD hath said, and in the remnant whom the LORD shall call.

—Joel 2:28–32

But this is that which was spoken by the prophet Joel; And it shall come to pass in the last days, saith God, I will pour out of my Spirit upon all flesh: and your sons and your daughters shall prophesy, and your young men shall see visions, and your old men shall dream dreams: And on my servants and on my handmaidens I will pour out in those days of my Spirit; and they shall prophesy: And I will shew wonders in heaven above, and signs in the earth beneath; blood, and fire, and vapour of smoke: The sun shall be turned into darkness, and the moon into blood, before that great and notable day of the Lord come: And it shall come to pass, that whosoever shall call on the name of the Lord shall be saved.

—Acts 2:16–21

As with the other passages, we find that there are events that were prophesied by Joel to take place that did not take place at this pentecostal outpouring. This reveals the *dual* fulfillment of Joel chapter *two*. In contrast to the Holy Spirit being poured out on the Gentiles in the last days, the Bible indicates that this latter day outpouring will be on Israel (Ezekiel 37).

The number two as a symbol of division

As we scan our Bibles we find more interesting details about the use of the number two. As you will see, it is also a number that represents *division*.

On the *second* day of creation, God made the firmament that ". . . divided the waters . . . from the waters . . ." (Genesis 1:6–8). Also during the creation, God made *two* lights that divided the day from the darkness. Notice what the Scriptures reveal to us from the book of Genesis.

> And God made two great lights; the **greater light** to rule the day, and the **lesser light** to rule the night: he made the stars also.
>
> —Genesis 1:16

In this verse we find the details of the creation of the sun and the moon. This is the seventh occurrence of the word "light" in the Scriptures. This in itself places an importance upon this particular passage. Notice the difference between these two lights; the greater light rules over the day, and the lesser light rules over the night. Even a babe in Christ can easily understand the constant conflict (division) that is present in the Scriptures between good and evil, God and the devil, represented by light and darkness. The Scriptures clearly point out not only this conflict, but who it is that rules over the day and who it is that rules over the night.

> In him was life; and the life was the **light** of men. And the **light** shineth in darkness; and the darkness comprehended it not. There was a man sent from God, whose name was John. The same came for a witness, to bear witness of the **Light**, that all men through him might believe.
>
> —John 1:4–7

> Then spake Jesus again unto them, saying, I am the **light** of the world: he that followeth me shall not walk in **darkness**, but shall have the **light** of life.
>
> —John 8:12

> Ye are all the children of light, and the children of the day: we are not of the night, nor of darkness.
>
> —1 Thessalonians 5:5

For we wrestle not against flesh and blood, but against principalities, against powers, against the **rulers of the darkness** of this world,
against spiritual wickedness in high places.

—Ephesians 6:12

As Lord over the day, those who walk in His light are the children of
the day. It is Satan who is the prince of darkness. He is the one who
rules over the darkness of this world. They were symbolized in the
form of the sun and the moon. This idea could also explain why Jesus'
face "did shine as the sun" when he was transfigured in Matthew 17.

We have already mentioned that is was in Genesis 2 that Adam
was divided and made into two separate people. In the second book
of the Bible, Exodus, we find that Israel was divided from Egypt, and
it is also where we see the Red Sea divided so that Israel could be
saved from Pharaoh and his army. We also see in the book of Exodus
that Moses brought the children of Israel the Ten Commandments on
two different occasions. This shows the division of God's plan for
Israel. As Israel rejected God's Word in the form of the Ten Commandments at Sinai, so Israel rejected God's Word in the form of
Jesus at His first coming. However, we find in Exodus 34 that Moses
returns from the mountain of God with the *two* tables in his hand the
second time and Israel finally accepts this law. So it will be when
Christ returns to save Israel in the last days.

In Genesis 22, we find the story of Abraham taking his only begotten son (type of Christ) to Mt. Moriah to offer him up as a sacrifice. There are two of Abraham's servants that accompany them. This
shows the division of God's plan and is the basis for the idea of *typology*. A Bible *type* is a story or event contained in the pages of the
Scriptures that reveal details of various events surrounding the coming of Jesus Christ and the last days. In the case of Genesis 22, Abraham and his son Isaac portrayed the details of God's plan for the
salvation of man.

This great plan of salvation was offered first to Israel.

For I am not ashamed of the gospel of Christ: for it is the power of

God unto salvation to every one that believeth; to the Jew first, and also to the Greek.

—Romans 1:16

Israel, by their choosing a murderer, Barrabbas, over Christ, was removed temporarily from God's plan and kingdom, and was replaced by the Gentiles. There will come a time in the last days when the dispensation of the Gentiles will be finished, the Gentile believers will be translated to heaven at Christ's appearing, and God will restore the kingdom to Israel.

When we look to the Scriptures for our answers, we find that there is a continuous and consistent pattern that points us to the transfer of the kingdom from the Gentiles back to the Jews for whom it was intended. These patterns appear to us in the form of Bible *types*. They are biblical representations of latter day events. What we will notice in these typological stories is the use of the number *two*.

The first story we will examine is the story of Isaac and Ishmael. From the book of Genesis, we are told that Abraham was promised a son. It was through doubt, not faith that he went in to Hagar, Sarah's servant, and conceived a child by her, Ishmael. Later, when Isaac, by faith, was born, Hagar and her son Ishmael became despised in Sarah's sight and sent away into the wilderness. We pick up the story in Genesis chapter twenty-one.

And God said unto Abraham, Let it not be grievous in thy sight because of the lad, and because of thy bondwoman; in all that Sarah hath said unto thee, hearken unto her voice; for in Isaac shall thy seed be called. And also of the son of the bondwoman will I make a nation, because he is thy seed.

—Genesis 21:12–13

Even though the idea was Sarah's, God instructed Abraham to do what Sarah told him to do. We must realize then that this was part of some great plan that God had in preparation. God reaffirmed His promise that the chosen seed was going to be through Isaac. However, God reassured Abraham that the son of Hagar would also become a great nation, because he also was the seed of Abraham.

> And Abraham rose up early in the morning, and took bread, and a bottle of water, and gave it unto Hagar, putting it on her shoulder, and the child, and sent her away: and she departed, and wandered in the wilderness of Beersheba. And the water was spent in the bottle, and she cast the child under one of the shrubs. And she went, and sat her down over against him a good way off, as it were a bowshot: for she said, Let me not see the death of the child. And she sat over against him, and lift up her voice, and wept.
>
> —Genesis 21:14–16

Abraham sent Hagar and Ishmael into the wilderness with provisions of bread and water, but the provisions became spent. It appears that she and her son were going to die in the wilderness. Later on, we will see exactly what this *bread* and *water* were symbolic of.

> And God heard the voice of the lad; and the angel of God called to Hagar out of heaven, and said unto her, What aileth thee, Hagar? fear not; for God hath heard the voice of the lad where he is. Arise, lift up the lad, and hold him in thine hand; for I will make him a great nation. And God opened her eyes, and she saw a well of water; and she went, and filled the bottle with water, and gave the lad drink.
>
> —Genesis 21:17–19

On the verge of death, God hears the cry of the lad and his mother. Notice a very important detail contained in this passage. God opened her eyes to reveal to her the living water that she and her son needed to live. It actually uses the same term that Jesus used when he was speaking to another "woman at a well."

> But whosoever drinketh of the water that I shall give him shall never thirst; but the water that I shall give him shall be in him a well of water springing up into everlasting life.
>
> —John 4:14

According to the Scriptures, the well was there all the time. However, because of her spiritual blindness, she could not see it and would have simply died in the wilderness. But God wanted to save Hagar and her son and release them from the curse of death they were under. Hagar and her son represent none other than the children of Israel. Notice what the New Testament reveals about this incredible story.

> For it is written, that Abraham had *two sons*, the one by a bond-maid, the other by a freewoman. But he who was of the bondwoman was born after the flesh; but he of the freewoman was by promise. *Which things are an allegory: for these are the two covenants*; the one from the mount Sinai, which gendereth to bondage, which is Agar. For this Agar is mount Sinai in Arabia, and *answereth to Jerusalem which now is*, and is in bondage with her children. But Jerusalem which is above is free, which is the mother of us all. For it is written, Rejoice, thou barren that bearest not; break forth and cry, thou that travailest not: for the desolate hath many more children than she which hath an husband. *Now we, brethren, as Isaac was, are the children of promise*. But as then he that was born after the flesh persecuted him that was born after the Spirit, even so it is now. Nevertheless what saith the scripture? Cast out the bondwoman and her son: for the son of the bondwoman shall not be heir with the son of the free woman. So then, brethren, we are not children of the bondwoman, but of the free.
>
> —Galatians 4:22–31

Because of their rejection of Jesus their Messiah, the Jews are still under the curse of bondage and blindness. Salvation awaits them, and can be attained by them at any time. But they cannot see the well, because, as Paul pointed out for us, the veil of Moses is still on them (2 Corinthians 3:13–17). However, God promised Hagar that one of these days, her son would be a great nation. It is interesting to note that Ishmael also had *twelve* sons (Genesis 25:16), and Hagar is mentioned by this name *twelve* times. These, as well, point us to the fact that they are types of Israel.

Again, in the book of Genesis, we find that Isaac had *two* sons, Jacob and Esau. We know the very familiar story, how Esau, being the firstborn, was heir to the blessings and riches of his father, Isaac. However, because of his low esteem for his birthright, he sold that which was eternal for that which was temporary. So, rather than the birthright being given to the older, it was given to the younger.

In order to seal this arrangement, Rebekah knows that Jacob must receive the right hand blessing of Isaac. She instructs him to appear as the firstborn son, Esau, and receive the blessing at the hand of his father. Let's take a look at the blessing that Jacob received.

> Therefore God give thee of the dew of heaven, and the fatness of the earth, and plenty of corn and wine: Let people serve thee, and nations bow down to thee: be lord over thy brethren, and let thy mother's sons bow down to thee: cursed be every one that curseth thee, and blessed be he that blesseth thee.
>
> —Genesis 27:28–29

Jacob's blessing was to receive the dew of heaven. This is how the manna was described in Exodus 16. He also receives the promise that was given to Abraham: that whoever blesses him would be blessed and whoever curses him would be cursed.

Esau's reaction upon hearing word of this was bitterness and fear. He begged Isaac to bless him as well. Notice what the Scriptures tell us.

> And Esau said unto his father, Hast thou but one blessing, my father? bless me, even me also, O my father. And Esau lifted up his voice, and wept.
>
> —Genesis 27:38

There is an amazing similarity between Esau's response and Hagar's plea. Because of their plight, they both lifted up their voices and wept. Their cries are cries of desperation. There is a very important scriptural reason why they are weeping bitterly.

Depart from me, all ye workers of iniquity; for the LORD hath heard *the voice of my weeping.* The LORD hath heard my supplication; the LORD will receive my prayer.

—Psalm 6:8–9

For his anger endureth but a moment; in his favour is life: *weeping* may endure for a night, but *joy cometh* in the morning.

—Psalm 30:5

For I have eaten ashes like bread, and mingled my drink with *weeping,* Because of thine indignation and thy wrath: for thou hast lifted me up, and cast me down. My days are like a shadow that declineth; and I am withered like grass. But thou, O LORD, shalt endure for ever; and thy remembrance unto all generations. *Thou shalt arise, and have mercy upon Zion: for the time to favour her, yea, the set time, is come.* For thy servants take pleasure in her stones, and favour the dust thereof. So the heathen shall fear the name of the LORD, and all the kings of the earth thy glory. *When the LORD shall build up Zion, he shall appear in his glory.*

—Psalm 102:9–16

For the people shall *dwell in Zion at Jerusalem: thou shalt weep no more*: he will be very gracious unto thee at the voice of thy cry; when he shall hear it, he will answer thee. And though the Lord give you the *bread of adversity, and the water of affliction*, yet shall not thy teachers be removed into a corner any more, but thine eyes shall see thy teachers." *(What was it that Abraham gave to Hagar?!)*

—Isaiah 30:19–20

And I will rejoice in Jerusalem, and joy in my people: and the voice of *weeping shall be no more heard in her*, nor the voice of crying.

—Isaiah 65:19

A voice was heard upon the high places, *weeping* and supplications of the children of Israel: for they have perverted their way, and they have forgotten the LORD their God. *Return, ye backsliding children,* and I will heal your backslidings. Behold, we come unto thee; for thou art the LORD our God.

—Jerermiah 3:21–22

They shall *come with weeping,* and with supplications will I lead them: I will cause them to walk by the rivers of waters in a straight way, wherein they shall not stumble: for I am a father to Israel, and Ephraim is my firstborn.

—Jeremiah 31:9

In those days, and in that time, saith the LORD, the children of Israel shall come, they and the children of Judah together, *going and weeping:* they shall go, and seek the LORD their God. They shall ask the way to Zion with their faces thitherward, saying, *Come, and let us join ourselves to the LORD in a perpetual covenant that shall not be forgotten.*

—Jeremiah 50:4–5

You see that the restoration and salvation of Israel in the last days is brought on as a result of their weeping and crying to the Lord. The Lord, even to this day, honors those who weep over their lost condition. He is touched by our infirmities and heals us with His hand of salvation. When Esau wept before Isaac, Isaac heard his son's sorrow, and answered accordingly.

And Isaac his father answered and said unto him, Behold, thy dwelling shall be the fatness of the earth, and of the dew of heaven from above; And by thy sword shalt thou live, and shalt serve thy brother; and it shall come to pass when thou shalt have the dominion, that thou shalt break his yoke from off thy neck.

—Genesis 27:39–40

You will notice that there is little difference between the blessings of Jacob and Esau. Notice also that Isaac prophesied that Esau would have dominion, but only when Jacob's yoke is broken off of his neck. Jacob's dominion must be removed before he can receive these blessings. It will be at this time that Esau will be reinstated as the rightful firstborn son.

After Esau hears the blessing and the curse from Isaac, the Bible tells us what his reaction was.

> *And Esau hated Jacob because of the blessing wherewith his father blessed him*: and Esau said in his heart, The days of mourning for my father are at hand; then will I slay my brother Jacob.
>
> —Genesis 27:41

Esau was jealous of his brother and the blessing he received. Once again we turn to the New Testament for a greater understanding of this jealousy.

> But I say, Did not Israel know? First Moses saith, *I will provoke you to jealousy by them that are no people, and by a foolish nation I will anger you.*
>
> —Romans 10:19

> What then? Israel hath not obtained that which he seeketh for; but the election hath obtained it, and *the rest were blinded* (According as it is written, God hath given them the spirit of slumber, eyes that they should not see, and ears that they should not hear;) unto this day. And David saith, Let their table be made a snare, and a trap, and a stumblingblock, and a recompense unto them: Let their eyes be darkened, that they may not see, and bow down their back alway. I say then, *Have they stumbled that they should fall? God forbid: but rather through their fall salvation is come unto the Gentiles, for to provoke them to jealousy.* Now if the fall of them be the riches of the world, and the diminishing of them the riches of the Gentiles; *how much more their fulness?*
>
> —Romans 11:7–12

The kingdom was taken away from Israel at the time of Christ, and through their fall, a foolish nation, the Gentiles, are blessed with salvation. This was done to provoke Israel to jealousy, just as Esau was provoked. The terrible events that await them during the Tribulation will cause them to cry out to God for salvation and restoration. God will certainly hear their prayers.

As we continue to move through the book of Genesis, we see that it was Jacob who is now on the receiving end of one of these *divisions*. Jacob had fallen in love with Rachel, the daughter of Laban. However, when Jacob went in to his new bride, whom he thought was Rachel, we find that she had been switched with Leah, her older sister. Here we have the first-chosen replaced by the firstborn. Is all hope lost for poor Rachel, Jacob's first love? Notice what the Scriptures say.

> And it came to pass, that in the morning, behold, it was Leah: and he said to Laban, What is this thou hast done unto me? did not I serve with thee for Rachel? wherefore then hast thou beguiled me? And Laban said, It must not be so done in our country, to give the younger before the firstborn. *Fulfil her week*, and we will give thee this also for the service which thou shalt serve with me yet seven other years. *And Jacob did so, and fulfilled her week: and he gave him Rachel his daughter to wife also.*
>
> —Genesis 29:25–28

Notice in this passage, we see that the switch that has taken place is a direct result of Laban's *beguilement*. In the garden of Eden, it was Satan who beguiled Eve. Likewise, in Jerusalem, it was Satan who beguiled Israel as they chose a murderer over their Savior. In order for Jacob to have his first-chosen, Rachel, he must fulfill *seven* days (*seven years?*) with Leah. It would seem that the Scriptures are revealing a time frame for the Rapture and the subsequent completion of the restoration of Israel, spanning a period of seven years. At the beginning of this *seven*-year period, Christ receives Leah (Gentile church) and at the close, Rachel (Israel). The Scriptures do clearly indicate that the Bride of Christ, New Jerusalem, consists of both the

Gentiles and the Jews (Revelation 21). As further evidence of this, we look to the book of Ruth. Naomi and Ruth are representative of the Jewish and the Gentile churches respectively. Here is what was said about these two in the book of Ruth.

> And all the people that were in the gate, and the elders, said, We are witnesses. The LORD make the woman that is come into thine house like *Rachel and like Leah, which two did build the house of Israel*: and do thou worthily in Ephratah, and be famous in Bethlehem.
>
> —Ruth 4:11

In yet another interesting story found in Genesis, we find Jacob once again being involved in a blessing that was switched. When Jacob came into the land of Goshen at the request of Joseph, Joseph brought his two sons, Manasseh and Ephraim, to Jacob to be blessed. Manasseh, the firstborn, should have received the right-hand blessing and Ephraim the blessing of the left hand. This is how Joseph presented them to his blind father. By direction of the Holy Spirit, Jacob crossed his arms and placed his right hand on Ephraim and his left hand on Manasseh. When Joseph protested, this is what Jacob had to say.

> The angel which redeemed me from all evil, bless the lads; and let my name be named on them, and the name of my fathers Abraham and Isaac; and let them grow into a multitude in the midst of the earth. And when Joseph saw that his father laid his right hand upon the head of Ephraim, it displeased him: and he held up his father's hand, to remove it from Ephraim's head unto Manasseh's head. And Joseph said unto his father, Not so, my father: for this is the firstborn; put thy right hand upon his head. And his father refused, and said, I know it, my son, I know it: *he also shall become a people, and he also shall be great: but truly his younger brother shall be greater than he, and his seed shall become a multitude of nations*.
>
> —Genesis 48:16–19

Once again, although the primary blessing was given to Ephraim the younger, a similar blessing is given to Manasseh the older. Even though the Gentiles now have custody of the kingdom of God, this kingdom is going to be given back to Israel (Manesseh) in the last days. It is interesting to note that in the list of the twelve tribes given in Revelation 7, Manasseh has replaced Dan, and Ephraim is not mentioned. I believe this indicates to us that Israel, in the form of Manesseh is restored to his rightful place, and Ephraim, representing the Gentile church, is no longer present.

As we have seen thus far, these stories all carry the same theme of rejection followed by restoration. I believe that each one of them speaks of God's plan of redemption for Israel, who rejected Christ at His first coming, but will receive Him at His second coming. However, before Israel can claim the kingdom that is rightfully theirs, the Gentiles must be removed. Here is how the New Testament reveals this truth.

> For I would not, brethren, that ye should be ignorant of this mystery, lest ye should be wise in your own conceits; that *blindness in part is happened to Israel, until the fulness of the Gentiles be come in.* And so all Israel shall be saved: as it is written, There shall come out of Sion the Deliverer, and shall turn away ungodliness from Jacob.
>
> —Romans 11:25–26

To see exactly how this is going to be accomplished, we look once again to the story of Elijah and Elisha. Before Elijah's departure in the whirlwind (a type of the Rapture), he turns to Elisha and asks him if there was anything he could do for him before he departs. Elisha responded: ". . . I pray thee, let a **double portion** of thy spirit be upon me" (2 Kings 2:9). This "spirit" that Elisha refers to is the power of the Holy Spirit that Elijah had on him. The "double portion" refers to the second outpouring of the Holy Spirit that is going to come on Israel in the last days.

The summation of all that we have examined in this section is that there will indeed be a translation of the Gentile church. This translation comes as a result of the fulfillment of the office that Jesus placed in our charge, namely the evangelization of the world prior to His return. When, and only when, this task is achieved, will the dispensation of the Gentiles become complete, and they will be removed to make way for the restoration of God's firstborn, Israel.

The Two Witnesses

This brings us to the final theme of the number two, the theme of *witnessing*. As in all things, our understanding of the number two and its connection with this theme comes directly from the Scriptures.

> At the mouth of two witnesses, or three witnesses, shall he that is worthy of death be put to death; but at the mouth of one witness he shall not be put to death.
>
> —Deuteronomy 17:6

> One witness shall not rise up against a man for any iniquity, or for any sin, in any sin that he sinneth: at the mouth of two witnesses, or at the mouth of three witnesses, shall the matter be established.
>
> —Deuteronomy 19:15

> But if he will not hear thee, then take with thee one or two more, that in the mouth of two or three witnesses every word may be established.
>
> —Matthew 18:16

> This is the third time I am coming to you. In the mouth of two or three witnesses shall every word be established.
>
> —2 Corinthians 13:1

In these verses we find the minimum requirement for bringing an accusation, or establishing a word or doctrine. In the case of doctrinal matters, no genuine doctrine can stand alone on the basis of just one verse; it must have a biblical witness. The concept of numbers and counting things in the Bible as a doctrinal principle is based upon two verses (Revelation 13:18; Ecclesiastes 7:27) therefore, the doctrine has biblical merit.

In Isaiah 28, God revealed through the prophet this same idea. Notice in these verses, not only the dual concepts, but also the poetic way it is given by repeating several statements twice.

> Whom shall he teach **knowledge**? and whom shall he make to understand **doctrine**? them that are weaned from the milk, and drawn from the breasts. For precept must be upon precept, precept upon precept; line upon line, line upon line; here a little, and there a little.
>
> —Isaiah 28:9–10

From this passage we understand that all scripture must be interpreted in the light of all other scripture. We build our foundation of doctrinal and theological knowledge by searching the entire Bible, not just one passage or book. No verse, chapter, or book can be totally understood in its own context, but rather in the context of the entire Bible. The two witnesses of the Bible, the Old and New Testament, must be understood together and not separate, for they both declare the same thing. God pointed this out to Israel in the same chapter from Isaiah.

> For with stammering lips and another tongue will he speak to this people. To whom he said, This is the rest wherewith ye may cause the weary to rest; and this is the refreshing: yet they would not hear. But the word of the LORD was unto them precept upon precept, precept upon precept; line upon line, line upon line; here a little, and there a little; that they might go, and fall backward, and be broken, and snared, and taken.
>
> —Isaiah 28:11–13

Because of the Jews' refusal to regard the New Testament as they regard the Old Testament, they cannot come to a full knowledge and understanding of God and their Messiah, Jesus Christ. Only when they receive the second witness of Matthew through Revelation will they know in full and believe.

Currently, the knowledge of God through the two testaments has been given to the Gentiles. We as the Gentile church have a mandate from Christ Himself that we are to go into all the world and be witnesses of the good news of the gospel; to preach salvation to all who are lost. When Jesus sent forth the seventy disciples in Luke 10, this is how he sent them.

> After these things the Lord appointed other seventy also, and sent them **two and two** before his face into every city and place, whither he himself would come.
>
> —Luke 10:1

Even to this very day, those who go forth from their local church to witness to the lost generally go in groups of two. It can be assumed from this and other clear patterns in the Scriptures that this age of witnessing to the world will last **two thousand** years.

The sending forth of the **seventy** in groups of two is a typological revelation concerning the two witnesses mentioned in Revelation 11.

> And I will give power unto my two witnesses, and they shall prophesy a thousand two hundred and threescore days, clothed in sackcloth.
>
> —Revelation 11:3

From all the things that we have seen concerning witnessing and the number two, we understand the nature and the role of these witnesses. As Paul revealed to us in 2 Corinthians 13, all the words that God has spoken will be established at the mouth of two witnesses. Though their exact identity can only be speculated, their role seems to be that of proclaiming to the world and the satanic powers that are in control during this time, that God is going to fulfill all that He spoke in His Word, including His wrath upon the wicked of the world and the destruction of the Beast and False Prophet. Remember what was spoken in Deuteronomy 17:6 and 19:15. Only at the mouth of two witnesses can a murderer or one who commits iniquity be put to death.

> A man that is an heretick after the first and second admonition reject.
>
> —Titus 3:10

These two witnesses will proclaim the accusations of God against a wicked world and the eternal judgment that will befall them for their sins. As with many of the Old Testament prophets, these latter day prophets will be put to death for their words, but this will not halt the wrath of Almighty God.

The Number Three

The pages of the Scriptures indicate to us that there are a few numbers that are associated with perfection and completion. When these numbers are present in the various passages, you will always find this theme brought out. The number three is such a number.

The number three
representing completion and divinity

An exhaustive study of the use of the number three and its representation of perfection and the Godhead would fill many pages. What is presented here are but a few of the many examples of how this number is used in the Bible. Often this number does not appear in the text of a particular passage, but in distinct patterns.

First, we see the number three as a direct representation of the person of God. There can be no mistaking that God is God in three persons, Father, Son, and Holy Spirit. First John 5:7 gives us a very direct account of this. It is obvious to the Bible reader that you will not find the word "trinity" in the Scriptures, rather the Bible uses the word "Godhead." By the very design of God Himself, this word is mentioned only three times in the Scriptures (Acts 17:29; Romans 1:20; Colossians 2:9). In Acts 17:29, we see that the Godhead cannot be represented by three things.

> Forasmuch then as we are the offspring of God, we ought not to think that the Godhead is like unto **gold, or silver**, or stone, graven by art and man's device.
>
> —Acts 17:29

In spite of the above statement, we find that the Godhead can be represented by one thing, the person of Jesus Christ. This is the third occurrence of the word "Godhead."

> For in him dwelleth all the fulness of the Godhead bodily.
>
> —Colossians 2:9

In Isaiah 6:3 and Revelation 4:8 we have an account of angelic creatures offering their continuous rounds of praise to God. They do so in this fashion.

> And the four beasts had each of them six wings about him; and they were full of eyes within: and they rest not day and night, saying, **Holy, holy, holy, Lord God Almighty, which was, and is, and is to come.**
>
> —Revelation 4:8

Notice the textual patterns of three contained in this verse. First is their declaration of God's holiness. Each time the word "holy" was spoken, it was given to each person of the Godhead, hence it is given thrice. Notice secondly that God's title is expanded to three titles, "Lord God Almighty." And finally we see God's eternalness represented by the three expressions of time—past, present, and future. The sum of these descriptions in this verse is three expressions in one verse, because God is three in one.

Other occasions where all three members of the Godhead are specifically listed in the same verse are Matthew 28:19, 2 Corinthians 13:14, 1 Peter 1:2, and 1 John 5:7.

In the wilderness tabernacle, there were three pieces of furniture that represented each person of the Godhead. The candlestick, or menorah, represented the revelation light of the Holy Spirit. The table of shewbread on which lay twelve loaves of bread represented Jesus, the Son, the living bread from Heaven. And finally, the Ark of the Covenant, behind the veil, which was a duplicate of the throne in heaven upon which God the Father sat (Exodus 35:12–14).

All of these items were to be earthly representations of what was in the temple of God in heaven. The scriptures declare to us that there are three heavens.

> I knew a man in Christ above fourteen years ago, (whether in the body, I cannot tell; or whether out of the body, I cannot tell: God knoweth;) such an one caught up to the **third heaven**.
>
> —2 Corinthians 12:2

The first heaven consists of the upper atmosphere of planet earth. The second heaven is composed of the regions of outer space. The third heaven is the dwelling place of God Almighty. It is no wonder then that God chose as the special dwelling place for mankind the third planet from the sun, earth, and it is where He will bridge the gap between God and man by way of that holy city, New Jerusalem (Revelation 21:2).

In his book *Aleph-Bet Soup*, Chuck Thurston shows that the three persons of the Godhead are revealed in the creation process as contained in Genesis 1:1. In this first verse of the Bible we see the three main parts of the universe: time, space, and matter.

> In the beginning [time] God created the heaven [space] and the earth [matter].
>
> —Genesis 1:1

Their exact and perfect order of creation are also revealed in the grammatical structure of this verse. Time is the essential law of the universe; nothing exists outside of the laws of time. Before there can be matter, there must be space to put it in; therefore, time, space, and matter are in their perfect order. The opposite of this is the worldly-satanic view of the origin of the universe called "the big bang theory." This theory starts with matter, which explodes and expands into space over time. In these three parts of the universe, we also find that each one of them only exists in three different forms. Time is always represented in the concepts of *past, present,* and *future.* Space only has three dimensions; *length, width,* and *height.* All matter exists in one of three forms: *solid, liquid,* and *gas.*

In the person of Jesus Christ we find the fullness of the three persons of the Godhead. Accordingly, Christ is given three descriptions of His Divine office, that of Prophet, Priest, and King.

> Many of the people therefore, when they heard this saying, said, Of a truth this is the Prophet.
>
> —John 7:40

> Wherefore, holy brethren, partakers of the heavenly calling, consider the Apostle and High Priest of our profession, Christ Jesus.
>
> —Hebrews 3:1

> Which in his times he shall shew, who is the blessed and only Potentate, the King of kings, and Lord of lords.
>
> —1 Timothy 6:15

Also, we find that at the birth of Christ, the wise men from the East presented the infant Jesus with three gifts: gold, frankincense, and myrrh (Matthew 2:11). In the book of Isaiah, Christ is given three different offices. Notice what the Scriptures reveal.

> For the LORD is our **judge,** the LORD is our **lawgiver,** the LORD is our **king;** he will save us.
>
> —Isaiah 33:22

In this verse, we see that in Christ rest the three systems of divine government. It is of noted interest that the greatest nation in modern times, the United States of America, follows this same divine system of government with its three branches: executive (king), legislative (lawgiver), and judicial (judge). This form of government was without a doubt extracted by the founding fathers of America directly from the pages of the Word of God.

According to Deuteronomy 16, the Israelites were specifically instructed to practice and maintain three holy feasts during the year.

> Three times in a year shall all thy males appear before the LORD thy God in the place which he shall choose; in the **feast of unleavened bread**, and in the **feast of weeks**, and in the **feast of tabernacles**: and they shall not appear before the LORD empty.
>
> —Deuteronomy 16:16

In this most revealing passage, we can see the perfection of the Godhead in each of these feasts. The feast of unleavened bread was the feast of Passover. It was at the Passover that Christ, the Lamb, was slain for the sins of Israel and the world. The feast of weeks is the feast that was held fifty days after the Passover, which was Pentecost. It was at this feast that the Holy Spirit was poured out on the disciples in the upper room, and to the whole world. The Feast of Tabernacles is the "unfulfilled feast." It represents God the Father dwelling in all His fullness with His people Israel, and the world. Seeing that God perfectly fulfilled, not only the true meaning of the first two feasts, but also the exact time of these feasts, is it not reasonable to assume that God will also use His perfect time frame to fulfill and accomplish the last as well?

The number 3 and the resurrection

". . . Lazarus, come forth."

With these three words did our Savior, the Word of God made flesh, resurrect Lazarus, who was in the fifth day of being dead. In a side note to this story from the Gospel of John, we see that Lazarus immediately responded and obeyed the voice of the Master of the universe, and the Scriptures in their divine perfection record the following seven words.

And he that was dead came forth. . . .

—John 11:44

The theme of the resurrection and its association with the number three seems to be connected by the idea of the power of God. The phrase "his mighty power" is mentioned exactly three times in the Scriptures, and the third time this phrase is used we see its connection with the resurrection.

And what is the exceeding greatness of his power to us-ward who believe, according to the working of **his mighty power**, Which he wrought in Christ, when **he raised him from the dead**, and set him at his own right hand in the heavenly places.

—Ephesians 1:19–20

It was on the third day of the creation that the power of God was displayed in the following manner.

And God said, Let the waters under the heaven be gathered together unto one place, and let the **dry land** appear: and it was so. And God called the **dry land** Earth; and the gathering together of the waters called he Seas: and God saw that it was good.

—Genesis 1:9–10

Thus on the third day of creation God manifested His power by bringing the dry land up out of the water. In this scene we instantly recognize that on three occasions God separated dry land from water. In the first occasion we have the famous story of Moses leading God's people across the Red Sea. This event is marked with the number three, for we find by counting in Numbers 33, that Israel camped in three places before crossing the dry land of the Red Sea (Numbers 33:5–8). The second place in which this occurs is in the book of Joshua. In Joshua chapter **three**, we are told that God, after three days of Israel being camped along the banks of the Jordan River, instructs Joshua and the Levites to bear the Ark of the Covenant to the banks of the river. As soon as their feet touch the water, the river parts and Israel is led into their promised inheritance on dry land.

In 2 Kings 2, beginning in verse **three**, we see that three separate groups of the "sons of the prophets" act as witnesses to the rapture of Elijah and the translation of the office of prophet to Elisha. The third group of these sons of the prophets witness the following event.

> And fifty men of the sons of the prophets went, and stood to view afar off: and they two stood by Jordan. And Elijah took his mantle, and wrapped it together, and smote the waters, and they were divided hither and thither, so that they two went over on **dry ground**.
> —2 Kings 2:7–8

In the occasion of the Red Sea crossing, Paul reveals to us that this was a symbol of baptism, and was a foreshadowing of things to come.

> Moreover, brethren, I would not that ye should be ignorant, how that all our fathers were under the cloud, and all passed through the sea; And were all **baptized unto Moses** in the cloud and in the sea. . . . Now all **these things** happened unto them for ensamples: and they are written for our admonition, upon whom the ends of the world are come.
> —1 Corinthians 10:1–2,11

The act of baptism itself shows the resurrection from the dead into eternal life (Romans 6:3–6). It was for this reason that the number three is so prominent in the Scriptures concerning the baptism of Jesus Christ. First, we see that in only three passages, Matthew 3:16, Mark 1:10–11, and Luke 3:22, do all three persons of the Godhead manifest themselves at Jesus' baptism. The parallel story given to us in John 1:32 does not include the voice of the Father from heaven. Seeing that this and many other patterns relate the number three with baptism, we must therefore precisely heed Christ's command concerning baptism.

> Go ye therefore, and teach all nations, baptizing them in the name
> of the *Father*, and of the *Son*, and of the *Holy Ghost*.
>
> —Matthew 28:19

From Genesis 1, we also see that God performed another act of creation related to the idea of resurrection.

> And God said, Let the earth bring forth grass, the herb yielding
> seed, and the fruit tree yielding fruit after his kind, whose seed is
> in itself, upon the earth: and it was so.
>
> —Genesis 1:11

Notice that God follows His divine order by categorizing His creation of plant life into three groups: grass, herb yielding seed, and fruit. It is in the seed that we continue to see this perfect plan, for a seed has three main parts: embryo, endoshell, and endosperm. In 1 Corinthians 15 (3 x 5), Paul explains the relationship that a seed has with resurrection.

> But some man will say, How are the dead raised up? and with what
> body do they come? Thou fool, that which thou sowest is not quick-
> ened, except it die: And that which thou sowest, thou sowest not
> that body that shall be, but bare grain, it may chance of wheat, or of
> some other grain: But God giveth it a body as it hath pleased him,
> and to every seed his own body. . . . So also is the resurrection of the
> dead. It is sown in corruption; it is raised in incorruption: It is sown
> in dishonour; it is raised in glory: it is sown in weakness; it is raised
> in power: It is sown a natural body; it is raised a spiritual body.
> There is a natural body, and there is a spiritual body.
>
> —1 Corinthians 15:35–38,42–44

It is interesting to note that the act of burying (planting) a dead body in the ground is a biblical witness to the fact that one day, God will call that body from the ground on the day of judgment to be given an eternal home, either heaven or hell.

The book of Genesis reveals that the bodies of Abraham, Isaac, Jacob, Sarah, Rebekah, and Leah are buried in the cave of Machpelah, six (3 x 2) in all. That they will be raised out of this cave and resurrected is evident by the statement Jesus made to those who doubt the resurrection. In Luke 20:37 Jesus said, "Now that the dead are raised, even Moses shewed at the bush, when he calleth the Lord the God of Abraham, and the God of Isaac, and the God of Jacob." You will notice that Christ seems to prove His point about the resurrection, not just with the language of the verse, but with the exact number of men that are named, three.

Seeing that God consistently uses the number three in association with the resurrection, we then must take the following prophecy in a very literal fashion.

> After two days will he revive us: in the **third day** he will raise us up, and we shall live in his sight.
>
> —Hosea 6:2

As with the Red Sea crossing, Joshua and the camp of Israel crossing the Jordan River, and Elisha being given the mantle and crossing the Jordan River, the prophecy of Hosea 6:2 is a prophecy concerning dead Israel. By the two witnesses of Psalm 90:4 and 2 Peter 3:8 that reveal to us that a prophetic day equals one thousand years, we can clearly see not only God's plan for Israel in Bible prophecy, but also the time frame that God is going to use in order to accomplish His plan. As Christ rose from the dead on the third day, typifying the rapture and the resurrection of Israel, so must this "third day" time prophecy be fulfilled at the coming of our Lord. Once God establishes a pattern that is as clear and concise as this one, it is against His nature to change from it.

From the lessons we have learned on the number two, it becomes quite clear that God will fulfill a period of two days, or two thousand years, in which the saving work of the Lord is to be performed by the witness of the Gentile church. At the close of this two-day period, the Gentile church will be removed in preparation for the revival of Israel

on the third day. Notice what our Savior said concerning this prophetic truth.

> And he said unto them, Go ye, and tell that fox, Behold, I cast out
> devils, and I do cures to day and to morrow, and the third day I shall
> be perfected.
>
> —Luke 13:32

Those who doubt these very specific time prophecies and numerical
principles must do so against the Scriptures and not with the Scriptures.

When we focus a Bible search of just the phrase "third day," we
find some very specific revelations concerning the coming of Christ
and His plan for Israel and the world. Notice this wonderful event
recorded for us in Exodus 19.

> And the LORD said unto Moses, Go unto the people, and sanctify
> them to day and to morrow, and let them wash their clothes, And
> be ready against the **third day**: for the **third day** the LORD will
> come down in the sight of all the people upon mount Sinai. And
> thou shalt set bounds unto the people round about, saying, Take
> heed to yourselves, that ye go not up into the mount, or touch the
> border of it: whosoever toucheth the mount shall be surely put to
> death: There shall not an hand touch it, but he shall surely be stoned,
> or shot through; whether it be beast or man, it shall not live: **when
> the trumpet soundeth long, they shall come up to the mount.**
> And Moses went down from the mount unto the people, and sanc-
> tified the people; and they washed their clothes. And he said unto
> the people, Be ready against the **third day**: come not at your wives.
> And it came to pass on the **third day in the morning**, that there
> were thunders and lightnings, and a thick cloud upon the mount,
> and the voice of the trumpet exceeding loud; so that all the people
> that was in the camp trembled. And Moses brought forth the peo-
> ple out of the camp to meet with God; and they stood at the nether
> part of the mount.
>
> —Exodus 19:10–17

In this typological story we are given a very clear picture of the return of Christ and the salvation of His people, Israel. This event foreshadowed the third day resurrection of Israel mentioned in Hosea 6:2. We also see from verse sixteen, that it took place at the exact same time of the day as Christ's resurrection: early in the morning. It is interesting, yet consistent with the use of apocalyptic language in the Scriptures that we find in verse eleven that the Lord *will come down in the sight of all people*, speaking prophetically of the revealing of Jesus to the world at His second coming (Revelation 1:7). Notice as well that the coming of the Lord in this passage is also accompanied with the familiar trumpet blast, declaring His descent from heaven (1 Corinthians 15:52; 1 Thessalonians 4:16). In the book of Hebrews, Paul explains to us why Israel was not to come near the mountain on that day.

> For ye are not come unto the mount that might be touched, and that burned with fire, nor unto blackness, and darkness, and tempest, And the sound of a trumpet, and the voice of words; which voice they that heard entreated that the word should not be spoken to them any more: (For they could not endure that which was commanded, And if so much as a beast touch the mountain, it shall be stoned, or thrust through with a dart: And so terrible was the sight, that Moses said, I exceedingly fear and quake:) But ye are come unto mount Sion, and unto the city of the living God, the heavenly Jerusalem, and to an innumerable company of angels.
>
> —Hebrews 12:18–22

Because of the weakness of the law, man was not allowed to come near unto God because of his many sins. Yet through the salvation of the cross, Jew and Gentile alike can approach the real mountain of God, heavenly Zion, the city of the living God.

Moving ahead in the Scriptures, we find that it was on the "third day" that the kingdom was finally taken out of the hands of Saul, and translated to David, from which came Christ (2 Samuel 1:2). In 1 Kings 12:12–14, it is on the third day that Jeroboam is told by Rehoboam, the evil king (type of Antichrist) that he would be chastised with *scorpions*, a prophetic utterance to be fulfilled in the last days according to Revelation 9:3–5. In 2 Kings 20:5–6 Hezekiah is told to present himself at the temple on the third day and God would grant him a fifteen-year (3 x 5) extension on his life. And finally, according to John 2, the seventieth chapter of the New Testament, it is on the third day that the *marriage* of Cana took place. It is at this wedding feast that Jesus performed his first miracle by taking the six (six thousand years since Adam) waterpots which were for the *purification of the Jews*, filling them with water, symbolic of the flood of Noah and the Red Sea crossing, and turning this water into the *new wine* of the Holy Spirit. Truly, our blessed Savior will perform this very act once again at His second coming, on the third day!

What is so special about the two meanings for the number three is that both of them are brought together in the resurrection of the Lord Jesus Christ. He was raised on the third day (Matthew 12:38–40) by the Divine Three in the Godhead: God the Father raised Him (Galatians 1:1), Jesus raised Himself (John 2:19-21), and the Holy Spirit raised Him (Romans 8:11). In the Lord Jesus Christ dwells *"all the fullness of the Godhead bodily,"* (Colossians 2:9). How beautifully our living Lord, who is the great Mathematician and Maker of all numbers, brings together or completes all numbers in His finished work!

The number three and Calvary

On a final note, we see God's message of hope displayed for us at Golgatha's hill on the day that Christ was sacrificed for our sins. The crucifixion of Christ seemed to many of His disciples to be the end of all that they had hoped for, their hope for salvation gone, and the promise of being part of His glorious kingdom, vanished. However, with God, there is always not only the promise of hope, but the fulfillment of hope. As Calvary's onlookers viewed the cross, the accusation, the darkness, as they heard His final words, they should have recognized the hope of resurrection. There were three crosses, three inscriptions of His accusation, three hours of darkness, and the last utterance from our Savior's mouth were three simple words, "It is finished." Because of His death, there truly is the hope of our resurrection.

The Number Four

The number four is generally recognized as the number for the world or creation. We will show various biblical patterns that relate to this theme. However, what we will also clearly see is its perfect relation to the Gospel of Jesus Christ. In fact, it may be said that whenever you see the number four in the pages of the Scripture, you will see a fascinating revelation of the four gospels, and their message.

The number 4 and the creation

As with all the numbers, their various meanings are extracted from the plain text of the Scriptures themselves. We see the correlation between the world, the creation, and the number four in various passages. The Scriptures mention the "four corners" of the earth (Isaiah 11:12; Revelation 7:1). Jeremiah 49:36 mentions the "four quarters" of heaven, while Revelation 20:8 speaks of the "four quarters" of the earth. From the four quarters of heaven, come the "four winds" of heaven (Daniel 7:2, 8:8, 11:4; Zechariah 2:6).

In the book of Colossians, the Scriptures reveal to us that Jesus is the Creator of all that is, and because of this, He is the Lord over all that is. We find this teaching in chapter one, verse sixteen (4 x 4). Notice the patterns of the number four in this passage.

> For by him were all things **created**, that are in (1) heaven, and that are in (2) earth, (3) visible and (4) invisible, whether they be (1)

thrones, or (2) dominions, or (3) principalities, or (4) powers: all things were created by him, and for him.

—Colossians 1:16

Nature itself teaches the association between the number four and the creation of God. On the earth, there are four directions: north, south, east, and west. There are four seasons that divide the earth's rotation around the sun: summer, autumn, winter, and spring. On the fourth day of creation, God created the sun, moon, and stars. These were given to man "for signs, and for seasons, and for days, and years" (four things) (Genesis 1:14). There are four periods of a day that are mentioned in the Scriptures: morning, noon, evening, and midnight. They are equally divided into groups of six hours apiece, a total of twenty-four hours in one day. The moon has four phases of visibility and circles the earth from west to east approximately every twenty-eight (4 x 7) days.

God's title of "Creator," with a capital C, is mentioned exactly four times in the Scriptures (Ecclesiastes 12:1; Isaiah 40:28; Romans 1:25; 1 Peter 4:19). God's title of "Judge," again with a capital J, is mentioned four times as well, and the connection between this title and the earth is given in the following verse.

That be far from thee to do after this manner, to slay the righteous with the wicked: and that the righteous should be as the wicked, that be far from thee: Shall not the Judge of all the earth do right?

—Genesis 18:25

The Scriptures indicate that God's creative act is not limited to the current heaven and earth that we see with our eyes, but a new heaven and earth.

For, behold, I create new heavens and a new earth: and the former shall not be remembered, nor come into mind.

—Isaiah 65:17

For as the new heavens and the new earth, which I will make, shall remain before me, saith the LORD, so shall your seed and your name remain.

—Isaiah 66:22

Nevertheless we, according to his promise, look for new heavens and a new earth, wherein dwelleth righteousness.

—2 Peter 3:13

And I saw a new heaven and a new earth: for the first heaven and the first earth were passed away; and there was no more sea.

—Revelation 21:1

You will notice that the Bible speaks of this new heaven and earth in exactly four verses. Along with this new heaven and earth, is the new Holy City of God, New Jerusalem. It is a city that is described as being "foursquare" (Revelation 21:16).

The number four and the Gospel

The elementary student of the Bible will instantly recognize that there are four books in the Bible that reveal the story of Christ's life, ministry, miracles, death, and resurrection. They are the books of Matthew, Mark, Luke, and John—the Gospels. The very word "gospel" or "gospels" is mentioned one hundred and four (4 x 26) times in the Scriptures. What we will see in this section is that there is a clear reason why there are four gospel stories in our Bibles, and the many places elsewhere where we can see the number four and the beautiful story of the Gospel of Jesus Christ.

In the fourth book of the Bible, the book of Numbers, we find the following story.

And the LORD sent fiery serpents among the people, and they bit the people; and much people of Israel died. Therefore the people came to Moses, and said, We have sinned, for we have spoken against the LORD, and against thee; pray unto the LORD, that he take away

the serpents from us. And Moses prayed for the people. And the
LORD said unto Moses, Make thee a fiery serpent, and set it upon a
pole: and it shall come to pass, that every one that is bitten, when
he looketh upon it, shall live. And Moses made a serpent of brass,
and put it upon a pole, and it came to pass, that if a serpent had
bitten any man, when he beheld the serpent of brass, he lived.

—Numbers 21:6–9

Jesus revealed to us in the fourth book of the New Testament, the
Gospel of John, that this was a type of His sacrificial death on the
cross.

And as Moses lifted up the serpent in the wilderness, even so must
the Son of man be lifted up: That whosoever believeth in him should
not perish, but have eternal life. For God so loved the world, that
he gave his only begotten Son, that whosoever believeth in him
should not perish, but have everlasting life.

—John 3:14–16

Jesus' title of "Lamb" is given him exactly twenty-eight (4 x 7) times
as well, the first time being found in the fourth gospel book, John.

The next day John seeth Jesus coming unto him, and saith, Behold
the Lamb of God, which taketh away the sin of the world.

—John 1:29

The connection between the Gospel and the theme of the world should
be obvious to any student of the Gospel, as evident in these verses.

And this gospel of the kingdom shall be preached in all the world
for a witness unto all nations; and then shall the end come.

—Matthew 24:14

And he said unto them, Go ye into all the world, and preach the
gospel to every creature.

—Mark 16:15

The very centerpiece of the Gospel message is the cross. The place of Jesus' crucifixion was called "Golgotha" three times (Matthew 27:33; Mark 15:22; John 19:17), and "Calvary" one time (Luke 23:33), giving a total of four. The word "cross" is mentioned exactly twenty-eight (4 x 7) times in the Bible. A cross has four points that point in four directions. As they laid Jesus on that cross and began to nail his hands and his feet to it, the cross would have been pointing to all the nations of the world as a witness.

Above the cross, the Scriptures record that the accusation against Christ was printed on a plaque of some kind. Liberal theologians have always had a "field day" with the fact that in each of the four gospels, the exact wording of this inscription is different. This, they say, proves that the Bible cannot be counted on to be an accurate representation of what really happened at Calvary. They are, however, misguided. Let us look at the inscriptions that are recorded for us

Matthew 27:37—*THIS IS JESUS THE KING OF THE JEWS*
Mark 15:26—*THE KING OF THE JEWS*
Luke 23:38—*THIS IS THE KING OF THE JEWS*
John 19:19—*JESUS OF NAZARETH THE KING OF THE JEWS*

The total number of words in all four inscriptions is **twenty-eight (4 x 7)**.

When they took the cross and set it in the ground, it is apparent that they would have done so with Jesus facing south, toward Jerusalem and in the general direction of Mt. Sinai. This is where the law was given. Jesus, whose face shone like the sun at the Transfiguration (Matthew 17) would seem to be shining the much needed light of revelation on the law, showing that He had come to fulfill it. There are several instances in the Scriptures where Satan is associated with the north (Isaiah 14:13; Jeremiah 1:14; Ezekiel 38:15). The northern most constellation is that of Draco, the Dragon. As Jesus was on the cross, his back would have been turned against the north, thus fulfilling Jesus' statement on three occasions, "Get thee behind me, Satan." His left hand would have been pointing east, and His right hand pointing west. This would fulfill the prophecy in Psalm 103:12: "As far as the east is from the west, so far hath he removed our transgressions from us."

It is also important to note that his right hand is the one pointing west. Take note of what the Scriptures reveal about Christ's right hand.

> Thou wilt show me the path of life: in thy presence is fulness of joy; at thy right hand there are pleasures for evermore.
>
> —Psalm 16:11

> Shew thy marvellous lovingkindness, O thou that savest by thy right hand them which put their trust in thee from those that rise up against them.
>
> —Psalm 17:7

> Now know I that the LORD saveth his anointed; he will hear him from his holy heaven with the saving strength of his right hand.
>
> —Psalm 20:6

> For they got not the land in possession by their own sword, neither did their own arm save them: but thy right hand, and thine arm, and the light of thy countenance, because thou hadst a favour unto them.
>
> —Psalm 44:3

> According to thy name, O God, so is thy praise unto the ends of the earth: thy right hand is full of righteousness.
>
> —Psalm 48:10

Many more verses could be cited that follow this same context. Notice that the Scriptures reveal that salvation and righteousness are at the right hand of Christ. This points us to a very revealing teaching concerning the wilderness tabernacle. It is apparent from the Scriptures that the tabernacle was a replica of the true tabernacle of God in heaven. As the high priest entered the outer court of the tabernacle, he would have done so by the only gateway into the court on the east side. In order to make his way to the most holy place where the Ark of the Covenant was, he would enter through three entrances, the gate at the outer court, the veil of the sanctuary, and the veil of the most holy place. These are typical of the three heavens, the third heaven being where the throne of God is. As the high priest travels, he travels west to the Ark of the Covenant, which is on the west side of the tabernacle. The Ark was a four-sided box upon which sat the Mercy Seat. Once a year, the high priest would enter into the most holy place and sprinkle blood on the mercy seat to atone for the sins of Israel. This is a type of Christ offering His blood as the atonement for the sins of man, not once a year, but only once. "Neither by the blood of goats and calves, but by his own blood he entered in once into the holy place, having obtained eternal redemption for us" (Hebrews 9:12). Truly, salvation is at the westward pointing, right hand of Jesus Christ.

It is also interesting to note that in the sanctuary of the tabernacle, the menorah, which represents the light of the Holy Spirit, is on the south side. This menorah was the only source of light in the tabernacle itself. This would seem to confirm the idea of Christ's countenance facing south, shining light upon the law. Also, the table of shewbread was specifically placed on the north side. This not only confirms our earlier idea of Jesus turning his back to Satan on the north, but also points to the location of the salvation of Israel, Calvary being on the north side of the city of Jerusalem.

Before the blood of sacrifice could be carried into the Ark of the Covenant, the sacrifice had to take place. This was done in the court area of the tabernacle at the *brazen altar*. The exact specifications for this altar were given to Moses on Mt. Sinai.

> And thou shalt make an altar of shittim wood, five cubits long, and five cubits broad; the altar shall be **foursquare**: and the height thereof shall be three cubits. And thou shalt make the **horns of it upon the four corners** thereof: his horns shall be of the same: and thou shalt overlay it with brass.
>
> —Exodus 27:1–2

First we note that God specifically told Moses, even though the length and the width were identical, that the altar had to be *foursquare*. We will look a little later at something else that is foursquare in the Bible, but for now, we also see that horns were to be placed on the *four corners* of the altar. These four corners of the altar directly correspond to the four corners that the earth has. Here again, we see the message of the four gospels going to the four corners of the earth, and being preached to the whole world. In the book of Leviticus, God gives an interesting instruction to the priests who would be performing sacrifices on this brazen altar. Notice the instruction given when a priest sacrifices a lamb on the altar.

> And if his offering be of the flocks, namely, of the sheep, or of the goats, for a burnt sacrifice; he shall bring it a male without blemish. And he shall kill it **on the side of the altar northward** before the LORD: and the priests, Aaron's sons, shall sprinkle his blood round about upon the altar.
>
> —Leviticus 1:10–11

There are two things that we will note about this passage. First, we see again the correlation between the location of the sacrifice of the lamb and the location of the crucifixion of Jesus, on the north side of Jerusalem. Second, the priest was instructed to sprinkle the blood of the lamb round about the altar, or in every direction so that north, south, east, and west would be covered by the sacrificial atoning blood of the lamb. The Calvary fulfillment of this *type* was prophesied by Isaiah.

> As many were astonied at thee; his visage was so marred more than any man, and his form more than the sons of men: **So shall he sprinkle many nations**; the kings shall shut their mouths at him: for that which had not been told them shall they see; and that which they had not heard shall they consider.
>
> —Isaiah 52:14–15

There is yet another, very interesting thing to note about the blood that was shed at the altar of sacrifice. In nearly every instance in the law when an animal was sacrificed on the brazen altar, a majority portion of that blood was either sprinkled or poured out on the ground at the base of the altar. We will see the significance of this in the following scriptures. From the fourth gospel story, we find that immediately after Jesus gave up the ghost on the cross, a Roman soldier took his spear and pierced His side. "But one of the soldiers with a spear pierced his side, and forthwith came there out **blood** and water" (John 19:34). By no stretch of the imagination can we say that there must have been a large amount of blood that came out of the Jesus' side on that day. This blood would have literally been poured out on the ground at the base of Calvary's altar of sacrifice, the cross.

This takes us, then, to the fourth chapter of the Bible, Genesis 4. In this passage we have the well known story of Cain and Abel. Truly this story is a microcosm of the gospel message, and it is only through the pages of Scriptures themselves that we may understand what is being portrayed in Genesis 4. First, let's look at the relevant portion of this chapter.

> And Adam knew Eve his wife; and she conceived, and bare Cain, and said, I have gotten a man from the LORD. And she again bare his brother Abel. And Abel was a keeper of sheep, but Cain was a tiller of the ground. And in process of time it came to pass, that Cain brought of the fruit of the ground an offering unto the LORD. And Abel, he also brought of the firstlings of his flock and of the fat thereof. And the LORD had respect unto Abel and to his offering: But unto Cain and to his offering he had not respect. And Cain was very wroth, and his countenance fell. And the LORD said unto Cain, Why art thou wroth? and why is thy countenance fallen? If thou doest well, shalt thou not be accepted? and if thou doest not well, sin lieth at the door. And unto thee shall be his desire, and thou shalt rule over him. And Cain talked with Abel his brother: and it came to pass, when they were in the field, that Cain rose up against Abel his brother, and slew him. And the LORD said unto Cain, Where

is Abel thy brother? And he said, I know not: Am I my brother's keeper? And he said, What hast thou done? the voice of thy brother's blood crieth unto me from the ground. And now art thou cursed from the earth, which hath opened her mouth to receive thy brother's blood from thy hand.

—Genesis 4:1–11

Now let's take a really close look at some of the details that will reveal to us this amazing gospel story. First, we see that verse two mentions that Abel was a keeper of sheep, a shepherd, as was David, and the Good Shepherd, Jesus. We also see that Abel, without future knowledge of the Mosaic law, brought exactly what the law required as far as a sacrifice was concerned: the firstlings of the flock and the fat. There are many arguments as to exactly why Abel's sacrifice was better than Cain's, but one thing we do notice from this passage is that Cain's offering came from the *ground*. There is a problem that exists in relation to his ground offering. At this point, the ground had been cursed in Genesis 3.

And unto Adam he said, Because thou hast hearkened unto the voice of thy wife, and hast eaten of the tree, of which I commanded thee, saying, Thou shalt not eat of it: **cursed is the ground for thy sake;** in sorrow shalt thou eat of it all the days of thy life; **Thorns also and thistles shall it bring forth to thee;** and thou shalt eat the herb of the field.

—Genesis 3:17–18

While it was possible for Abel to offer an offering without blemish, it was not possible for Cain to do so, because of the curse that was upon the ground. Any offering that Cain would have made from the ground would have been saturated with *thorns and thistles*.

The New Testament reveals some of the important details concerning the offerings of Cain and Abel. First, since we are dealing with the relationship between Abel and the gospel, it is interesting to note that we find Abel mentioned twelve (4 x 3) times in the Old

Testament, and four times in the New Testament, a total of sixteen (4 x 4) times. First, we see that all of Abel's deeds were righteous, and all of Cain's deeds were evil.

> Not as Cain, who was **of that wicked one**, and slew his brother. And wherefore slew he him? Because his own works were evil, and his brother's righteous.
>
> —1 John 3:12

In this, we see the *types* more clearly. Cain would represent the kingdom of Satan, being of that Wicked one, Satan himself. Abel represents a type of Christ, whose deeds are righteous. With this understanding, let's look at what the Bible says about the sacrifice of Abel.

> By faith Abel offered unto God a more excellent sacrifice than Cain, by which he obtained witness that he was righteous, God testifying of his gifts: and by it **he being dead yet speaketh.**
>
> —Hebrews 11:4

Notice that in the context of the verse, we see a clear connection between the sacrifice of Abel and his own death. It can be said that the murder of Abel by his own brother carries a similarity to Joseph, who was betrayed by his brethren, them telling his father that a *beast* had killed him, and Jesus, betrayed, not just by his own disciple Judas, but by the whole house of Israel, and murdered on Golgatha. Truly, Abel was murdered as a result of the offering that he presented to the Lord. Now notice the exact language that Paul used in Hebrews 11:4, when he said that Abel, "being dead yet speaketh." There is something about the death of Abel that speaks to us even today. Now let's go back to the Genesis story to see what it is that is speaking.

> And he said, What hast thou done? **the voice of thy brother's blood crieth unto me from the ground.**
>
> —Genesis 4:10

It is the blood of Abel that is his testimony. Just as the priest was instructed to sprinkle or pour the blood of the sacrifice on the ground around the altar, and as Jesus' own blood was poured out on the ground at the base of the cross, so Abel's blood was poured out on the ground, as a testimony to what would be done by Jesus at Calvary. Of this very idea, Paul once again expounds for us its true meaning in the book of Hebrews.

> And to Jesus the mediator of the new covenant, and to the **blood of sprinkling, that speaketh better things than that of Abel.**
>
> —Hebrews 12:24

Truly, Abel's blood speaks, but Christ's blood speaks better! It is the blood of Christ that is the center of the Gospel message. Without the blood, there can be no remission of sins (Matthew 26:28). In the temple of the human body, the main organ of the life-blood of all human beings is the heart. It is with the heart that man believes the Gospel message and is saved. The heart has four chambers.

One final note concerning the "gospel preaching" blood of Abel. It is mentioned in Genesis 4:11 that the earth ". . . hath opened her mouth to receive thy brother's blood from thy hand." The Scriptures reveal to us in Matthew 27:50 that Jesus cried with a loud voice and yielded up the ghost. John records for us that at this precise time, a Roman soldier pierced His side, issuing forth the water and the blood. Now according to Matthew 27:51, as soon as these events took place, the veil ripped in the Temple, an earthquake took place, and the rocks were torn apart. Could it not be that at the base of the cross, the rocks opened up and allowed the blood that was at the base of the cross to seep in, the earth literally opening her mouth to receive His blood? Since the blood of Christ is a spiritual cleansing agent, this would have the effect of eliminating the curse that was upon the ground, thus making the ground underneath the cross *holy ground*.

In Genesis 2, we see that there is a river that flows out of the land of Eden. Verse ten tells us that this river watered the garden of Eden, and then parted into four heads. This would be typical of the "river of water of life" that flows out of the throne of God in Revelation 22:1. It parts into four heads because it is the gospel message that flows to the four corners of the earth. In Ezekiel 37 we have the famous "dry bones" prophecy. This is a prophecy concerning the revival of the nation of Israel in the last days. As instructed by God, Ezekiel prophesies to these dry bones and they join together, being covered with flesh and sinew. But there is one thing that is lacking that these bones desperately need.

> Then said he unto me, Prophesy unto the **wind**, prophesy, son of man, and say to the wind, Thus saith the Lord GOD; Come from the **four winds**, O breath, and breathe upon these slain, that they may live. So I prophesied as he commanded me, and the breath came into them, and they lived, and stood up upon their feet, an exceeding great army.
>
> —Ezekiel 37:9–10

The wind represents the Holy Spirit. There are four winds because they represent the four gospels. Currently, Israel has become a nation once again, the dry bones have come together. Part of this prophecy has been fulfilled. However, they have not the breath of the Holy Spirit in them by way of the Gospels because of their blindness and refusal to hear the gospel message. Before Jesus the Messiah can reign over His people Israel, they must accept His sacrificial atonement for their sins.

In Matthew 24:31, we see these four winds used again to gather together the *elect*, those that have been saved by the gospel of Jesus Christ. In Mark 2 there was a man who was sick of the palsy, who was brought to Jesus for healing. He was let down through the roof, whereupon Christ immediately forgave his sins. He was "borne of four." According to Exodus 25:14, the Ark of the Covenant was to be "borne" by staves with **four** priests from the tribe of Levi. As in the case of Uzzah (2 Samuel 6) carrying the Ark, any other way was a violation of the law and resulted in death. Accordingly, there is no other way of salvation other than through the message of the **four** gospels. Any other way is death.

Although it is commonly recognized that Jacob had two wives through which came the twelve tribes of Israel, this is not the whole picture. Both Rachel and Leah each had one handmaid which they gave to Jacob as wives. This means that the twelve tribes of Israel were also "born of four," wives that is.

In Genesis 15, God reveals to Abram two significant things that relate to Israel receiving the Gospel. First He tells Abram that his seed will go into captivity in Egypt and be afflicted **four hundred** years, then afterward they will "come out with great substance." He also tells him that this will take place in the **fourth** generation.

In my first book, *By Divine Order,* the use of the number forty is described in the following way.

> The number forty is the number for *probation, testing, trials, and purification.* It is the product of **eight** (new beginnings, new life) and five (grace). The number forty is not intended to represent final judgment, but judgment unto repentance that will allow God's grace to bring about a new beginning.

This was the generally recognized meaning of the number forty. Now, when we focus on this number's exact and precise *prophetic* meaning, we see that it differs very little from this general meaning. In fact, what we see, since it is based on the number **four,** is its perfect relationship to the above described representation and the four-gospel message. In the following references we can clearly see the Gospel message in the plain text use of the number forty.

1. The forty days of the flood. This had the effect of killing off the old world and bringing in the new world. Acts 10 tells us that the clean animals are a type of Israel, and the unclean animals are a type of the Gentiles. It also tells us that the unclean Gentile animals are carried on a sheet with **four** corners. Noah takes in two of each on the unclean animals, for they are saved during the two thousand years after Christ's first coming. The Jewish clean animals are taken in by sevens, indicating that they will be saved in

the seventh millenium during the seven years of tribulation. The
ark is a *foursqaure* box. Genesis 7 tells us that at the end of the
forty days, Moses sends forth a dove which returns with an olive
leaf (Genesis 8; Romans 11).

2. In Genesis 50, the Scriptures tell us that Jacob has died and they
prepared his body for forty days. His instruction is that his body
is to be taken to the cave of Machpelah and buried there with
Abraham, Sarah, Isaac, Rebekah, and Leah. This cave was purchased by Abraham in Genesis 23 for **four hundred** shekels of
silver. Because of the resurrection power of the Gospel, all of these
bodies will rise out this cave and live again. Christ made this plain
in Luke 13:28–29: "There shall be weeping and gnashing of teeth,
when ye shall see **Abraham**, and **Isaac**, and **Jacob**, and **all the
prophets**, in the kingdom of God, and you yourselves thrust out.
And they shall come from the **east**, and from the **west**, and from
the **north**, and from the **south**, and shall sit down in the kingdom of God."

3. In Exodus 24, Moses went up into the mountain of God and there
waited forty days. After this period, God showed Moses the patterns of the tabernacle and gave him the Ten Commandments.
Moses then came down from the mountain with this holy book in
his hand, but Israel rejected this first coming of the Gospel message in the Ten Commandments. He then ascends the mountain
once more, and for forty days has nothing to eat or drink (sound
familiar?). He receives the commandments of God once more,
and descends from the heavenly mountaintop. This time, his face
shines as bright as the sunshine. At this point, the Word of God
in the form of the Ten Commandments is received by Israel and
placed in the four-cornered Ark of the Covenant.

4. In Numbers 13:25, twelve spies are sent into Canaan land to spy
it out. They return after a forty-day period. Ten of the spies are
afraid and reject the notion of entering the Promised Land. Two
of the spies (Gentile church) have no fear of the antichrist giants
and are ready to possess the land. For the children of Israel's disobedience, they must wander through the wilderness for **forty**

years. During this time, the old generation of Israel dies off, and a new generation is born. It could be said that Israel was *born again* as a result of this **forty-year** journey. The only exception is Joshua and Caleb; they do not see death before entering the Promised Land! Exodus 16, the sixty-sixth chapter of the Bible, tells us that the children of Israel ate bread that came down from heaven (manna) for this **forty-year** period.

5. Joshua 4:13 tells us of forty thousand men who were prepared for war. These are the men who marched around the city of Jericho (*Babylon the Great*). Only the power of the gospel can bring an end to this Mother of Harlots.

6. In 1 Samuel 17, Israel's reproach is lifted off of them after Goliath stands against them for **forty** days.

7. Second Samuel 5:4 tells us that David reigned over Israel for **forty** years. He reigned in Hebron for seven years and in Jerusalem for thirty-three years. Christ the Messiah reigned as King of the Jews for thirty-three years. He will reign as King of the Jews during the seven-year Tribulation during which they receive the gospel in order to fulfill this **forty** year prophetic *type*. In relation to this, Leviticus 12 tells us that a woman who gives birth to a *man child* is unclean for seven days, followed by the eighth day circumcision, then another thirty-three days, giving us a total forty days for purification. During this time, she is purified by *blood*! Immediately following this, the woman begins her monthly menstrual cycle. Approximately every **twenty-eight** (4 x 7) days, her secret place of the womb is purified by *blood* (Hebrews 9:22).

8. In 1 Kings 19:8, the Angel of the Lord (Jesus) gave food to Elijah the prophet and instructed him to eat it. Elijah went in the strength of that meat for **forty** days.

9. In Jonah 3:4 we are told that Ninevah is given **forty** days to repent or God will destroy them. Ninevah repented and was saved.

10. In Matthew 4:2, Mark 1:13, and Luke 4:2, we are told that Jesus fasted for **forty** days and nights. During this time he is tempted of Satan and overcomes the tempter. After the forty days, the Bible in Luke 4:14 tells us that ". . . Jesus returned in the power of

the Spirit. . . ."

11. Acts 1:3 tells us that Jesus appeared to many for **forty** days after His resurrection, "speaking of the things pertaining to the kingdom of God."

12. After Malachi's prophecy, God left off speaking to His people for a period of **four hundred** years. During this time, the uninspired Apocrypha was penned, but no prophet was raised up. After this **four hundred** years of silence, God once again began to speak to His people by His own Son, Jesus. This was undertaken in the **forthieth** book of the Bible, the first of the **four** gospels, the book of Matthew.

So many more references could be cited. The reader is encouraged to do his own study. However, the use of the number in the text of the Scriptures is now plain, and very revealing. Christ will save Israel in the last days with the **Four-Gospel** message of the cross.

In Revelation 4, John sees a vision of the throne of God. Circling the throne were twenty-four (4 x 6) elders. These elders cast their crowns before the throne of God and proclaim, "Thou art worthy, O Lord, to receive glory and honour and power: for thou hast **created** all things, and for thy pleasure they are and were **created**" (vs. 11). In the midst of the throne, John sees four heavenly beasts, cherubim, which he describes in the following manner.

> And the first beast was like a lion, and the second beast like a calf, and the third beast had a face as a man, and the fourth beast was like a flying eagle. And the four beasts had each of them six wings about him; and they were full of eyes within: and they rest not day and night, saying, Holy, holy, holy, Lord God Almighty, which was, and is, and is to come.
>
> —Revelation 4:7–8

These same cherubim make an appearance in Isaiah 6. In this chapter, Isaiah is instructed to go and deliver the message of repentance and salvation to Israel. Ezekiel is also allowed to see these same four creatures (Ezekiel 1). In chapters two and three, Ezekiel is likewise instructed to give this gospel message to Israel, who will not hear it.

As we saw earlier, Moses was instructed to build the altar of sacrifice *foursquare*. This reminds us of a city that is to be built foursquare, New Jerusalem. This is the holy city of God, from which He will reign over His people for all eternity. New Jerusalem is described as having twelve foundations and twelve gates. This is the number for the Godhead (three) times the number for the gospel (four). The twelve foundations are the foundations of the teachings of the apostles (Ephesians 2:20; Revelation 21:14). This city can only be built and based upon the gospel message, and only those who have accepted the gospel can enter into its gates. It can be said that New Jerusalem is only possible because of the blood atonement of Jesus Christ for the sins of the world. This is why it is a city built *foursquare*.

As we saw earlier in this chapter, it was on the fourth day of creation that God created the "greater light" that rules over the day. This is a type of Christ in many ways, more will be presented on this in the chapter on the number twenty-two. Suffice it to say that Jesus verified this and confirmed the association with the number four when He said: "Then spake Jesus again unto them, saying, **I am the light of the world**: he that followeth me shall not walk in darkness, but shall have the light of life" (John 8:12). Along with this verse, we find that the gospel itself is a light that shines on the world: "In whom the god of this world hath blinded the minds of them which believe not, lest the **light of the glorious gospel of Christ**, who is the image of God, should shine unto them" (2 Corinthians 4:4). The fourth thing that was created, after time, space, and matter in Genesis 1 was light. To do this, God spoke four words, "Let there be light," and it was fulfilled in four words, "and there was light." In the fourth gospel, the book of John, chapter one, Jesus is given the title of "Light" exactly four times.

The number 4 and the vengeance of the gospel

And to you who are troubled rest with us, when the Lord Jesus shall be revealed from heaven with his mighty angels, In flaming

fire taking vengeance on them that know not God, and that obey
not the gospel of our Lord Jesus Christ.

—2 Thessalonians 1:7–8

As we can see from the above verse, there is a heavenly vengeance that awaits all those who do not obey the gospel of Jesus Christ. Those who have received this wonderful gift of salvation and forgiveness cannot understand the mind that will not allow the love of God into their life. After all, the gospel message is truly summed up in John 3:16 when Jesus said, "For God so loved the world. . . ." If you are reading this book, and you have never asked Jesus to wash all your sins away, and through faith, be born again into the wonderful kingdom of Christ, you are missing God's richest blessings. Furthermore, as the old preachers say, "there is a heaven to gain, and a hell to shun" by repenting of your sins and calling on the name of the Lord. Those who will not open the door for Christ to enter in are doomed to face the eternal judgment of God.

In the various judgments mentioned for us in the book of Revelation, the association that the number four shares with the vengeance of the gospel is now clear. In Revelation 6, Christ begins by opening the seven-sealed book (*see the chapter on the number seven for more information concerning this book*). By opening these seven seals, there are seven corresponding events that take place. The first four seals that are opened release a concurring number of judgments to be sent forth to a **fourth** part of the earth: death by the sword, by famine, by pestilence, and by wild beasts of the earth (Revelation 6:1–8). These are exactly identical to the "four sore judgments" referred to in Ezekiel 14. Notice what the Scriptures reveal.

Though Noah, Daniel, and Job, were in it, as I live, saith the Lord
GOD, they shall deliver neither son nor daughter; they shall but
deliver their own souls by their righteousness. For thus saith the
Lord GOD; How much more when I send my **four sore judgments**
upon Jerusalem, the **sword**, and the **famine**, and the **noisome beast**,
and the **pestilence**, to cut off from it man and beast? Yet, behold,

therein shall be left a remnant that shall be brought forth, both sons and daughters: behold, they shall come forth unto you, and ye shall see their way and their doings: and ye shall be comforted concerning the evil that I have brought upon Jerusalem, even concerning all that I have brought upon it. And they shall comfort you, when ye see their ways and their doings: and ye shall know that I have not done without cause all that I have done in it, saith the Lord GOD."

—Ezekiel 14:20–23

Notice that in the above text, the main concentration of these four gospel avenging judgments are aimed at Jerusalem, the center of God's people Israel. They rejected the gospel of Jesus Christ and therefore must be the recipients of these judgments. There is, however, a saving purpose in these judgments. Verses twenty-two and twenty-three reveal that through these judgments, a remnant of Israel is brought forth who will serve their soon coming Messiah, Jesus Christ. This remnant is the same remnant of seven thousand spoken of in 1 Kings 19:18 who have not defiled themselves with the image of the beast. They are those of the children of Israel who believe and accept the gospel in the last days.

In Revelation 8:12, the **fourth** angel sounds his trumpet, causing the sun, moon, and stars to be stricken with darkness. You might remember that it was on the fourth day of creation that the sun, moon, and stars were created. The sun was referred to as the "greater light" that rules over the day. This would seem to point us directly to Jesus Himself, who is "the light of the world" (John 8:12), and to the "light of the glorious gospel" (2 Corinthians 4:4). When the light of the gospel of Christ is allowed to shine, it illuminates the entire world, showing to them the salvation message. When this light is stricken, the message is no longer available to a sinful and wicked world.

In Revelation 16:8, once again the **fourth** angel pours out his vial of wrath upon the sun. This has the effect of scorching the wicked men of the earth with fire. This, of course, brings us right back to 2 Thessalonians 1:8 which says, "In **flaming fire** taking **vengeance** on them that know not God, and **that obey not the gospel** of our Lord Jesus Christ." This idea was alluded to by Jesus Himself in Mark 4. In this chapter, Jesus reveals that the seed (the Word of God) which was sown on stony ground, because it had no root, was scorched by the sun and burnt up. These are those who receive the word, but through the scorching effect of persecution and affliction wither away (Mark 4:17).

The number four
and the fourth kingdom of the Beast

Now that we have a firm grasp on the number four and its gospel message, we now examine its dynamic opposite. Isaiah 14:14 tells us that Satan has a goal of being "like the most High." What we begin to see with this understanding as our foundation, is that Satan is the Great Copycat. His *modus operandi* is to mimic and pervert what he sees God do, becoming the *anti-god*, or the replacement of God. The full force of Satan's replacement theology will be manifest in the last days. As God builds His foursquare holy city of Jerusalem on the foundation of the true gospel of Jesus Christ, Satan will build his kingdom (city) upon a false gospel.

Turning back to Genesis 4, we find this theme when we look at the details. Verse eleven tells us that Cain is now cursed because of the murder of his brother, Abel. This would mean that the generations of Cain would be cursed in a similar manner. There is a biblical implication in this, for God swears that He would visit the iniquity of the fathers unto the **fourth** generation (this idea is expressed in exactly four passages: Exodus 20:5, 34:7; Numbers 14:18; Deuteronomy 5:9). Cain left the presence of the Lord, took a wife, and conceived a child, whom they named Enoch. After Enoch was born, Cain built a city (kingdom) and named it after his son, Enoch. The book of Psalms has an interesting thing to say about those who build cities and name them after themselves.

That he should still live for ever, and not see corruption. For he seeth that wise men die, likewise the fool and the brutish person perish, and leave their wealth to others. Their inward thought is, that their houses shall continue for ever, and their dwelling places to all generations; they call their lands after their own names.

—Psalm 49:9–11

The ones being spoken of in this passage are those who put their trust in riches (vs. 6). The theme of these verses is how the wicked attempt to find eternal life, a central theme of the real gospels. Verse ten tells us that they look around them and see that rich people that die have to leave all their riches to others, an abhorrent idea if you are rich. Their alleged remedy is to build cities and name them after themselves. Verse twelve of this chapter tells us that this will not work.

Nevertheless man being in honour abideth not: he is like the beasts that perish.

—Psalm 49:12

The city named after Enoch in Genesis 4 is this prototypical kingdom of the Antichrist, where Satan promises, through the deceitfulness of riches and a false gospel, that if men will follow him, they will be as gods, hence, receive eternal life. Of note is that although each of the descendants of Seth in Genesis 5 (with the exception of Enoch) is described by their birth and their *death*, not one member of the lineage of Cain in Genesis 4 is ever described as dying. The answer to this puzzle will someday be revealed, but for now remains unsolved.

The next place we find this false gospel kingdom being built is in Genesis 10. Nimrod, who is the thirteenth descendant from Adam, builds his kingdom. Many details concerning Nimrod, his religion, and his evil activities are documented in various sources, including the classic *The Two Babylons* by Alexander Hislop. For now, we look at the kingdom that Nimrod built.

He was a mighty hunter before the LORD: wherefore it is said, Even as Nimrod the mighty hunter before the LORD. And the beginning of his kingdom was **Babel**, and **Erech**, and **Accad**, and **Calneh**, in the land of Shinar.

—Genesis 10:9–10

He built his kingdom, with him set up as its god, with **four** cities, including the infamous Babel, or Babylon. Revelation 17–18 tells us that that great wicked city of the last days is called "BABYLON THE GREAT." Nimrod is mentioned **four** times in the Scriptures.

Next we look at the book of Daniel. In Daniel 2, Daniel is interpreting the dream that Nebuchadnezzar received. In this dream, Nebuchadnezzar sees an image having four separate parts. Daniel explains that these are four kingdoms that shall arise. In verse forty, he describes the fourth kingdom of iron which shall subdue the entire world in the last days. This fourth kingdom of the Antichrist will be destroyed by the Stone cut without hands, Jesus Himself, who will set up His own kingdom (v. 44). The idea that this kingdom has a religious nature to it is established in chapter three. Nebuchadnezzar erects the image of gold, silver, brass, and iron in the plain of Dura. At his command, all the peoples of the kingdom are ordered to bow down to it. This is precisely what the *false prophet* of Revelation 13 does. He erects an image of the first beast and causes all to worship this image.

There are three dissenters to this New Age religion of the Antichrist, the three Hebrews: Shadrach, Meshach, and Abednego. Because they refuse, Nebuchadnezzar instructs that they are to be thrown into a furnace that is heated **seven times** hotter, indicative of the seven-year Tribulation. Notice exactly what the Scriptures reveal in this amazing prophecy.

Then Nebuchadnezzar the king was astonied, and rose up in haste, and spake, and said unto his counsellors, Did not we cast three men bound into the midst of the fire? They answered and said unto the king, True, O king. He answered and said, Lo, I see **four men loose**, walking in the midst of the fire, and they have no hurt; and the form of the *fourth is like the Son of God*.

—Daniel 3:24–25

Truly we can now see the salvation of the children of Israel and their acceptance of the gospels in the last days by the appearance of the fourth in the fiery furnace, the Savior Himself, Jesus Christ!

There is one very important issue that this author feels must be dealt with at this point. The Authorized Version is the *only* English translation of the Scriptures that renders verse twenty-five as "the fourth like the Son of God." Here is what some of the others have to say.

New International Version
    ". . . the fourth looks like a son of the gods."
New World Translation
    ". . . the appearance of the fourth one is resembling a son of the gods."
New Revised Standard Version
    ". . . the fourth has the appearance of a god."
Today's English Version
    ". . . and the fourth one looks like an angel."
The Living Bible
    ". . . and the fourth looks like a god."

Many statements could be made concerning these very disturbing passages. I will, however, let the reader draw his own conclusion.

In Daniel 7, Daniel gives us a description of an end times vision that he receives.

Daniel spake and said, I saw in my vision by night, and, behold, the four winds of the heaven strove upon the great sea. And four great beasts came up from the sea, diverse one from another. The first was like a **lion**, and had eagle's wings: I beheld till the wings thereof were plucked, and it was lifted up from the earth, and made stand upon the feet as a man, and a man's heart was given to it. And behold another beast, a second, like to a **bear**, and it raised up itself on one side, and it had three ribs in the mouth of it between the teeth of it: and they said thus unto it, Arise, devour much flesh.

> After this I beheld, and lo another, like a **leopard**, which had upon
> the back of it four wings of a fowl; the beast had also four heads;
> and dominion was given to it. After this I saw in the night visions,
> and behold a **fourth beast**, dreadful and terrible, and strong ex-
> ceedingly; and it had great **iron** teeth: it devoured and brake in pieces,
> and stamped the residue with the feet of it: and it was diverse from
> all the beasts that were before it; and it had ten horns.
>
> —Daniel 7:2–7

There are some interesting similarities between this fourth beast and
the fourth kingdom that Daniel interpreted in chapter two, in that
they are both kingdoms associated with the strength of iron, and that
it seems to devour and overtake the entire world. We also notice that
the three former beasts that arise out of the great sea are the same
beasts that John saw when he described the beast of Revelation 13.

> And I stood upon the sand of the sea, and saw a **beast rise up out
> of the sea**, having seven heads and **ten horns**, and upon his horns
> ten crowns, and upon his heads the name of blasphemy. And the
> beast which I saw was like unto a **leopard**, and his feet were as the
> feet of a **bear**, and his mouth as the mouth of a **lion**: and the dragon
> gave him his power, and his seat, and great authority.
>
> —Revelation 13:1–2

This beast that John sees is a composite of the beasts that Daniel saw
in his vision; all four beasts rolled up into one great and terrible beast.
The four-beast creature that John sees is described as having "a mouth
speaking great things and blasphemies" (Revelation 13:5). When we
examine the Holy Scriptures for our understanding, we find the precise nature of what it is this four-beast creature speaks. The first thing
we look at is the phrase, "great things." In Daniel 7:8, we see that
Daniel's fourth beast also speaks "great things." This phrase is mentioned exactly twenty-eight (4 x 7) times in the Bible. Its overall use
points us to the central theme of the gospel message.

Only fear the LORD, and serve him in truth with all your heart; for consider how **great things** he hath done for you.

—1 Samuel 12:24

And what one nation in the earth is like thy people, even like Israel, whom **God went to redeem for a people to himself**, and to make him a name, and to do for you **great things** and terrible, for thy land, before thy people, which thou redeemedst to thee from Egypt, from the nations and their gods?

—2 Samuel 7:23

And the king talked with Gehazi the servant of the man of God, saying, Tell me, I pray thee, all the **great things** that Elisha hath done. And it came to pass, as he was telling the king **how he had restored a dead body to life**, that, behold, the woman, whose son he had restored to life, cried to the king for her house and for her land. And Gehazi said, My lord, O king, this is the woman, and this is her son, whom Elisha restored to life.

—2 Kings 8:4–5

Howbeit **Jesus** suffered him not, but saith unto him, Go home to thy friends, and tell them how **great things the Lord hath done for thee**, and hath had compassion on thee.

—Mark 5:19

Although all the occurrences of this phrase are not listed here, almost all of them carry this same theme of salvation. There is a noted exception listed for us in the book of James that seems to point to what the beast is saying.

Even so the tongue is a little member, and **boasteth great things.** Behold, how great a matter a little fire kindleth!

—James 3:5

It would seem then that this four-beast creature speaks a message of salvation to all the world. Truly this is a blasphemy to speak such a thing if you are not the one and true God of salvation. There are other interesting verses that reinforce the idea that this beast is speaking a false gospel.

> And the scribes and the Pharisees began to reason, saying, Who is this which **speaketh blasphemies? Who can forgive sins, but God alone?**
>
> —Luke 5:21

> The Jews answered him, saying, For a good work we stone thee not; but for **blasphemy**; and because that thou, **being a man, makest thyself God**.
>
> —John 10:33

First, we see that Christ was accused of speaking blasphemy because He said He could *forgive sins*. Then, we also see that He was accused of blasphemy because He, as a man, made Himself God. While it is true that only God can forgive sins, since Jesus was God, it was not blasphemy. However, there is coming one, the Antichrist, who will show himself to the world that he is God (Ezekiel 2:2; 2 Thessalonians 2:4) and will present to the world a false gospel and a false salvation. Notice that in John 10:33 the Jews were about to stone Christ for His alleged offense. This was directly according to the levitical law.

> And **he that blasphemeth** the name of the LORD, he shall surely be put to death, and all the congregation shall certainly stone him: as well the stranger, as he that is born in the land, when he blasphemeth the name of the LORD, shall be put to death.
>
> —Leviticus 24:16

The direct punishment for the man that blasphemed God was to be killed with stones. This takes us, then directly to Daniel 2. The fourth-antichrist kingdom arises in the last days and conquers the entire earth. Do you remember what destroys this last days kingdom?

> Then was the iron, the clay, the brass, the silver, and the gold, broken to pieces together, and became like the chaff of the summer threshingfloors; and the wind carried them away, that no place was found for them: and the stone that smote the image became a great mountain, and filled the whole earth.
>
> —Daniel 2:35

The stone that smote it is Jesus, who establishes the mountain of the Lord's house in the last days and rules the whole earth for one thousand years. This same idea is presented to us in the story of David and Goliath. Goliath defies the army of God for forty days, until David, who comes in the name of the Lord, smites the giant Goliath . . . with a *stone*.

In Hosea 13, we also see another connection between the four-beast creature and the idea of a false gospel, or a false savior. God begins the chapter by declaring His anger at Ephraim for falling into Baal worship. Notice what God says to them because of their wickedness.

> Therefore I will be unto them as a lion: as a leopard by the way will I observe them: I will meet them as a bear that is bereaved of her whelps, and will rend the caul of their heart, and there will I devour them like a lion: the wild beast shall tear them.
>
> —Hosea 13:7–8

Aside from the fact that the exact same four beasts are mentioned here, the most important thing to note about this passage is the exact words that begin verse seven. God says, "I will be unto them as. . . ." This clearly points out to us that though mankind thinks he is worshipping God, because God will send them strong delusion (2 Thessalonians 2:11), they will actually be worshipping the false Christ of the last days.

This last days false gospel kingdom governed by the entire realm of demonic hosts will be given free reign to deceive and destroy mankind. These demonic spirits are divided into four categories: principalities, powers, rulers of the darkness of this world, and spiritual wickedness in high places (Ephesians 6:12). This false gospel that will come has been prophesied and warned about in four places in the Bible.

> For if he that cometh preacheth another Jesus, whom we have not preached, or if ye receive another spirit, which ye have not received, or another gospel, which ye have not accepted, ye might well bear with him.
>
> —2 Corinthians 11:4

> I marvel that ye are so soon removed from him that called you into the grace of Christ unto another gospel. . . . But though we, or an angel from heaven, preach any other gospel unto you than that which we have preached unto you, let him be accursed. As we said before, so say I now again, If any man preach any other gospel unto you than that ye have received, let him be accursed.
>
> —Galatians 1:6,8–9

This last days false gospel will be preached by another beast who arises up out of the cursed earth in Revelation 13:11. He is called the *false prophet* and this phrase is also mentioned precisely four times in the Scriptures. The exact wording of this last days *false gospel* may not be clearly revealed as yet, but its precise nature and tone can be summed up in this very familiar four word phrase: ". . . *Yea, hath God said*. . . ."

The Number Five

There are several themes connected with the number five. We will look at its general themes of grace and redemption, then focus on its prophetic themes of the Rapture of the Gentile church and the salvation of Israel in the last days.

The number five and grace

As with so many of the numbers that we will cover in this book, we use the biblical principles of counting (Revelation 13:18; Ecclesiastes 7:27) in order to find the things that a number is associated with. The fifth time Noah's name is mentioned in the Scriptures is found in Genesis 6:8, saying, ". . . Noah found **grace** in the eyes of the LORD." The fifth time Ruth is mentioned is in Ruth 2:2 where she seeks to find grace in the eyes of Boaz. The fifth time Boaz is mentioned is in Ruth 2:8, whereupon Ruth realizes she has found grace in his sight (vs. 10). The word "grace" is given in three different forms in the Bible: "grace," "gracious," and "graciously." They are found a total of two hundred and five (5 x 41) times in the Bible.

In the first five books of the New Testament, the word "grace" is mentioned exactly fifteen (5 x 3) times. Our Savior received five wounds on the cross, two in His hands, two in His feet, and one in His side. It was from this wound in His side that the blood of reconciliation and forgiveness of sins flowed. Because of this fifth wound, salvation is possible. It was also a wound in Adam's side that brought forth Eve, his wife. From this wound, God took a rib, probably the fifth rib. The word "rib" is mentioned five times, and in four occasions it is mentioned as being the fifth rib.

In Isaiah 9:6, Jesus is given the titles of "Wonderful, Counselor, the Mighty God, the everlasting Father, the Prince of Peace." Hebrews 10:5 tells of what Jesus said when He came to the world. His appearing to the world the first time took place at the beginning of the fifth millenium, or fifth day, from Adam. This was done in order to shed light on a very interesting pattern that is present in Genesis 5.

The first thing that is mentioned in Genesis 5 is the genealogy of Adam, given to us in a book called "The book of the generations of Adam." This is somewhat significant, for it is the first time that the word "book" is mentioned in the Bible. The very first New Testament occurrence of the word "book" is the following.

> The **book** of the generation of Jesus Christ, the son of David, the son of Abraham.
>
> —Matthew 1:1

This describes the coming, or birth, of Jesus at the beginning of the **fifth** millenium from Adam. You will also notice that in Genesis 5:1, it refers to the generations (plural) of Adam, and in Matthew 1:1 the generation (singular) of Jesus. Some would say that this might amount to the biblical equivalent of "nit-picking," until we look at a verse that brings these puzzle pieces together and tells us why "every word of God is pure."

> For as in Adam all die, even so in Christ shall all be made alive.
>
> —1 Corinthians 15:22

In Adam, the need for many generations is obvious: all die. The Old Testament, especially the five books of Moses, the law, is a book of death. It is for this reason that Israel is dead in their trespasses and sins (Romans 8:2). By the way, all the mentions of the word "death" including "death," "deaths," "die," "died," "diest," and "dieth" total nine hundred twenty-nine times. There are nine hundred twenty-nine chapters in the Old Testament. However, in Christ, there is only a need for one generation, the generation of those who live forever and never die. The New Testament with the blood-red words of Christ is the book of life, eternal life. This is the grace of God.

Let us look even deeper into these two books and see their relationship to the number five and the grace of God. Let us examine the first five verses of Genesis 5.

> This is the book of the generations of Adam. In the day that God created man, in the likeness of God made he him; Male and female created he them; and blessed them, and called their name Adam, in the day when they were created. And Adam lived an hundred and thirty years, and begat a son in his own likeness, after his image; and called his name Seth: And the days of Adam after he had begotten Seth were eight hundred years: and he begat sons and daughters: And all the days that Adam lived were nine hundred and thirty years: and he died."
>
> —Genesis 5:1–5

Most people, for obvious reasons, generally choose to skip over the various lineage listings that are given in the Scriptures. However, there is a very precise and revealing pattern to these incredible verses. When Adam is *first* mentioned (vs. 1), it goes without saying that the *book* of his generations begins the very moment he *first* came into the world. The *second* time Adam is mentioned (vs. 2), his name is actually given to he and his wife Eve. This, of course, points us to the general meaning of the number two. The third time Adam is mentioned (vs. 3), Adam's son, Seth, is born. It mentions that Seth was in the likeness and image of Adam, thus Adam, who will die, is resurrected in a sense in his son, Seth. The fourth time Adam is mentioned, we find that "he begat sons and daughters." It is through the saving grace of the four gospels that God is able to say to us that He ". . . will be a Father unto you, and ye shall be my sons and daughters, saith the Lord Almighty" (2 Corinthians 6:18).

This brings us to the fifth mention of Adam's name in Genesis 5. It is found in verse five.

> And all the days that Adam lived were nine hundred and thirty years: and he died.
>
> —Genesis 5:5

As we examine the entire chapter, we will clearly see that this name pattern is followed precisely on every generation of Adam all the way down to Noah. The only exception is Enoch. We will discuss him later. For now, we concentrate on the fact that death occurs the fifth time each one is named in Genesis 5. For answers to this mystery we go to the Book of the Generation of Jesus Christ, the New Testament. Naturally, the precise place we would look would almost surely have something to do with the number five. Let us look in the forty-fifth (5 x 9) book of the Bible, Romans 5.

> For if, when we were enemies, we were reconciled to God by the death of his Son, much more, being reconciled, we shall be saved by his life.
>
> —Romans 5:10

This verse is clear in that it tells us that we are reconciled to God by the death of His "only begotten Son," this phrase being mentioned exactly five times in the Bible. The fifth time it is mentioned is in 1 John 4:9 and says, ". . . God sent his only begotten Son into the world, that we might live through him." This is precisely what Romans 5:10 tells us, that we are saved by the death and life of Christ. Yet, the Bible speaks even more amazing things than this as we continue to look at Romans 5.

> Wherefore, as by one man sin entered into the world, and death by sin; and so death passed upon all men, for that all have sinned: (For until the law sin was in the world: but sin is not imputed when there is no law. Nevertheless death reigned from Adam to Moses,

even over them that had not sinned after the similitude of Adam's transgression, who is the figure of him that was to come.

—Romans 5:12–14

The "one man" spoken of in verse twelve is, of course, Adam. Now, it says that death reigned from "Adam to Moses." Adam died in the first book of the Bible, in the fifth chapter and fifth verse. Moses died in the fifth book of the Bible, Deuteronomy, in verse five of chapter thirty-four. Now notice the following verses.

> But not as the offence, so also is the free gift. For if through the offence of one many be dead, much more the grace of God, and the gift by grace, which is by one man, Jesus Christ, hath abounded unto many.
>
> —Romans 5:15

> Moreover the law entered, that the offence might abound. But where sin abounded, grace did much more abound.
>
> —Romans 5:20

It is through the offense of Adam that death entered into him and to the rest of the world, even though they did not commit Adam's sin. The law entered into the world, by way of the five books of Moses (Genesis–Deuteronomy), so that the offense that causes death may abound. Paul calls it in Romans 8:2 the "law of sin and death." But now, through Christ, who came to fulfill the five books of the law, grace has abounded to many. For where sin abounded through the five books of the law, grace much more abounds in the sacrifice of Jesus Christ, the only begotten Son, who came at the beginning of the fifth millennium, and was pierced five times on the cross.

In the previous chapter, we saw how the number four was related to the evil world empire of the Beast in the last days. This terrible empire will consume the entire world, and no power on earth will be its equal. Nebuchadnezzar dreamed that this empire would finally be destroyed by a **fifth** empire.

Thou sawest till that a **stone** was cut out without hands, which
smote the image upon his feet that were of iron and clay, and brake
them to pieces. Then was the iron, the clay, the brass, the silver,
and the gold, broken to pieces together, and became like the chaff of
the summer threshingfloors; and the wind carried them away, that
no place was found for them: and the stone that smote the image
became a great mountain, and filled the whole earth. . . . And in the
days of these kings shall the God of heaven set up a kingdom, which
shall never be destroyed: and the kingdom shall not be left to other
people, but it shall break in pieces and consume all these kingdoms,
and it shall stand for ever. Forasmuch as thou sawest that the stone
was cut out of the mountain without hands, and that it brake in
pieces the iron, the brass, the clay, the silver, and the gold; the great
God hath made known to the king what shall come to pass hereafter: and the dream is certain, and the interpretation thereof sure.

—Daniel 2:34–35,44–45

Of a surety, this **fifth** kingdom, established by God Himself, is the
millennial reign of the King of Kings, Jesus Christ. If you will notice
the above passage from Daniel, in verse forty-five it says that the
stone broke in pieces the iron, brass, clay, silver and gold—five things.
In our King James Bible, the word "Christ" is mentioned exactly **five
hundred fifty-five** times! When Jesus presented himself to the world
the first time, it was some four thousand years after the creation, at
the beginning of the fifth millennium.

In one of the most recognized stories of the Bible, that of David's
battle with Goliath, we can now clearly see this illustrated for us.
David rejected the armor that was given him by Saul to defeat Goliath. Notice what the Scriptures say David picked as his weapon of
choice.

And he took his staff in his hand, and chose him **five smooth stones**
out of the brook, and put them in a shepherd's bag which he had,
even in a scrip; and his sling was in his hand: and he drew near to
the Philistine. . . . And David put his hand in his bag, and took

thence a stone, and slang it, and smote the Philistine in his forehead, that the stone sunk into his forehead; and he fell upon his
face to the earth. So David prevailed over the Philistine with a
sling and with a stone, and smote the Philistine, and slew him; but
there was no sword in the hand of David.

—1 Samuel 17:40,49–50

Thus Goliath, a type of the Beast, is destroyed by the fifth stone. It
appears that the stone sunk in the exact spot that the Mark of the
Beast would be, and when this happens, Goliath, who is facing David
(Christ), falls on his face to the earth. Generally speaking, when a
person in the Bible falls on their face to the earth, they are doing so in
an act of worship. At the final judgment, every knee shall bow before
the mighty Jesus Christ. God seems to have a sense of ironic humor.

In 1 Samuel 5, the lords of the Philistines take custody of the Ark
of the Covenant, the throne of God. They take the Ark to the temple
of Dagon, a half-man, half-sea serpent god, figurative of Satan's power and spirit in the beast of Revelation 13. The obvious indication is
that the five lords of the Philistines were supposing that the God of
the Hebrews would stand before Satan, in the form of Dagon. The
end result was just the opposite. "And when they arose early on the
morrow morning, behold, **Dagon was fallen upon his face to the
ground before the ark of the LORD**; and the head of Dagon and
both the palms of his hands were cut off upon the threshold; only the
stump of Dagon was left to him" (1 Samuel 5:4). It is interesting to
note at this point that contained inside the Ark of the Covenant was
the Ten Commandments, written on two tables of **STONE**, **five** on
one table, **five** on the other.

These five lords of the Philistines should have learned their les-
son from their forefathers. The book of Joshua tells us another story
that reveals a few more details of the dominion of the fifth kingdom
of Christ. In chapter ten, Joshua and his armies pursue and capture
the five lords of the Philistines. Notice what is done with these kings.

Then said Joshua, Open the mouth of the cave, and bring out those
five kings unto me out of the cave. And they did so, and brought

forth those five kings unto him out of the cave, the king of Jerusalem, the king of Hebron, the king of Jarmuth, the king of Lachish,
and the king of Eglon. And it came to pass, when they brought out
those kings unto Joshua, that Joshua called for all the men of Israel,
and said unto the captains of the men of war which went with him,
Come near, **put your feet upon the necks of these kings.** And
they came near, and put their feet upon the necks of them. And
Joshua said unto them, Fear not, nor be dismayed, be strong and of
good courage: **for thus shall the LORD do to all your** *enemies*
against whom ye fight.

—Joshua 10:22–25

This is highly reminiscent of the promise in Genesis 3:15: "And I will
put enmity between thee and the woman, and between thy seed and
her seed; it **shall bruise thy head,** and thou shalt bruise his heel." It
will be according to Joshua's words that Christ will conquer all His
enemies and dash them in pieces. The Philistines have always been
the mortal enemies of God's people. Once again we see a connection
between the Philistines as the enemies of God and the number five.
Joshua commands the captains of the men of war to put their feet on
the necks of these five kings. (See the chapter on the number ten
concerning their feet.) This coincides with the promise of Genesis
3:15 and Paul's blessing for the Church in Romans 16:20. Joshua promises that God will do this to all of the enemies of God's people, not
just the Philistines. What do these five Philistine kings represent?

For he must reign, till **he hath put all enemies under his feet.**
The last enemy that shall be destroyed is **death.**

—1 Corinthians 15:25–26

As we have already seen from the previous portions of this chapter,
the relationship between the number five and death under the law is
obvious. These five Philistine kings represent Death himself, who is
defeated by Christ. I will mention at this point the exact word "Philistines" is mentioned two hundred fifty-five times, or 5 x 51 times in
the Bible. (To see the importance of the number fifty-one in this equa-

tion, see the chapter on the number seventeen in this book.) The question is now raised, just exactly how does Christ defeat this eternal mortal enemy of God's people, death? The answer is given to us in the proceeding verses from Joshua 10. Please put on your *prophecy* glasses and see God's wonderful plan as you read these verses.

> And afterward Joshua smote them, and slew them, and hanged them on five trees: and they were hanging upon the trees until the evening. And it came to pass at the time of the going down of the sun, that Joshua commanded, and they took them down off the trees, and cast them into the cave wherein they had been hid, and laid great stones in the cave's mouth, which remain until this very day.
>
> —Joshua 10:26–27

It is my sincere hope that the reader can clearly see the absolute precision of the Word of God, and that it has indeed been preserved for our understanding in the last days. The events that we see taking place in the above verses are precisely what took place at Calvary. It was Christ Himself who hung on a tree, a curse according to Galatians 3:13. The four gospels are careful to record for us that they made sure to take Christ's body down from the tree before sunset that day. They immediately took His body and placed it in a tomb, literally a cave belonging to Joseph of Arimathaea. A great stone was rolled in place to seal off the cave. The only difference between this story and Christ's fulfillment at Calvary is the fact that to this day, the stones remain in front of the cave where the five kings of death were buried. Christ's stone was rolled away, signifying the defeat of the great enemy, Death.

From this passage we see that Christ defeated Death, and all of our enemies for that matter, by taking them with Him when He died on the Cross. Of this, 2 Corinthians 5:21 tells us that God made Christ ". . . to be sin for us, who knew no sin; that we might be made the righteousness of God in him." The result of Christ becoming sin for us was that when Christ died, sin died as well. When Christ died, death died. When Christ died, He took on all these curses in His flesh so that the curse would die with Him, and so we would be made the righteousness of God in Him. I will also mention at this point as well that as "Christ" is mentioned five hundred fifty-five times in the Bible, so all the forms of the word "righteous" are mentioned exactly five hundred fifty-five times in the Bible.

There is yet another story from the pages of our perfect Bible that also involves the "death" lords of the Philistines and their defeat. This Bible *type* points directly to the idea that although Christ died, He took all His enemies with Him. The story is the story of Samson.

> Then the **lords of the Philistines** gathered them together for to offer a great sacrifice unto Dagon their god, and to rejoice: for they said, Our god hath delivered Samson our enemy into our hand. . . . Now the house was full of men and women; and **all the lords of the Philistines** were there; and there were upon the roof about three thousand men and women, that beheld while Samson made sport. And Samson called unto the LORD, and said, O Lord GOD, remember me, I pray thee, and strengthen me, I pray thee, only this once, O God, that I may be at once avenged of the Philistines for my two eyes. And Samson took hold of the two middle pillars upon which the house stood, and on which it was borne up, of the one with his right hand, and of the other with his left. And Samson said, **Let me die with the Philistines**. And he bowed himself with all his might; and the house fell upon the lords, and upon all the people that were therein. **So the dead which he slew at his death were more than they which he slew in his life.**
>
> —Judges 16:23,27–30

In Samson's last great effort in defeating the enemies of the children of God, we see Samson reaching out to grab the two pillars of the house of Dagon, extending out his right and left hands as Christ did on the cross. Thus with his own death, destroying all of his enemies forever. What a magnificent picture our Father has drawn for us in the pages of our Bibles so that we could understand just what He has done for our sakes. By the way, I will point out that in Judges 16:5 the Scriptures reveal to us that these five lords of the Philistines paid Delilah eleven hundred pieces of silver each to entice Samson. This amounts to a total of **fifty-five hundred** pieces of silver that bought and paid for Samson's death. This perfectly coincides with the fact that we find "Satan" exactly fifty-five times in the Bible, "devils" is mentioned fifty-five times, and the Antichrist is mentioned exactly five times in the Scriptures. These are all the enemies of Christ that will be defeated in the last days. Could it be more than a coincidence that Satan's primary symbol is a *pentagram*, a five-pointed star.

Christ gave us the promise in Matthew 16:28 that ". . . there be some standing here, which shall not **taste of death**, till they see the Son of man coming in his kingdom." In fact, this promise is given to us in the Scriptures exactly five times (Matthew 16:28; Mark 9:1; Luke 9:27; John 8:52; Hebrews 2:9). The fifth place it is mentioned it is mentioned with the grace of God. "But we see Jesus, who was made a little lower than the angels **for the suffering of death**, crowned with glory and honour; that he by the **grace of God** should **taste death for every man**" (Hebrews 2:9).

Seeing that Christ's death on the cross accomplished the defeat of our enemy, Death, it surely is the signature of Almighty God, the Author of order, when we see what is in the **five hundredth** chapter of the Holy Bible.

> My God, my God, why hast thou forsaken me? . . . All they that see me laugh me to scorn: they shoot out the lip, they shake the head, saying, He trusted on the LORD that he would deliver him: let him deliver him, seeing he delighted in him. . . . they pierced my hands and my feet. . . . They part my garments among them, and cast lots upon my vesture.
>
> —Psalm 22:1,7–8,16,18

The number five and the Rapture

What we have seen so far is that God manifests His unending grace over mankind by giving Him victory over our mortal and final enemy,

Death. This is the true nature of grace. The Scriptures tell us in Titus that ". . . the grace of God that bringeth salvation hath appeared to all men" (Titus 2:11). And that this grace teaches us five things: "Teaching us that, **denying ungodliness** and **worldly lusts**, we should live **soberly**, **righteously**, and **godly**, in this present world" (Titus 2:12). This is in preparation for ". . . that blessed hope, and the glorious appearing of the great God and our Saviour Jesus Christ" (Titus 2:13).

Much debate among those interested in the specifics of Bible prophecy is centered on the idea of the future translation of the Gentile church into heaven. It is commonly referred to as the Rapture. Some say that this event will never occur, and many others believe that it will assuredly occur, but the exact timing of this Rapture creates its own set of debates. The commonly held view is that the Rapture occurs just prior to a seven-year period before the thousand-year reign of Christ, the time in which Israel will be saved. It is this view that I believe has the most merit. In the following discourse, we will see, first, that the Rapture is associated heavily with the number five, we will learn why it is associated with the number five, and we will also see the clear connection between the Rapture of the Gentile church and the subsequent salvation of Israel.

First, let us look at the most familiar passage that teaches us about the translation of the church into heaven.

> For the Lord himself shall descend from heaven with a shout, with the voice of the archangel, and with the trump of God: and the dead in Christ shall rise first: Then we which are alive and remain shall be caught up together with them in the clouds, to meet the Lord in the air: and so shall we ever be with the Lord.
>
> —1 Thessalonians 4:16–17

You will notice that there are exactly five things that happen when the Lord descends: a shout, the voice of the archangel, the trump of God, the raising of the dead in Christ, and then those who are alive will be caught up to meet the Lord in the air. Also, I believe it is important to not just count the number of things that happen, but look individually at the things that happen when Christ appears in the clouds. We see a shout, a trumpet, a voice of an angel, etc. We will look at just a few places where these events are referred to in other parts of the Scriptures, and how they point directly to the salvation of Israel after the Rapture of the Gentile church.

> And it came to pass at the **seventh time**, when the priests blew with the **trumpets**, Joshua said unto the people, **Shout**; for the LORD hath given you the city.
>
> —Joshua 6:16

This is in reference to the destruction of Jericho. The city of Jericho is a *type* of that wicked city, Babylon the Great in the last days. For more on this, see the chapter on the number thirteen. Joshua and the armies of Israel are commanded to circle Jericho once a day for six days and remain quiet. In the morning of the seventh day (seventh millennium) they blow trumpets and shout and circle the city seven times (seven years of God's judgment on Babylon). The only one saved out of this destruction is Rahab, the harlot. She is a type of Israel who has sold herself into spiritual adultery (Ezekiel 16), but is saved during the final seven years. Rahab is mentioned in the book of Joshua exactly five times. She is redeemed from a sure death in Jericho.

> So David and all the house of Israel brought up the ark of the LORD with **shouting**, and with the **sound of the trumpet**.
>
> —2 Samuel 6:15

The ark of the Lord is the Ark of the Covenant which contains the two tables of stone that I mentioned earlier. The ark is a replica of the throne in heaven that God sits on. It represents God's authority, God's Word, and His mercy. It was on the Mercy Seat that the blood of a bullock and the blood of a goat of the sin offering was sprinkled seven times. This was done once a year by the high priest for the salvation of Israel. The parallel passage to this story, found in 1 Chronicles 15, mentions that when the priests began to bring the ark, they sacrificed seven bullocks and seven rams. In 2 Samuel 6:5 the Scriptures tell us that the ark was accompanied into Jerusalem by five types of instruments: harps, psalteries, timbrals, cornets, and cymbals. The entrance of the ark into Jerusalem, the holy city, symbolizes the restoration of the kingdom and salvation to Israel during a period of seven years.

> So they gathered themselves together at Jerusalem in the third month, in the fifteenth year of the reign of Asa. And they offered unto the LORD the same time, of the spoil which they had brought, **seven** hundred oxen and **seven** thousand sheep. And they entered into a covenant to seek the LORD God of their fathers with all their heart and with all their soul; That whosoever would not seek the LORD God of Israel should be put to **death**, whether small or great, whether man or woman. And they sware unto the LORD with a loud voice, and with **shouting**, and with **trumpets**, and with cornets. And all Judah rejoiced at the oath: for they had sworn with all their heart, and sought him with their whole desire; and he was found of them: and the LORD gave them rest round about.
>
> —2 Chronicles 15:10–15

In this passage, Asa the king leads Judah into a covenant with God, sealing this covenant with a sacrifice of seven hundred oxen and seven thousand sheep. The oath that the people make to God is resounded by shouting and trumpets. By doing this, God spares Asa from war for thirty-five (7 x 5) years (vs. 19).

Ezra 3:11 tells us that Israel shouted with a great shout when Zerubbabel laid the foundation of the Lord's house after the seventy-year Babylonian captivity. Psalm 47 begins with, ". . . O clap your hands, all ye people; shout unto God with the voice of triumph." The following verses tell of God conquering the nations of the world and restoring the inheritance to Israel. It is in verse **five** that we find, "God is gone up with a shout, the LORD with the sound of a trumpet." This is just a sample of the details we can find when we understand that God has given us a "sure word of prophecy."

The next place we will look at to see the relationship between the number five and the Rapture involves the word "mystery." The first occurrence of this word sets the overall theme of its use in the Bible. "And he said unto them, Unto you it is given to know the mystery of the kingdom of God: but unto them that are without, all these things are done in parables" (Mark 4:11). This same theme is repeated several times throughout the Bible; the Gentiles have the mystery of salvation revealed to them that Jesus Christ is the Messiah, but to Israel, this mystery is still a secret. The second occurrence of the word "mystery" reveals this truth.

> For I would not, brethren, that ye should be ignorant of this mystery, lest ye should be wise in your own conceits; that blindness in part is happened to Israel, until the fulness of the Gentiles be come in.
>
> —Romans 11:25

When, and only when, the dispensation of the Gentiles is over will Israel receive the revelation that Jesus is their Savior, thus eliminating their partial blindness. I might add at this point that Israel is only partially blinded because they only read one testament of the Bible. When any Jew accepts and believes the New Testament, their blindness is lifted and they walk in the light of the glorious Gospel.

This brings us the fifth occurrence of the word "mystery." It is found in 1 Corinthians.

> Behold, I shew you a **mystery**; We shall not all sleep, but we shall all be changed, In a moment, in the twinkling of an eye, at the last trump: for the trumpet shall sound, and the dead shall be raised incorruptible, and we shall be changed.
>
> —1 Corinthians 15:51–52

These verses reveal the mystery behind the Rapture of the Gentile church. It promises us that the dead in Christ will be raised "incorruptible." This word is used in various forms exactly five times in this chapter. In verse fifty-four we see that this event fulfills an Old Testament prophecy. "So when this corruptible shall have put on incorruption, and this mortal shall have put on immortality, then shall be brought to pass the saying that is written, **Death is swallowed up in victory**" (1 Corinthians 15:54). This prophecy is recorded for us in Isaiah 25 (5 x 5), verse eight. It is in verse **fifty-five** of 1 Corinthians 15 that we see **death** and the **grave** defeated. "O death, where is thy sting? O grave, where is thy victory?"

There is yet another occurrence of the word "mystery" that points us to the theme of the Rapture, and it is also associated with the number five. In the fifty-fifth verse of the Bible, here is what is written. "Therefore shall a man leave his father and his mother, and shall cleave unto his wife: and they shall be one flesh" (Genesis 2:24). This is the union of Adam, the son of God, and Eve, whom God brought to him. Paul explains this amazing type by using the same words as are found in the fifty-fifth verse of the Bible. He does so in the tenth (5 x 2) book of the New Testament, Ephesians, in the fifth chapter.

> For this cause shall a man leave his father and mother, and shall be joined unto his wife, and they two shall be one flesh. This is a great **mystery**: but I speak concerning **Christ and the church.**
>
> —Ephesians 5:31–32

In the twenty-fifth (5 x 5) chapter of the New Testament, Matthew 25, Jesus tells us of the parable of the five wise virgins and the five foolish ones. The five wise virgins await the coming of the Bridegroom Jesus, with their lamps trimmed and full of oil (the Holy Spirit). The five foolish ones are without oil. The oil is readily available to them, but they cannot depend on others to give it to them, they must acquire it from the source, God. In verse ten, the Bridegroom comes and receives the five wise virgins, but shuts the door and rejects the five foolish ones. This is a picture of those who will be taken in the Rapture, and those who are left behind.

In 1 Samuel 25 (5 x 5) we have the story of Abigail who is married to Nabal, a son of Belial, and the enemy of David. When Abigail revealed to Nabal that David sought to kill him, God smote him and his heart became as a stone. Here, once again, the Stone is responsible for destroying His enemies. Ten days later, he died, which freed Abigail to remarry according to the law (Romans 7:3). Abigail went after David (type of Christ) to marry him, accompanied by her five damsels (vs. 42).

Let's look now at Enoch. He is the seventh from Adam, being part of the lineage of death that was mentioned earlier from Genesis 5. There is, of course, one noticeable difference about Enoch. He does not die. The fifth time Enoch is mentioned it says, "And all the days of Enoch were three hundred sixty and five years: And Enoch walked with God: and he was not; for God took him" (Genesis 5:23–24). The only other place in the Bible that it speaks of Enoch being taken to heaven by God without seeing death is in Hebrews 11:5. Here is what it says.

> By faith Enoch was translated that he should not see death; and was not found, because God had translated him: for before his translation he had this testimony, that he pleased God.

As many have pointed out, the word Rapture is not in the Bible. The book of Hebrews uses the word "translate" to describe what took place with Enoch. It follows the pattern of the number five to note that this word is used exactly five times in the Scriptures. It says that Enoch was translated by faith. The word "faith" is mentioned exactly two hundred forty-five (49 x 5) times in the New Testament.

Earlier, we saw from the book of Daniel that the fifth Stone kingdom of Jesus was symbolized as a "great mountain." It is obvious to the reader of the Bible that many of the great things that God has done have taken place on a mountain. These are figurative of the kingdom of God. Isaiah 2:2 refers to the "mountain of the LORD's house" being established in the last days. With this in mind, please notice the exact language of the following verse and its relationship between the gathering of God's elect and the number five. This is the first verse of the fifth chapter of the New Testament.

> And seeing the multitudes, he went up into a mountain: and when
> he was set, his disciples came unto him.
>
> —Matthew 5:1

Along with this we might also look at Psalm 50:5.

> Gather my saints together unto me; those that have made a cove-
> nant with me by sacrifice.

Now we turn our attention to Matthew 24. It was here that Jesus
gave us a glimpse of what the future would hold, and described various signs of His Second Coming. It was here that Jesus told us that
His coming would be "As the days of Noe were. . . ." You may notice
that in the King James Bible that in a few instances, Noah's name is
spelled "Noe." I will just simply mention here that it is spelled this
way exactly five times.

> But as the days of Noe were, so shall also the coming of the Son of
> man be. For as in the days that were before the flood they were
> eating and drinking, marrying and giving in marriage, until the day
> that Noe entered into the ark.
>
> —Matthew 24:37–38

> Which was the son of Cainan, which was the son of Arphaxad, which
> was the son of Sem, which was the son of Noe, which was the son
> of Lamech.
>
> —Luke 3:36

> And as it was in the days of Noe, so shall it be also in the days of the
> Son of man. They did eat, they drank, they married wives, they were
> given in marriage, until the day that Noe entered into the ark, and
> the flood came, and destroyed them all.
>
> —Luke 17:26–27

It is interesting that in four of the five instances of this pattern, it
points us directly to the "days" of Noe. From Genesis 7 we find that
from the time that the rains began to descend, the "seventeenth day

of the second month," to the time the ark rested on the mountain of Ararat, on the "seventeenth day of the seventh month," was exactly five months. This would be a literal interpretation of what Jesus said in the New Testament, and would follow the same pattern of the number five that we have seen so far.

Seeing, as we have so far, that the Rapture is closely associated with the number five, we also can now clearly see *why* the Rapture of the Gentile church is associated with this number. As we learned, the number five is associated with the victory that Christ gained over all His enemies, Death being the final one, by His sacrificial death on the cross of Calvary. The generation that is still alive at His glorious appearing in the clouds will not see death, but will be translated into heaven to ever be with the Lord. This seems to be what is portrayed by the five-month boat ride Noah and his family made. While God was busy destroying all flesh by water, Noah, his family and the animals on the ark did not see death and stepped out of the ark into a new world in Genesis 8.

The same could be said of Joshua and Caleb. From the previous chapter of this book, we learned that all of Israel (save Joshua and Caleb), including Moses, died before entering into the land of promise. Joshua and Caleb, two witnesses that seemed to be associated with the time of the Gentiles (see the chapter on the number two), actually make it through the fifth book of the Bible, Deuteronomy, and live in the Promised Land.

The final passage that we will look at concerning the Rapture is found in 2 Kings 2. Here we have the story of Elijah and Elisha. Again, let's look at the Scriptures.

> And fifty men of the sons of the prophets went, and stood to view afar off: and they two stood by Jordan. And Elijah took his mantle, and wrapped it together, and smote the waters, and they were divided hither and thither, so that they two went over on dry ground. And it came to pass, when they were gone over, that Elijah said unto Elisha, Ask what I shall do for thee, before I be taken away from thee. And Elisha said, I pray thee, let a **double portion of thy**

spirit be upon me. And he said, Thou hast asked a hard thing: nevertheless, if thou see me when I am taken from thee, it shall be so unto thee; but if not, it shall not be so. And it came to pass, as they still went on, and talked, that, behold, there appeared a chariot of fire, and horses of fire, and parted them both asunder; and Elijah went up by a whirlwind into heaven.

—2 Kings 2:7–11

In this we have a perfect picture of the various themes we have seen so far. Elijah escapes the grasp of death because of his walk with God and is translated into heaven by way of a whirlwind. We see the number five in the fifty sons of the prophets that are witnesses to this magnificent event. Elisha is going to have the kingdom and the ministry of Elijah translated to him by way of the mantle that fell from Elijah. For this office, Elisha is going to need the power of God's Spirit on him. The double portion of this Spirit represents the second mighty outpouring of God's Spirit that will be poured out on Israel in the latter days. If you will notice, the number of prophets that view this event is the exact number of days that passed from the Passover when Christ was crucified to the day of Pentecost, fifty, when the Holy Spirit was poured out to the disciples in Acts 2. Do you remember what the disciples heard as this event took place? It would seem that they were hearing the rushing, mighty whirlwind of the Rapture as the Holy Spirit was poured out to them.

The presence of this number fifty in association with the Rapture and the outpouring of the Holy Spirit on Israel in the last days points us directly to the year of Jubilee, which was to take place every fifty years. We find this teaching in Leviticus 25 (5 x 5).

And thou shalt number seven sabbaths of years unto thee, seven times seven years; and the space of the seven sabbaths of years shall be unto thee forty and nine years. Then shalt thou cause the **trumpet** of the jubilee to sound on the tenth day of the seventh month, in the day of atonement shall ye make the **trumpet sound** throughout all your land. And ye shall hallow the **fiftieth** year, and proclaim **liberty** throughout all the land unto all the inhabitants thereof: it shall be a jubilee unto you; and ye shall return every man unto his possession, and ye shall return every man unto his family. A jubilee shall that fiftieth year be unto you: ye shall not sow, neither reap that which groweth of itself in it, nor gather the grapes in it of thy vine undressed. For it is the jubilee; it shall be holy unto you: ye shall eat the increase thereof out of the field. In the year of this jubilee ye shall return every man unto his possession.

—Leviticus 25:8–13

Notice that the event that signals the beginning of the Jubilee year is a trumpet blast. Surely, the Rapture of the Gentile church will send a signal to Israel that their time is at hand, and God will do all His good will to them. The main theme of this Jubilee is mentioned in verse ten, that of proclaiming liberty throughout the land of Israel. The word "liberty" is mentioned in twenty-five (5 x 5) verses of the Bible. This is what Christ came to proclaim to Israel at His first coming in Isaiah 61:1. In Exodus 34, the Bible reveals that as Moses came down from Mount Sinai the second time (figurative of Christ's second coming) his face shown so much so that they had to put a veil over it. Second Corinthians 3:14–15 tells us that every time the Jews read the Old Testament, the veil of Moses is still there, hiding who is really underneath it.

Verses sixteen and seventeen reveal, "Nevertheless when it shall turn to the Lord, the vail shall be taken away. Now the Lord is that Spirit: and where the Spirit of the Lord is, there is liberty." When the Spirit of the Lord is poured out unto Israel, the veil will be lifted and they will recognize Jesus as their real Lawgiver.

By understanding these and many other various symbols in the Bible, the Scriptures are clear as to the nature of the Rapture. The Rapture will most assuredly take place as a result of the completion of the Gentile age, and the mission work of the Church being accomplished. As we, the Church, are translated to heaven on that glorious day, God will begin His seven-year process of restoring Israel to her inheritance, filling her with His Spirit, and saving her with the gospel of Jesus Christ.

The Number Six

Many of the various numbers in the Bible seem to be very closely related to measurements of time and specific time prophecies. That God not only reveals what He is going to perform throughout the pages of the Scriptures, but also when He is going to do them, is evident. Many of the numbers that we examine in this book deal specifically with time prophecies; the principle being that what God is going to do, in accordance with a particular number is directly related to the specific time period that He is going to do it in. These numerical time prophecies are given as numbers of years, length of days or years, certain months of the year, certain days of the month, specific days of the week, and even hours in a day. In the previous chapters of this book, we have taken note of certain time prophecies that relate to the theme of the number given. An example of this would be that since the number three represented Divine completion and resurrection, then this is precisely why Christ was resurrected on the third day from His death, and why we could expect the resurrection of dead Israel on the third day of prophetic time (one day = one thousand years).

Such is the case with the number six. We will examine the various themes that are commonly associated with the number six, and we will also see a new understanding of this number and its relation to Bible time prophecies.

The number six and man

The number six seems to be consistently linked with man or mankind. The Scriptures reveal to us that it was on the sixth day that man was created (Genesis 1:26–31). The sixth time the word "man" is mentioned is found in Genesis 2:8, and tells that God put man in the garden of Eden. Eden is mentioned six times in the book of Genesis. The word "man" is mentioned one thousand, seven hundred and forty-six (6 x 291) times in the Old Testament. The word "mankind" is mentioned exactly six times in the whole Bible. Beginning in Genesis 2:23, you will find "Man" with a capital M exactly twelve (6 x 2) times in the Scriptures. The word "man" is mentioned six times in Genesis 6. It is also mentioned six times in Joshua 6, 2 Chronicles 6, Romans 6, and Galatians 6.

Jesus' most common title, and seemingly His favorite was *Son of Man*. He referred to himself this way eighty-four (6 x 14) times in the Gospels. In the whole of the New Testament, this phrase is mentioned eighty-eight times, but in eighty-four verses. His name of *JESUS*, in all capital letters, is mentioned exactly six times. The phrase "behold the man" is mentioned exactly six times in the Bible. Here is the sixth time it is mentioned.

> Then came Jesus forth, wearing the crown of thorns, and the purple robe. And Pilate saith unto them, Behold the man!
>
> —John 19:5

When Paul explained to Timothy the ministry of Christ's first coming, he described six things that Jesus did as the Man.

> And without controversy great is the mystery of godliness: God was (1) **manifest in the flesh**, (2) **justified in the Spirit**, (3) **seen of angels**, (4) **preached unto the Gentiles**, (5) **believed on in the world**, (6) **received up into glory**.
>
> —1 Timothy 3:16

The sixth commandment declares, "Thou shalt not kill." This is in reference to the murder of a man. You will also find this same commandment in Genesis 9:**6**.

> Whoso sheddeth man's blood, by man shall his blood be shed: for in the image of God made he man.
>
> —Genesis 9:6

Abel was the first man on the earth to die. He was murdered by his own brother, Cain. The sixth time Abel is mentioned in the Bible is in the following verse.

> And Cain talked with Abel his brother: and it came to pass, when they were in the field, that Cain rose up against Abel his brother, and slew him.
>
> —Genesis 4:8

The number six and the Beast

> Here is wisdom. Let him that hath understanding count the number of the beast: for it is the number of a man; and his number is six **hundred threescore and six.**
>
> —Revelation 13:18

It has long been contemplated, the meaning of the enigmatic 666 and its complete relationship to the identity of the Beast of Revelation 13. What we will examine in this section is not a definitive understanding, but rather a few more pieces to the puzzle.

The first puzzle piece is found in Genesis 6.

> And it came to pass, when men began to multiply on the face of the earth, and daughters were born unto them, That the sons of God saw the daughters of men that they were fair; and they took them wives of all which they chose. And the LORD said, My spirit shall not always strive with man, for that he also is flesh: yet his days shall be an hundred and twenty years. There were giants in the earth in those days; and also after that, when the sons of God came

in unto the daughters of men, and they bare children to them, the same became mighty men which were of old, men of renown.

—Genesis 6:1-4

A lengthy argument as to the proper identification of the "sons of God" will not be presented here. Suffice it to say that there is no instance in the Old Testament that this phrase ever referred to any person or group other than the angels of heaven. This mingling between the angelic and the human represented an abomination to God and produced a race of men on earth known as the giants. The idea that the Antichrist would somehow be associated with the idea of Satan or some other fallen angel mating with a human woman and producing a mixed offspring is supported by such titles given in the Bible as "son of Belial" (1 Samuel 25:17), "child of the devil" (Acts 13:10), "son of perdition" (John 17:12; 2 Thessalonians 2:3), and Cain, who was "of that wicked one" (1 John 3:12). It may also be seen as the ultimate form of blasphemy: the idea that Mary conceived Christ by way of the Holy Spirit being copied by Satan performing a similar act to produce Antichrist. This of course is only speculation; however, there does seem to be a numerical connection between the giants and the person of Antichrist.

It is in Genesis 6 that we see these giants first making an appearance. The most famous of the giants is, of course, Goliath. You will find Goliath mentioned exactly six times in the Scriptures. Goliath stands just over six cubits tall. His spear head weighed six hundred shekels of iron (1 Samuel 17:4–7). In Revelation 13, John describes the Antichrist in the following manner.

And the beast which I saw was like unto a leopard, and his feet were as the feet of a bear, and his mouth as the mouth of a lion: and the dragon gave him his power, and his seat, and great authority.

—Revelation 13:2

Now notice how David described his upcoming defeat over Goliath.

> Thy servant slew both the lion and the bear: and this uncircum-
> cised Philistine shall be as one of them, seeing he hath defied
> the armies of the living God.
>
> —1 Samuel 17:36

John also describes the Antichrist in Revelation 13 as having a mouth that spoke great blasphemies, and he seeks to make war with the saints of God. This Goliath also does by cursing David by his gods, and defying the armies of the living God. We also take note of the exact order and circumstances by which Goliath was defeated.

> And David put his hand in his bag, and took thence a stone, and
> slang it, and smote the Philistine in his forehead, that the stone
> sunk into his forehead; and he fell upon his face to the earth. So
> David prevailed over the Philistine with a sling and with a stone,
> and smote the Philistine, and slew him; but there was no sword in
> the hand of David. Therefore David ran, and stood upon the Philis-
> tine, and took his sword, and drew it out of the sheath thereof,
> and slew him, and cut off his head therewith. And when the Phi-
> listines saw their champion was dead, they fled.
>
> —1 Samuel 17:49–51

In Revelation 13, John describes the beast he sees as having seven heads and ". . . one of his heads as it were wounded to death; and his deadly would was healed . . ." (Revelation 13:3). Goliath also received a deadly head wound, but the Scriptures are sure to indicate that there was still a final defeat that must take place over Goliath. David, who had no sword of his own, uses Goliath's own sword to take his head off, killing him for good. In relation to this, Revelation 13 also tells us, "He that leadeth into captivity shall go into captivity: he that killeth with the sword must be killed with the sword. Here is the patience and the faith of the saints" (Revelation 13:10).

As the beast of Revelation 13 had seven heads, so there are seven giants specifically referred to in the Scriptures. These giants are list-ed below.

1. Og, the king of the giants (Deuteronomy 3:10)
2. Goliath
3. Ishbibenob, a brother of Goliath (2 Samuel 21:16)
4. Saph or Sippai, a brother of Goliath (2 Samuel 21:18; 1 Chronicles 20:4)
5. An Egyptian of great stature, killed with his own spear (1 Chronicles 11:23)
6. Lahmi, a brother of Goliath (1 Chronicles 20:5)
7. Man of great stature, a brother of Goliath, had six fingers on each hand and six toes on each foot (1 Chronicles 20:6)

Finally, in Revelation 13, we see that the False Prophet causes all the people of the earth to build an image of the first beast that John saw.

> And deceiveth them that dwell on the earth by the means of those miracles which he had power to do in the sight of the beast; saying to them that dwell on the earth, that they should make an image to the beast, which had the wound by a sword, and did live. And he had power to give life unto the image of the beast, that the image of the beast should both speak, and cause that as many as would not worship the image of the beast should be killed.
>
> —Revelation 13:14–15

This is identical to the passage in the book of Daniel in which Nebuchadnezzer erects an image in the plain of Dura and causes his entire kingdom to fall and worship it or they will lose their life. The call to worship this image was brought on by the playing of six instruments (Daniel 3:7). The exact dimensions for this image are given for us.

> Nebuchadnezzar the king made an image of gold, whose height was **threescore cubits**, and the breadth thereof **six cubits**: he set it up in the plain of Dura, in the province of Babylon.
>
> —Daniel 3:1

The number six
and the preparation for the coming of Christ

By far, the most significant prophetic theme associated with the number six is the theme of *preparation* for the coming of Jesus Christ to the earth. As with the meanings of all the numbers we will examine in this book, our primary source for the meaning of a number comes from its corresponding Genesis chapter. When we look once again to Genesis 6, here is what we find.

> Make thee an ark of gopher wood; rooms shalt thou make in the ark, and shalt pitch it within and without with pitch.
>
> —Genesis 6:14

God instructs Noah to begin to make preparations for the coming flood that is going to take place in Genesis 7. Noah did just as the Lord commanded him to. He did so until he was **six hundred** years old.

> And Noah was six hundred years old when the flood of waters was upon the earth.
>
> —Genesis 7:6

Jesus warned us that His coming would be directly connected to the *days of Noah*. In fact, we find exactly six references in the Scriptures connected to the preparation *days of Noah*.

> And all the **days of Noah** were nine hundred and fifty years: and he died.
>
> —Genesis 9:29

> But as the **days of Noe** were, so shall also the coming of the Son of man be. For as in the days that were before the flood they were eating and drinking, marrying and giving in marriage, until **the day that Noe** entered into the ark.
>
> —Matthew 24:37–38

And as it was in the **days of Noe**, so shall it be also in the days of
the Son of man. They did eat, they drank, they married wives, they
were given in marriage, until the **day that Noe** entered into the
ark, and the flood came, and destroyed them all.

—Luke 17:26–27

Which sometime were disobedient, when once the longsuffering of
God waited in the **days of Noah**, while the **ark was a preparing**,
wherein few, that is, eight souls were saved by water.

—1 Peter 3:20

It is noted that the dimensions of the ark, three hundred by fifty by
thirty cubits, give us an area of four hundred fifty thousand square
cubits, a number divisible by six. It is also important to note that the
ark of Noah is specifically mentioned exactly thirty times (6 x 5) in
the Scriptures.

The sixth time the phrase "God said" is found, is in Genesis 1:20–
21 when the Scriptures tell that God made *great whales* in the ocean.
Jesus said that it was a whale that swallowed Jonah (Matthew 12:40).
The following verse describes how this happened.

Now the LORD had **prepared** a great fish to swallow up Jonah. And
Jonah was in the belly of the fish **three days and three nights** [a
total of **six** time periods].

—Jonah 1:17

In the book of Revelation, we have three sets of events taking place:
the opening of the seven-sealed book, the blowing of seven trumpets,
and the pouring out of seven vials of wrath. When we look at the
sixth phase of each event, we see that they are associated with the
theme of preparation.

And I beheld when he had opened the **sixth seal**, and, lo, there was
a great earthquake; and the sun became black as sackcloth of hair,
and the moon became as blood.

—Revelation 6:12

The book of Joel reveals to us that this is the event that prepares the great and terrible day of the Lord.

> The sun shall be turned into darkness, and the moon into blood, before the great and the terrible day of the LORD come.
>
> —Joel 2:31

In both the sixth trumpet and the sixth vial we can clearly see that they are used as preparatory.

> And the **sixth angel** sounded, and I heard a voice from the four horns of the golden altar which is before God, Saying to the sixth angel which had the trumpet, Loose the four angels which are bound in the great river Euphrates. And the four angels were loosed, **which were prepared** for an hour, and a day, and a month, and a year, for to slay the third part of men.
>
> —Revelation 9:13–15

> And the **sixth angel** poured out his vial upon the great river Euphrates; and the water thereof was dried up, that **the way of the kings of the east might be prepared**.
>
> —Revelation 16:12

The sixth book of the Bible is the book of Joshua. The name of Joshua is mentioned two hundred sixteen (6 x 6 x 6) times in the Bible, including Joshua 6:6. This book is divided into twenty-four (6 x 4) chapters. The theme of this book is the conquests of Joshua and the armies of Israel over the wicked Canaanites, including the six-day march around Jericho in preparation for the seventh and final day, which is mentioned in chapter six. All of these things were done in preparation for the tribes of Israel to receive their portion of the promised land. This theme is spelled out for us in the first chapter of Joshua.

> Pass through the host, and command the people, saying, **Prepare** you victuals; for within three days ye shall pass over this Jordan, to

go in to possess the land, which the LORD your God giveth you to
possess it.

—Joshua 1:11

The word "prepare" is mentioned in seventy-eight (6 x 13) verses of
the Bible. When we look at this word in the plain text of the Scriptures, we find several very interesting things. First, in Exodus 16:5,
Israel is told to gather the manna for six days, and on the sixth day,
they are told to gather twice as much and prepare it for the seventh
day. Exodus 16 is the sixty-sixth chapter of the Bible. In Leviticus 25,
Israel is told to plant crops for six years and rest on the seventh year.
On the sixth year, God would prepare enough at harvest time to see
them through the sabbath year. In 1 Chronicles 9:32, the sons of the
Kohathites were employed to prepare the shewbread in the Temple
before the sabbath day, on the sixth day. This shewbread was laid out
in two rows of six loaves. In Isaiah 21:5, the word "prepare" is first in
a list of six things.

(1) Prepare the table, (2) watch in the watchtower, (3) eat, (4) drink:
(5) arise, ye princes, and (6) anoint the shield.

There are also exactly six verses in the Bible that specifically point to
a *day of preparation*. In the biblical week, this would have been the
preparation day before the Sabbath.

The shield of his mighty men is made red, the valiant men are in
scarlet: the chariots shall be with flaming torches in the **day of his**
preparation, and the fir trees shall be terribly shaken.

—Nahum 2:3

Now the next day, that followed the **day of the preparation**, the
chief priests and Pharisees came together unto Pilate.

—Matthew 27:62

And now when the even was come, because it was the **preparation**,
that is, the day before the sabbath.

—Mark 15:42

And that day was the preparation, and the sabbath drew on.

—Luke 23:54

The Jews therefore, because it was the preparation, that the bodies should not remain upon the cross on the sabbath day, (for that sabbath day was an high day,) besought Pilate that their legs might be broken, and that they might be taken away. . . . There laid they Jesus therefore because of the Jews' preparation day; for the sepulchre was nigh at hand.

—John 19:31,42

What we see in the verses from the New Testament is that the preparation day was the sixth day of the week, or Friday. The phrase "sixth day" is mentioned six times in the Bible. This is the day of Christ's crucifixion at Calvary. What is interesting is the way God incorporated two of the themes of the number six: the theme of preparation and the theme of killing an innocent man, i.e. the sixth commandment and Genesis 9:6. Although Jesus laid down His life willingly, it is also clear from the Scriptures that He was murdered unjustly by wicked people. The Scriptures also warn us that there is a curse upon those who do not wish to regard with reverence the shed blood of Jesus.

Whoso sheddeth man's blood, by man shall his blood be shed: for in the image of God made he man.

—Genesis 9:6

For as often as ye eat this bread, and drink this cup, ye do shew the Lord's death till he come. Wherefore whosoever shall eat this bread, and drink this cup of the Lord, unworthily, shall be guilty of the body and blood of the Lord.

—1 Corinthians 11:26–27

We also see these two themes brought together through the account given to us in the gospel of John.

> And it was the preparation of the passover, and about the sixth hour: and he saith unto the Jews, Behold your King! But they cried out, Away with him, away with him, crucify him. Pilate saith unto them, Shall I crucify your King? The chief priests answered, We have no king but Caesar.
>
> —John 19:14–15

The things that God performed in the person of Jesus Christ are mentioned for us in 1 Timothy. There are six things listed.

> And without controversy great is the mystery of godliness: (1) God was manifest in the flesh, (2) justified in the Spirit, (3) seen of angels, (4) preached unto the Gentiles, (5) believed on in the world, (6) received up into glory.
>
> —1 Timothy 3:16

You might notice that there doesn't seem to be any visible connection between these six things and the theme of preparation. However, if we were to notice the sixth thing Jesus did, being received up into glory, we just might remember what Jesus Himself told us as to exactly why He was leaving this earth.

> In my Father's house are many mansions: if it were not so, I would have told you. I go to prepare a place for you. And if I go and prepare a place for you, I will come again, and receive you unto myself; that where I am, there ye may be also.
>
> —John 14:2–3

The sixth act of Jesus, returning to heaven, is done to make ready a place for us to dwell with Him. This is in preparation for the seventh thing that Christ will perform, His return to this world to receive His disciples unto him. We also see this same pattern displayed for us in the gospel of Luke.

> And there was delivered unto him the book of the prophet Esaias. And when he had opened the book, he found the place where it was

written, The Spirit of the Lord is upon me, because he hath anointed me to (1) preach the gospel to the poor; (2) he hath sent me to
heal the brokenhearted, (3) to preach deliverance to the captives,
(4) and recovering of sight to the blind, (5) to set at liberty them
that are bruised, (6) To preach the acceptable year of the Lord. And
he closed the book, and he gave it again to the minister, and sat
down. And the eyes of all them that were in the synagogue were
fastened on him. And he began to say unto them, This day is this
scripture fulfilled in your ears.

—Luke 4:17–21

More details of this fascinating story are given in other chapters in
this book. For now, notice that Jesus reads a portion of the book of
Isaiah, and proclaims that God has sent Him to perform six things.
He then closes the book and reveals to the world that this particular
Scripture is fulfilled. However, when we look at the passage in Isaiah,
we find that He not only proclaims the acceptable year of the Lord,
but also comes to proclaim something else, a seventh item.

The spirit of the Lord GOD is upon me; because the LORD hath anointed me to preach good tidings unto the meek; he hath sent me to
bind up the brokenhearted, to proclaim liberty to the captives, and
the opening of the prison to them that are bound; To proclaim the
acceptable year of the LORD, **and the day of vengeance of our
God**; to comfort all that mourn.

—Isaiah 61:1–2

It was at this very point that Jesus closed the book, to show that the
proclamation of the day of vengeance of God was not given yet. This
proclamation will come in the last days when the Book is opened
once again by Jesus Himself.

In Matthew 17:1–8, we find that there are six days that lead up to
the transfiguration of Jesus Christ (vs. 1). There are also six people
present at this event: Jesus, Peter, James, John, Moses and Elijah.

In Matthew 25, we find that there are six things that the sheep and the goats either do or don't do in order to be separated into their respective prepared places.

> Then shall the King say unto them on his right hand, Come, ye blessed of my Father, inherit the kingdom **prepared** for you from the foundation of the world: (1) For I was an hungred, and ye gave me meat: (2) I was thirsty, and ye gave me drink: (3) I was a stranger, and ye took me in: (4) Naked, and ye clothed me: (5) I was sick, and ye visited me: (6) I was in prison, and ye came unto me.
>
> —Matthew 25:34–36

In Ephesians **6**, we see that there are exactly six things that a Christian should arm himself with in preparation for war against the devil.

> Stand therefore, (1) having your loins girt about with truth, (2) and having on the breastplate of righteousness; And (3) your feet shod with the **preparation** of the gospel of peace; Above all, (4) taking the shield of faith, wherewith ye shall be able to quench all the fiery darts of the wicked. And (5) take the helmet of salvation, (6) and the sword of the Spirit, which is the word of God.
>
> —Ephesians 6:14–17

Since we have seen several significant associations with the first advent of Christ and the number six, it is very interesting then to see that the King James translators have written Jesus' name in all capital letters exactly six times.

> And she shall bring forth a son, and thou shalt call his name JESUS: for he shall save his people from their sins. . . . And knew her not till she had brought forth her firstborn son: and he called his name JESUS.
>
> —Matthew 1:21,25

> And set up over his head his accusation written, THIS IS JESUS THE KING OF THE JEWS.
>
> —Matthew 27:37

And, behold, thou shalt conceive in thy womb, and bring forth a son, and shalt call his name JESUS.

—Luke 1:31

And when eight days were accomplished for the circumcising of the child, his name was called JESUS, which was so named of the angel before he was conceived in the womb.

—Luke 2:21

And Pilate wrote a title, and put it on the cross. And the writing was, JESUS OF NAZARETH THE KING OF THE JEWS.

—John 19:19

Jesus was our Lord's name when He came to earth as a *man* the first time. When He comes the second time, He will be called by a new name.

And I saw heaven opened, and behold a white horse; and he that sat upon him was called **Faithful and True**, and in righteousness he doth judge and make war. His eyes were as a flame of fire, and on his head were many crowns; and he had a name written, that no man knew, but he himself. And he was clothed with a vesture dipped in blood: and his name is called **The Word of God**.

—Revelation 19:11–13

In Isaiah 40 there are exactly six things mentioned in association with preparing the way for the coming of Jesus Christ.

The voice of him that crieth in the wilderness, **Prepare ye the way of the LORD**, make straight in the desert a highway for our God. (1) Every valley shall be exalted, and (2) every mountain and hill shall be made low: and (3) the crooked shall be made straight, and (4) the rough places plain: And (5) the glory of the LORD shall be revealed, and (6) all flesh shall see it together: for the mouth of the LORD hath spoken it.

—Isaiah 40:3–5

The above verse is a prophecy concerning the appearance of the prophet Elijah in the last days to proclaim and prepare the day of the coming of the Lord. In the New Testament of the Authorized Version, he is called *Elias*. He is given this name exactly thirty (6 x 5) times. Since God not only does things in a perfect order, but speaks them as well in a perfect order, this is why we find exactly six verses in the Scriptures that speak of Elijah preparing the way of the Lord.

> The voice of him that crieth in the wilderness, Prepare ye the way of the LORD, make straight in the desert a highway for our God.
>
> —Isaiah 40:3

> Behold, I will send my messenger, and he shall prepare the way before me: and the Lord, whom ye seek, shall suddenly come to his temple, even the messenger of the covenant, whom ye delight in: behold, he shall come, saith the LORD of hosts.
>
> —Malachi 3:1

> For this is he that was spoken of by the prophet Esaias, saying, The voice of one crying in the wilderness, Prepare ye the way of the Lord, make his paths straight.
>
> —Matthew 3:3

> The voice of one crying in the wilderness, Prepare ye the way of the Lord, make his paths straight.
>
> —Mark 1:3

> And thou, child, shalt be called the prophet of the Highest: for thou shalt go before the face of the Lord to prepare his ways.
>
> —Luke 1:76

> As it is written in the book of the words of Esaias the prophet, saying, The voice of one crying in the wilderness, Prepare ye the way of the Lord, make his paths straight.
>
> —Luke 3:4

At Jesus' first advent, John the Baptist was the *type* of the last days Elijah. His primary role in preparing the way for Christ, was to baptize him in preparation for Christ's ministry. It is the ordinance of baptism that prepares the Christian for service and a new walk in Christ. Again from the book of Joshua, the sixth book of the Bible, we see that Israel must once again be baptized in the Jordan River before entering into the Promised Land (Joshua 3). In the sixth book of the New Testament, the book of Romans, chapter six, we understand what baptism is all about.

> Know ye not, that so many of us as were baptized into Jesus Christ were baptized into his death? Therefore we are buried with him by baptism into death: that like as Christ was raised up from the dead by the glory of the Father, even so we also should walk in newness of life.
>
> —Romans 6:3–4

In 1 Samuel 7:3 the prophet Samuel compels a sinful Israel to prepare themselves to serve the Lord and put away all their idols. It is in verse six that the token of this covenant is given.

> And they gathered together to Mizpeh, and drew water, and poured it out before the LORD, and fasted on that day, and said there, We have sinned against the LORD. And Samuel judged the children of Israel in Mizpeh.
>
> —1 Samuel 7:6

In Mark 14 and Luke 22, Jesus instructs His disciples, who have asked Him about the preparation of the Passover, to go into Jerusalem where they will find a man bearing a pitcher of water. They are to follow this man who, ". . . will shew you a large upper room furnished and prepared: there make ready for us" (Mark 14:15).

This brings us to a greater understanding of a very important miracle that Jesus performed. This miracle has everything to do with the salvation of Israel in the last days. Notice exactly what the Scriptures reveal.

And the third day there was a marriage in Cana of Galilee; and the
mother of Jesus was there: And both Jesus was called, and his disciples, to the marriage. And when they wanted wine, the mother of
Jesus saith unto him, **They have no wine.** Jesus saith unto her,
Woman, what have I to do with thee? mine hour is not yet come.
His mother saith unto the servants, Whatsoever he saith unto you,
do it. And there were set there **six waterpots** of stone, after the
manner of the **purifying of the Jews**, containing two or three fir-
kins apiece. Jesus saith unto them, **Fill the waterpots with water.**
And they filled them up to the brim. And he saith unto them, Draw
out now, and bear unto the governor of the feast. And they bare it.
When the ruler of the feast had tasted **the water that was made
wine**, and knew not whence it was: (but the servants which drew
the water knew;) the governor of the feast called the bridegroom,
And saith unto him, Every man at the beginning doth set forth good
wine; and when men have well drunk, then that which is worse: but
thou hast kept the good wine until now.

—John 2:1–10

As we will clearly see in the chapter on the number twenty-two, wine,
especially new or good wine, is a symbol of the Holy Spirit. Since
these six waterpots are for the cleansing of the Jews, we see that as
the water was turned into wine, thus will God purify and cleanse
Israel in the last days in preparation for them receiving the gift of the
Holy Spirit, prophesied in Ezekiel 37 and other places. God will literally turn the water of baptism into the wine of the Holy Spirit.

The Number Seven

If there is to be one, quintessential number in the Scriptures that contains the very essence of God and His Word, it would have to be the number seven. Because of its many uses throughout Scripture, there is never any doubt in the mind of the scholar that the number seven represents perfection and completion. It is the number most often associated with God Himself.

God establishes these patterns in various ways. God established the measurement of time in a seven-day week (Genesis 2:2–3). The very words "week" or "weeks" are mentioned twenty-eight (7 x 4) times in the Scriptures. God used a measurement of weeks to determine the feast of weeks, or feast of Pentecost. This measurement was based upon a period of seven weeks, a total of forty-nine days (Deuteronomy 16:9–10). In the book of Daniel, we find the prophecy of the seventy weeks, a total of four hundred ninety days. In this prophecy, God declares that He will perform seven things.

> Seventy weeks are determined upon thy people and upon thy holy city, (1) to finish the transgression, and (2) to make an end of sins, and (3) to make reconciliation for iniquity, and (4) to bring in everlasting righteousness, and (5) to seal up the vision and (6) prophecy, and (7) to anoint the most Holy.
>
> —Daniel 9:24

In various places, God uses the measurement of years in conjunction with the number seven. Beginning in Genesis, we find that Jacob agreed to work seven years for the prize of Rachel, his first love (Genesis 29:18). In Genesis 41:29–30, Joseph reveals to Pharaoh a period of seven years of plenty in the land, followed by seven years of famine. It is this seven years of famine that seem to be a type of the seven years of great worldwide tribulation that shall come to the earth. It is during this seven years of famine that Joseph becomes the savior of his brethren, yet another type of Jesus becoming the Savior of Israel during the seven years of Tribulation.

It would appear that many of the uses of the number seven would indicate the seven-year period in which Jesus becomes the Lord and Savior of Israel in the last days, just prior to His thousand-year reign on the earth. In Genesis 33, Jacob bows himself to the ground seven times before his brother Esau. According to what we saw in the chapter on the number two, we saw how Jacob, a type of the Gentile church, received the blessing of Isaac before his older brother Esau, a type of the Jewish church. Esau received a similar blessing from Isaac, but Isaac declared that Esau would not receive this blessing until the yoke of the dominion of Jacob was removed. It would seem then that Jacob's bowing before Esau seven times indicates the seven years in which the Gentile church has been Raptured and now Israel can receive her full and complete blessing.

The same may also be said of the uses of the number seven in the tabernacle sacrifices. The high priest was directed to sprinkle the blood of the sin offering seven times on the altar and the Ark of the Covenant on the day of atonement according to Leviticus 16. The purpose of this seems to be clearly spelled out in the following verse. "And he shall sprinkle of the blood upon it with his finger **seven times**, and cleanse it, and hallow it from **the uncleanness of the children of Israel**" (Leviticus 16:19). Although Christ has fulfilled the actions of the high priest when He shed His blood on the altar of the cross, the primary recipients of this atonement, Israel, have not as a nation received this atonement, but have rejected it. It will be during these seven years, according to Daniel 9:24, that this will be accomplished.

And again, even the very words of Christ seem to speak of the same idea: that of the forgiveness of Israel during a seven-year period. When He spoke in Matthew 18 of forgiving His brother's sins, we can see the idea behind the seventy weeks of Daniel, and the sprinkling of blood seven times on the Ark of the Covenant.

> Then came Peter to him, and said, Lord, how oft shall my brother sin against me, and I forgive him? till **seven times**? Jesus saith unto him, I say not unto thee, Until seven times: but, Until seventy times seven.
>
> —Matthew 18:21–22

In Leviticus 25, a formula is given to determine the Jubilee year. God ordered Israel to measure seven times seven years, a total of forty-nine years. On the fiftieth year, liberty was proclaimed throughout the land, and all land that was taken from its original birthright owner was restored to its original owner. This Jubilee is a symbol of the future time when God will restore the land that He swore to Abraham.

The Seven-Sealed Book

> And I saw in the right hand of him that sat on the throne a book written within and on the backside, sealed with seven seals.
>
> —Revelation 5:1

Certainly much debate centers around this book, its contents, and its purpose. What I will present to you here is certainly not authoritative. However, as we have already seen, the exact language of the Bible is crucial to understanding certain symbols, and being able to tie them all together as far as meaning is concerned. The King James Bible, above all others, preserves these language clues, and this, among other reasons is why I recommend its use.

First, let's look at the numerical pattern that is associated with this book. In the Authorized Version, you will find the word *book* or *books* a total of *one hundred ninety-six* times. This number may not be apparently significant until you break it down. This equation is *49*

x 4 or 7 x 7 x 4. From the book *By Divine Order*, we find this association with that equation.

WORD OF GOD	49 TIMES
SON OF GOD	49 TIMES
MOST HIGH	49 TIMES
HOLY ONE	49 TIMES
PARABLES	49 TIMES
SON OF MAN	196 TIMES
JESUS CHRIST	196 TIMES
BOOK(S)	196 TIMES

There are several other significant numerical patterns that associate God's spoken and written Word with the number seven, showing both its perfection and completion. Our Savior was given the name of "Jesus" exactly nine hundred eighty (49 x 20) times in the Scriptures. The phrase "saith the lord" is used eight hundred fifty-four (7 x 122) times in the Bible. The word "word" is used in exactly one hundred ninety-six (49 x 4) verses in the New Testament. The words "words" or "word's" is used precisely ninety-eight (49 x 2) times in the New Testament. The phrase "every word" is spoken exactly seven times in the Bible, including the idea of "every word" that proceeds from the mouth of God (Deuteronomy 8:3; Matthew 4:4; Luke 4:4). Also all the forms of the words "speak," "spake," and "spoken" are found in the Authorized Version exactly one thousand, five hundred fifty-four times, which comes to 777 x 2!

There does seem to be a direct connection with the mentioning of *books* in the Bible, and the Word of God Himself, Jesus Christ. What we will look at in this section are the various places in the Scriptures where I believe the scriptures are referring to, and shedding light on this seven-sealed book and its contents.

To begin, let's take notice of the location of the book. It is in God's right hand. This is also where our Savior now sits in glory. Here again we see the biblical connection between Jesus and the Word of God, both of which are at the Father's right hand.

Jesus saith unto him, Thou hast said: nevertheless I say unto you, Hereafter shall ye see the *Son of man* sitting *on the right hand* of power, and *coming in the clouds of heaven.*

—Matthew 26:64

So then after the Lord had spoken unto them, he was received up into heaven, and *sat on the right hand of God.*

—Mark 16:19

Him hath *God exalted with his right hand* to be a Prince and a Saviour, for *to give repentance to Israel,* and forgiveness of sins.

—Acts 5:31

If ye then be risen with Christ, seek *those things which are above, where Christ sitteth on the right hand of God.*

—Colossians 3:1

Please notice, according to Acts 5:31, that the true purpose for Christ being at the right hand of the power of God, is so that He could grant forgiveness to *Israel.* Surely our God offers salvation to the Gentile world, but the primary gift of salvation was, and still is intended for the true seed of Abraham.

In the Scriptures, the *right hand* of God was used and mentioned in various ways. Since we now can clearly see the relationship that Jesus has with the *right hand* of God, let us once again turn to the pages of the Old Testament to see these awesome displays of God's power and authority performed by His *right hand,* Jesus Christ.

Thy *right hand,* O LORD, is become glorious in power: thy right hand, O LORD, *hath dashed in pieces the enemy.* . . . Thou stretchedst out thy *right hand,* the earth swallowed them. [*These verses are the Song that Moses sang after the dividing of the Red Sea.*]

—Exodus 15:6,12

And he said, The LORD came from Sinai, and rose up from Seir unto them; he shined forth from mount Paran, and he came with ten

thousands of saints: from his *right hand went a fiery law for them.*
[*This reveals that the Ten Commandments were written by God's right hand,
another connection between Christ and this book.*]

—Deuteronomy 33:2

Thou wilt shew me the path of life: in thy presence is fulness of joy;
at thy *right hand there are pleasures* for evermore.

—Psalm 16:11

Shew thy marvellous lovingkindness, O *thou that savest by thy right
hand* them which put their trust in thee from those that rise up
against them.

—Psalm 17:7

Thou hast also given me the shield of thy salvation: and thy *right
hand hath holden me up*, and thy gentleness hath made me great.

—Psalm 18:35

Now know I that the LORD saveth his anointed; he will hear him
from his holy heaven with the *saving strength of his right hand*.

—Psalm 20:6

Thine hand shall find out all thine enemies: *thy right hand shall
find out those that hate thee.*

—Psalm 21:8

For *they got not the land in possession* by their own sword, neither
did their own arm save them: *but thy right hand*, and thine arm, and
the light of thy countenance, because thou hadst a favour unto them.

—Psalm 44:3

According to thy name, O God, so is thy praise unto the ends of the
earth: thy *right hand is full of righteousness*. [*Both the word* Christ
and all the forms of the word righteousness *are found five hundred fifty-
five times in the KJV.*]

—Psalm 48:10

And he brought them to the border of his sanctuary, even to this
mountain, *which his right hand had purchased*.

—Psalm 78:54

Let *thy hand be upon the man of thy right hand*, upon the *son of man*
whom thou madest strong for thyself.

—Psalm 80:17

A Psalm. O sing unto the LORD a new song; for he hath done marvellous things: *his right hand*, and his holy arm, hath gotten him
the victory.

—Psalm 98:1

The Lord at thy *right hand* shall strike through kings in the *day of
his wrath*.

—Psalm 110:5

With the understanding that the *right hand* of God represents His
Son, Jesus, we can clearly understand from these verses how God
uses Him to put down all of His enemies and bring salvation to those
who desire it. All of these verses, and the many more not listed here,
speak of Christ's second coming.

In Revelation 5, a call goes out to find someone who is worthy to
open the *seven* seals that are on this *book*. These *seven* seals reveal to
us that this is in fact God's book, for *seven* is the number for completion and perfection, and we also see the scriptural reason why *book(s)*
are mentioned *one hundred ninety-six* times. No one can open the
seals, for no one is worthy. John begins to weep, as it seems that
there is no one to bridge the gap between God and man, until this
happens.

And one of the elders saith unto me, Weep not: behold, the *Lion of
the tribe of Juda, the Root of David*, hath prevailed to open the book,
and to loose the seven seals thereof. . . . And he came and *took the
book* out of the right hand of him that sat upon the throne.

—Revelation 5:5,7

Notice that it is in verse *seven* that Jesus takes the book out of God's right hand. What perfect placement for such a momentous and extraordinary event. Now Jesus, the Son of God, has been given everything that the Father has. It has been placed into His hand, and He alone is worthy to open and present the book. Notice what our Savior said about this event.

> *All things that the Father hath are mine*: therefore said I, that he shall take of mine, and shall shew it unto you. A little while, and ye shall not see me: and again, *a little while, and ye shall see me, because I go to the Father.*
>
> —John 16:15–16

> The Father loveth the Son, and hath given *all things into his hand.*
>
> —John 3:35

> Labour not for the meat which perisheth, but for that meat which endureth unto everlasting life, which the *Son of man shall give unto you*: for *him hath God the Father sealed.* . . . *All that the Father giveth me shall come to me*; and him that cometh to me I will in no wise cast out. For *I came down from heaven*, not to do mine own will, but the will of him that sent me. And this is the Father's will which hath sent me, that of *all which he hath given me I should lose nothing*, but should raise it up again at the last day. And this is the will of him that sent me, that every one which seeth the Son, and believeth on him, may have everlasting life: and I will raise him up at the last day.
>
> —John 6:27,37–40

> Jesus knowing that the *Father had given all things into his hands*, and that he was come from God, and went to God.
>
> —John 13:3

As you scan the various commentaries and prophecy books on this subject you will find a wide assortment of ideas concerning this seven-sealed book. Some say that it is the *Book of Life*, others say it is the title deed to the earth, and some say it is the book of Daniel. As I scanned the Scriptures for possible interpretations of this book, what I found is that this *book* represents many things; in fact, as you will see, this book represents *all things*. As we continue in this portion of our study, you will see the importance of this *book* and what it means for those who live in the last days.

One of the things that we notice about the book in Revelation 5 is that it has writing on both sides.

> And I saw in the right hand of him that sat on the throne *a book written within and on the backside*, sealed with seven seals.
>
> —Revelation 5:1

This book, written on both sides, has made a previous appearance in the Scriptures. Do you remember this story?

> And Moses turned, and went down from the mount, and the *two tables of the testimony* were *in his hand*: the tables were *written on both their sides; on the one side and on the other were they written*. And the tables were the work of God, and the *writing was the writing of God*, graven upon the tables.
>
> —Exodus 32:15–16

Of course we recognize one of the most important stories of the Scriptures, the giving of the Ten Commandments. And now, we are beginning to see what the *book* of Revelation 5 represents. The Ten Commandments symbolized God's divine authority over His people. It is the basis for establishing His reign over them. It was Moses who went up to God to receive the *book*, and likewise our Savior, after His resurrection, left this world to receive the *book* at the right hand of the Father. By the act of giving this *book* to Jesus, like Moses, Jesus now becomes the real Lawgiver, and is given the authority to lead His people into their promised inheritance.

These tables were not merely God's advice to mankind in the

form of the Ten Commandments. They were a token of the covenant that God had made with His people, Israel.

> And he gave unto Moses, when he had made an end of communing with him upon mount Sinai, *two tables of testimony*, tables of stone, written with the finger of God.
>
> —Exodus 31:18

> And he declared unto you *his covenant*, which he commanded you to perform, even *ten commandments*; and he wrote them upon two tables of stone.
>
> —Deuteronomy 4:13

Now let's look at another example of how this *book* is portrayed in the *Book of God*, the Holy Bible. Fitting with the theme of Christ putting down all of His enemies, we see that in Exodus 17, the *book* is mentioned in this fashion.

> And the LORD said unto Moses, Write this for a *memorial in a book*, and rehearse it in the ears of Joshua: for I will utterly put out the remembrance of Amalek from under heaven. And Moses built an altar, and called the name of it Jehovahnissi: For he said, Because the LORD hath sworn that the LORD will have war with Amalek from generation to generation.
>
> —Exodus 17:14–16

Because of their wickedness and unprovoked attack on Israel, Amalek became the arch enemy of Israel. In this story, we see that Moses sets himself on top of a mountain with the rod of God in his hand. This is a prefiguring of Christ who establishes the mountain of the Lord's house and rules with a *rod of iron* (Revelation 19:15). Amalek is figurative of Israel's enemies during the end times. God promised that He would eliminate Amalek for what they had done. In 1 Samuel 15, God commissioned Saul, the king of the Jews, to perform this task. However, Saul was unwilling to completely eliminate Amalek, and because of greed, left a remnant. Because of this, the Scriptures record that the kingdom was going to be taken away from Saul and given to another.

> And Samuel said unto Saul, I will not return with thee: for thou hast rejected the word of the LORD, and the LORD hath rejected thee from being king over Israel.
>
> —1 Samuel 15:26

It is at this time that Samuel was sent to anoint David as king of the Jews. We have a prophecy recorded for us in Ezekiel 37 that reveals to us who this new king is going to be.

> And *David* my servant shall be *king* over them; and they all shall have one *shepherd*: they shall also walk in my judgments, and observe my statutes, and do them. And *they shall dwell in the land* that I have given unto Jacob my servant, wherein your fathers have dwelt; and they shall dwell therein, even they, and their children, and their children's children for ever: and *my servant David shall be their prince for ever.*
>
> —Ezekiel 37:24–25

It is obvious that David the son of Jesse is not going to be reincarnated in the last days, but rather Jesus, the Son of David will assume his father's throne as King of the Jews. Notice what the Scriptures reveal in this matter.

> To *translate the kingdom from the house of Saul,* and to set up the *throne of David* over Israel and over Judah, from Dan even to Beersheba.
>
> —2 Samuel 3:10

> Their blood shall therefore return upon the head of Joab, and upon the head of his seed for ever: but upon David, and upon his seed, and upon his house, and upon *his throne,* shall there be peace *for ever* from the LORD.
>
> —1 Kings 2:33

And, behold, I purpose to build an house unto the name of the LORD my God, as the LORD spake unto David my father, saying, *Thy son, whom I will set upon thy throne in thy room, he shall build an house unto my name.*

—1 Kings 5:5

Then I will establish the *throne of thy kingdom upon Israel for ever*, as I promised to David thy father, saying, There shall not fail thee a man upon the throne of Israel. . . . Of the increase of his government and peace there shall be no end, *upon the throne of David*, and upon his kingdom, to order it, and to establish it with judgment and with justice from henceforth even for ever. The zeal of the LORD of hosts will perform this.

—1 Kings 9:5,7

He shall be great, and shall be called the Son of the Highest: and the Lord God shall give unto him the throne of his *father David*: And he shall reign over the house of Jacob for ever; and of his kingdom there shall be no end.

—Luke 1:32–33

As we saw in 1 Kings 5, there is a very interesting teaching about God's plan for the last days. It tells us in verse five that the Son of David will sit on David's throne and will build the house of the Lord. Notice that it does not mention Solomon as being the one who does this. Of course we realize that Solomon did actually build the first temple in Jerusalem, but the true fulfillment of this prophecy does not occur until Jesus, the true Son of David builds the House of God for His people. Do you remember how long it took Solomon to build this first temple?

And in the eleventh year, in the month Bul, which is the eighth month, was the house finished throughout all the parts thereof, and according to all the fashion of it. So was he *seven years in building it.*

—1 Kings 6:38

During the seven years of what is commonly called the Tribulation period, Christ gathers the remnant of Israel, who then become His true Temple.

> Now of the things which we have spoken this is the sum: We have such an high priest, who is set on the right hand of the throne of the Majesty in the heavens; A minister of the sanctuary, and of the *true tabernacle, which the Lord pitched, and not man.*
>
> —Hebrews 8:1–2

Since we are beginning to see the relationship between this *book* and the King of Israel, we add to this idea an interesting passage out of the book of Deuteronomy.

> When thou art *come unto the land* which the LORD thy God giveth thee, and shalt possess it, and shalt dwell therein, and shalt say, *I will set a king over me,* like as all the nations that are about me; Thou shalt in any wise *set him king over thee, whom the LORD thy God shall choose*: one from among thy brethren shalt thou set king over thee: thou mayest not set a stranger over thee, which is not thy brother. . . . And it shall be, when *he sitteth upon the throne of his kingdom, that he shall write him a copy of this law in a book* out of that which is before the priests the Levites: *And it shall be with him,* and he shall read therein all the days of his life: that he may learn to fear the LORD his God, *to keep all the words of this law and these statutes, to do them.*
>
> —Deuteronomy 17:14–19

This commandment was from God Himself. When the Israelites came into the Promised Land, and they wanted a king to rule over them, they were to let God choose the king. We, of course, see that God has chosen His Son to be their King. The main requirement for this King is that when He sits on the throne over His people, he must have the *book.* It is the only way that He can perform all the words that are contained in it. It is now obviously clear why Jesus must receive this book from the Father's right hand: he must perform everything the Father has sent Him to do as King of the Jews. Many kings ruled over Israel and Judah. Many of them failed miserably in performing the work of the Lord according to the *book*. At times, as we will see later, several of the kings discovered the *book*, and it caused revival to break out in the land. It was during these times that Israel was invincible as a nation, and God prospered them.

In the book of Joshua, we see this *book* used in this manner.

> And the men went and passed through the land, and described it by cities into *seven parts in a book*, and came again to Joshua to the host at Shiloh. And Joshua cast lots for them in Shiloh before the LORD: and there *Joshua divided the land* unto the children of Israel according to their divisions.
>
> —Joshua 18:9–10

In this story, there are *seven* of the tribes of Israel that have not yet received their *inheritance*. Joshua sends three from each of these tribes to survey the land, write their findings in a *book*, and from the *book*, Joshua divides the land among the tribes so that they may receive their inheritance from the Lord. This is one of the things that Jesus will accomplish at His second coming, in that He will restore the promises and the inheritance to Israel. Notice here again the correlation between the *book* and the number *seven*.

The very first king who was anointed over Israel was Saul. In 1 Samuel 10, we see that after Saul was anointed as king, God gave him a new heart and made a new man out of him; a man that, at least in the beginning, wanted to do the will of God as spoken to Samuel the prophet (vs. 6). Later in this same chapter, we find the following passage.

> And Samuel said to all the people, See ye *him whom the LORD hath chosen*, that there is *none like him among all the people*? And all the people *shouted*, and said, *God save the king*. Then Samuel told the people the *manner of the kingdom, and wrote it in a book, and laid it*

up before the LORD. And Samuel sent all the people away, every man
to his house. And Saul also went home to Gibeah; and there went
with him a band of men, whose hearts God had touched. But the
children of Belial said, How shall this man save us? And they despised him, and brought him no presents. But he held his peace.

—1 Samuel 10:24–27

The *"manner of the kingdom"* referred to in verse twenty-five symbolizes all that Christ must perform as King of the Jews, similar to the
passage in Deuteronomy 17. These things were written in the ***book***,
showing that this ***book***, given to Jesus by the Father, represents the
divine authority to rule over Israel.

Truly when Christ is the chosen King, there will be no one like
Him. Only the children of Belial, who are types of those who follow
Satan, reject him as King. There will, however, be one who wishes to
be like Christ, and he will convince the world that there is no one like
him.

And they worshipped the dragon which gave power unto the beast:
and they worshipped the beast, saying, *Who is like unto the beast?*
who is able to make war with him?

—Revelation 13:4

As we mentioned earlier, this ***book*** did actually make it into the hands
of several of the kings of Israel. One particular place is found in the
book of 2 Kings 22.

And Hilkiah the high priest said unto Shaphan the scribe, *I have
found the book* of the law in the house of the LORD. And Hilkiah
gave the book to Shaphan, and he read it.

—2 Kings 22:8

Notice that the *book* was hidden, and has now been found. Here we
have a biblical principle that applies.

For there is *nothing covered*, that shall not be *revealed*; neither *hid*, that shall not be *known*.

—Luke 12:2

The Scriptures are very clear. All things will be revealed in the last days. This directly speaks to the identity of the *book* that is in the hand of Jesus. We will deal more with this theme later on. Notice also that we find this *book* uncovered and revealed in 2 Kings 22. As we will see later, the number *twenty-two* is the number for *revelation*. This is the very theme of this chapter: the book of the law that is uncovered. Interestingly, you will find this book mentioned in this chapter *seven* times. When Josiah hears this book read, he understands that it speaks of the judgment of Jerusalem. In verse sixteen, notice what it says.

Thus saith the LORD, Behold, I will bring evil upon this place, and upon the inhabitants thereof, even *all the words of the book* which the king of Judah hath read.

—2 Kings 22:16

The Scriptures tell us that God will perform all the words that have come from His mouth, they will accomplish everything that they have been sent forth to do. That is why we are not to add to, nor take away from these words. Jesus, as the Word of God, will do just that: perform all the words that have been spoken by God. That is His true purpose. This is another piece to the puzzle of the *book*, its relationship to Jesus, and why it will be opened.

In 2 Chronicles, it is King Jehoshaphat that is in possession of the *book*.

And they taught in Judah, and *had the book of the law* of the LORD with them, and went about throughout all the cities of Judah, and *taught the people*. And the fear of the LORD fell upon all the kingdoms of the lands that were round about Judah, so that they made no war against Jehoshaphat. Also some of the Philistines brought

Jehoshaphat presents, and tribute silver; and the Arabians brought him flocks, *seven* thousand and *seven* hundred rams, and *seven* thousand and *seven* hundred he goats.

—2 Chronicles 17:9–11

As in the case with Josiah, we find that because of King Jehoshaphat's righteousness, he sent out various people to teach Judah the Word of God. As a direct result of this, the enemy nations of Judah were afraid to wage any kind of war against Judah, and even sent gifts to their longtime mortal enemy. Notice here again the connection between this *book* and the number *seven*.

Because there were so many kings of Israel and Judah that did not govern according to the *book* of the law of God, the people began to live in wickedness. It was for this reason that God dispersed the *ten* northern tribes into Assyria, and sent Judah into bondage in Babylon for *seventy* years. Please notice what God has done here. Remember that God is a God of divine order, and the devil is the father of chaos. As you examine the Scriptures, you will see this consistent theme. Notice that God took Israel and dispersed her (a form of disorder, chaos) into Assyria. He then sent Judah into Babylon (remember *Babel*, confusion?) and there they mingled with other peoples. However, in the last days, Christ will reclaim those Jews that have been dispersed all these years, and gather them together into *one* nation once again.

In the books of Ezra and Nehemiah this theme is portrayed as the Jews return from their *seventy*-year captivity in Babylon. It was Cyrus, the *king* of Persia that the Lord God raised up to bring down Babylon the Great and set free the children of Israel. Even in someone such as Cyrus, a Gentile king, we see an image of Christ and His second coming. Notice what God revealed to Isaiah about Cyrus.

That saith of *Cyrus, He is my shepherd*, and *shall perform all my pleasure*: even *saying to Jerusalem, Thou shalt be built; and to the temple, Thy foundation shall be laid.*

—Isaiah 44:28

Thus saith the LORD to *his anointed, to Cyrus*, whose *right hand* I have holden, to *subdue nations before him*; and I will loose the loins of kings, to open before him the two leaved gates; and the gates shall not be shut; I will go *before thee, and make the crooked places straight*: I will break in pieces the gates of brass, and cut in sunder the bars of iron: And I will give thee the treasures of darkness, and hidden riches of secret places, that thou mayest know that I, the LORD, which call thee by thy name, am the God of Israel. For Jacob my servant's sake, and Israel mine elect, *I have even called thee by thy name*: I have surnamed thee, though thou hast not known me.

—Isaiah 45:1–4

Looking at the very revealing clues that are given us in this passage, there can be no mistaking that Cyrus was a *type* of Christ. From verse twenty-eight we see that Cyrus, like Christ, is a *shepherd*, that he is going to perform all of God's will, and even pronouncing that Jerusalem and the Temple will be rebuilt! He is God's anointed, from where the word *messiah* comes from. He will subdue all the nations, and even before he comes, all the crooked places will be made straight, just exactly like the coming of Christ.

As the Jews made their way back into Jerusalem, they did indeed begin the task of rebuilding Jerusalem and the Temple. However, God made a pronouncement to them as they began the work of restoring the Temple of God.

The glory of this latter house shall be greater than of the former, saith the LORD of hosts: and in this place will I give peace, saith the LORD of hosts.

—Haggai 2:9

God promised that the *latter* house would be more glorified than the first Temple ever was. However, we know that this wasn't the case with this particular Temple. First, we do not have a record of the Glory of the Lord coming down to this Temple like it did in the days

of the Temple of Solomon. Secondly, a few very important furnish-
ings are missing from this second Temple, namely the Ark of the Covenant, the table of shewbread, and the menorah. Without these items,
each of which represent the three persons of the Godhead—Father,
Son, and Holy Spirit—there can be no real dwelling place for God
among His people. It is obvious, then, that God was referring to a
latter days Temple, that would be built by Jesus Himself, a Temple not
made with hands, the Temple of the body of Jewish believers in the
last days.

Along with the rebuilding of this Temple, God raised up several
men as leaders of the people during this time: Ezra, Nehemiah, Haggai, Zechariah, and Zerubbabel. I will not dwell on the various details
of each of these men, and their importance to the theme of Christ's
second coming. However, in the context of the theme of the *book* that
is in Christ's hand, let's look at a very interesting story about Ezra,
the scribe.

> And all the *people gathered* themselves together *as one man* into the
> street that was before the water gate; and they spake unto Ezra the
> scribe to *bring the book* of the law of Moses, which the LORD had
> commanded to Israel. And Ezra the priest brought the law before
> the congregation both of men and women, and all that could hear
> with understanding, upon the first day of the seventh month. And
> he read therein before the street that was before the water gate
> from the morning until midday, before the men and the women,
> and those that could understand; and the *ears of all the people were
> attentive* unto *the book* of the law. And Ezra the scribe stood upon a
> pulpit of wood, which they had made for the purpose; and beside
> him stood Mattithiah, and Shema, and Anaiah, and Urijah, and Hilki-
> ah, and Maaseiah, on his right hand; and on his left hand, Pedaiah,
> and Mishael, and Malchiah, and Hashum, and Hashbadana, Zecha-
> riah, and Meshullam. And *Ezra opened the book* in the sight of all
> the people; (for *he was above all the people*;) and when he opened it,
> *all the people stood up*: And Ezra blessed the LORD, the great God.
> And all the people answered, Amen, Amen, *with lifting up their*

hands: and they bowed their heads, and worshipped the LORD with
their faces to the ground.

—Nehemiah 8:1–6

Notice Ezra's *typological* actions as he **opened the book**. It is interesting that we find that immediately when the book is opened, the people began to worship the Lord. Such is the awesome power of the
Word of God, and specifically of the power of God through the Word.
In the last days, when Christ appears and opens this *book*, all those
who are His will truly worship Him and have the Word revealed to
them who used to walk in darkness.

In Jeremiah 30, we find that the *book* is directly related to the
gathering of Israel in the last days into the land of their inheritance.

Thus speaketh the LORD God of Israel, saying, Write thee all the
words that I have spoken unto thee in a *book.* For, lo, the days come,
saith the LORD, that I will **bring again the captivity of my people**
Israel and Judah, saith the LORD**: and I will cause them to return to**
the land that I gave to their fathers, and they shall possess it.

—Jeremiah 30:2–3

This also fits in with what we have seen so far. God will accomplish
the Words of His Book, and as the Son of God is revealed in the last
days, so also will His full and complete plan for the world and for
Israel be accomplished.

One of the most significant teachings that we have in the Bible
concerning this *book* is found in Jeremiah 32. Incidentally, this chapter is the **seven hundred seventy-seventh** chapter of the Bible. Here is a
very significant prophecy of the last days.

And I bought the field of Hanameel my uncle's son, that was in
Anathoth, and weighed him the money, even seventeen shekels of
silver. And I **subscribed the evidence, and sealed it,** and took witnesses, and weighed him the money in the balances. So I took the evidence of the purchase, both *that which was sealed* according to the

law and custom, and that which was open: And I gave the evidence
of the purchase unto Baruch the son of Neriah, the son of Maasei-
ah, in the sight of Hanameel mine uncle's son, and in the presence
of the witnesses that subscribed the *book of the purchase*, before all
the Jews that sat in the court of the prison. And I charged Baruch
before them, saying, Thus saith the LORD of hosts, the God of Israel; Take these evidences, this evidence of the purchase, both which
is sealed, and this evidence which is open; and put them in an *earthen
vessel*, that they may *continue many days*. For thus saith the LORD of
hosts, the God of Israel; Houses and fields and vineyards *shall be
possessed again in this land*.

—Jeremiah 32:9–15

This event took place just prior to the destruction of Jerusalem. The
message that God wanted to send was that even though He planned
on destroying Jerusalem because of their idolatry and rebellion, the
inheritance of the land, in the form of the land that was bought by
Jeremiah, was going to remain theirs and restored to them in the last
days. Notice that two copies of the book were made, one sealed and
one opened, and that they were both placed in *earthen vessels*. What
was the purpose behind these two documents in the vessels?

But we have *this treasure in earthen vessels*, that the excellency of
the power may be of God, and not of us.

—2 Corinthians 4:7

In whom ye also trusted, after that ye heard the word of truth, the
gospel of your salvation: in whom also after that ye believed, *ye
were sealed with that holy Spirit of promise*, Which is the *earnest of
our inheritance until the redemption of the purchased possession*, unto
the praise of his glory.

—Ephesians 1:13–14

The open copy was for the Gentiles, who have already been given
their inheritance through the blood of Jesus Christ. To us, the Word

of God is revealed, as well as His mysteries. The sealed copy is re-
served for Israel in the last days when it is time to receive their inheritance. We as the Gentile church are the "earnest" of the inheritance;
we are the custodians and legal holders of this *book* of inheritance
until it is time to be redeemed, when the age or "fullness" of the
Gentiles is completed. When the *seven* seals are taken off this book,
Israel will once again be restored.

This idea is the central theme of the book of Ruth. Ruth, a Gentile, represents the Gentile church, and Naomi, a Jew, represents the
Jewish church who has lost the inheritance by the death of her husband. Through Boaz's redemption of the property and his marriage
to Ruth, Naomi is given *new life*. As a result of this union between
Ruth and Boaz, a son is born. Notice what the Scriptures reveal about
this spectacular event.

> So Boaz took Ruth, and she was his wife: and when he went in unto
> her, the LORD gave her conception, and *she bare a son*. And the
> women said unto Naomi, Blessed be the LORD, which hath not left
> thee this day without a kinsman, that *his name may be famous in
> Israel*. And he shall be unto thee *a restorer of thy life*, and a nourish-
> er of thine old age: for thy daughter in law, which loveth thee, which
> is better to thee than *seven sons*, hath borne him. And *Naomi took
> the child*, and laid it in her bosom, and became nurse unto it.
>
> —Ruth 4:13–16

The son born to Ruth is the restorer of the life of Naomi. Naomi
represents those dry bones of Israel who will be given new life according to the prophecy of Ezekiel 37. Later on in the book of Jeremiah we see that this book reveals the destruction of Babylon the Great.

> So Jeremiah wrote in a *book all the evil that should come upon Baby-
> lon*, even all these words that are written against Babylon. And Jer-
> emiah said to Seraiah, When thou comest to Babylon, and shalt see,
> and shalt *read all these words*; Then shalt thou say, O LORD, thou
> hast spoken against this place, to cut it off, that none shall remain

in it, neither man nor beast, but that it shall be desolate for ever. And it shall be, when thou hast made an end of *reading this book*, that thou shalt bind *a stone to it, and cast it into the midst of Euphrates*: And thou shalt say, *Thus shall Babylon sink*, and shall not rise from the evil that I will bring upon her: and they shall be weary. Thus far are the words of Jeremiah.

—Jeremiah 51:60–64

Students of Bible prophecy will recognize the similarity between what is being told here and what is seen in Revelation 18, the prophecy against Babylon the Great. The reading of these words indicate that the book is opened and Babylon's judgments are being revealed. This coincides with the *seven* trumpets that announce Joshua's destruction of Jericho, a type of Babylon the Great. When Jesus returns, God's people, Israel, will be restored, and Babylon the Great destroyed.

In the book of Isaiah, this theme is also very clearly revealed. Notice the similarities here with everything else we have seen so far.

And the multitude of all the nations that fight against Ariel, even all that fight against her and her munition, and that distress her, shall be as a dream of a night vision. . . . For the LORD hath poured out upon you the spirit of deep sleep, and hath closed your eyes: the prophets and your rulers, the seers hath he covered. And the vision of all is become unto you as the words of *a book that is sealed*, which men deliver to one that is learned, saying, Read this, I pray thee: and he saith, I cannot; for it is sealed: And the book is delivered to him that is not learned, saying, Read this, I pray thee: and he saith, I am not learned.

—Isaiah 29:7,10–12

Isaiah 29 predicts the destruction of Jerusalem, an event that has happened once, and will happen again in the last days, just prior to Jesus' second coming. Because Israel would not obey the Lord and walk in His ways, God gave them the spirit of slumber. The vision given to them is indiscernible, because it has been *sealed*. All of their learned men cannot comprehend the meaning of the prophecy. The Jews should have recognized their Messiah as He was hanging there on the cross, fulfilling Old Testament prophecies right before their very eyes. But because they had been put to sleep, the meaning was sealed. This is similar to the veil of Moses that hangs over the Old Testament for them. But, as is God's definite pattern, this book will be unsealed and revealed to them in the last days.

> Is it not yet a very little while, and Lebanon shall be turned into a fruitful field, and the fruitful field shall be esteemed as a forest? And in that day shall the *deaf hear the words of the book*, and the *eyes of the blind shall see out of obscurity*, and out of darkness. The meek also shall increase their joy in the LORD, and the poor among men shall rejoice in the Holy One of Israel.
> —Isaiah 29:17–19

From Revelation 5, we saw that the book in God's right hand contained writing on both sides. Ezekiel described this same book in his prophecy, and gives us more clues as to its overall nature.

> But thou, son of man, hear what I say unto thee; Be not thou rebellious like that rebellious house: open thy mouth, and eat that I give thee. And when I looked, behold, *an hand was sent unto me; and, lo, a roll of a book was therein*; And he spread it before me; and *it was written within and without: and there was written therein lamentations, and mourning, and woe.*
> —Ezekiel 2:8–10

> Moreover he said unto me, Son of man, *eat that thou findest; eat this roll*, and go speak unto the house of Israel. So I opened my mouth, and he caused me to eat that roll. And he said unto me, Son of man, cause thy belly to eat, and fill thy bowels with this roll that I give thee. *Then did I eat it; and it was in my mouth as honey for sweetness.* . . . So the spirit lifted me up, and took me away, and I went in bitterness, in the heat of my spirit; but the hand of the

LORD was strong upon me. Then I came to them of the captivity at Telabib, that dwelt by the river of Chebar, and I sat where they sat, and remained there *astonished among them seven days.*

—Ezekiel 3:1–3,14–15

Revelation 5 tells us that *the book* has writing on both sides, and in order to give the book to Ezekiel, a *hand* was sent to him containing the book. A careful study of the book of Ezekiel reveals a theme that is consistent with everything we have learned so far. This prophecy is given during the *seventy* years of Babylonian captivity, warnings about the rebellion of the Jews are given, promises of judgment and later blessings are revealed, prophecies against the *seven* nations of the world are delivered, and the promise of the restoration of Israel is foretold by the act of measuring the Temple. Compare this Ezekiel measuring with Revelation 11, and you will immediately see the correlation. There is a central theme to the book of Ezekiel. Repeatedly, God repeatedly explains why He carrying out the plans He has revealed to Ezekiel. It is so they will *"know that I am the LORD."* This statement is given exactly *sixty-three (7 x 9)* times in this book.

When we examine the first occurrence of the word *book* in the Bible, we find the following passage.

This is the *book of the generations of Adam.* In the day that God created man, in the likeness of God made he him.

—Genesis 5:1

What we find when we examine this passage is the repetition of the consistent numerical patterns that are found in the Authorized Version of the Bible. First, we notice that according to Genesis 5, there are exactly *ten* generations from Adam to the last generation of the earth before the flood began, Noah being the *tenth*. This reconciles us, as we will see later, with the patterns of *ten* associated with Christ coming as *King*. We also see an association with the number *seven*. In Luke 3 we find the lineage of Jesus Christ is traced all the way back to Adam, who is described as the "son of God." There are exactly *seven-*

ty-seven generations in this lineage. Incidentally, the *seventy-seventh* occurrence of the word *book* is found in 2 Chronicles 12:15. It is called a *book of genealogies*.

In an even more amazing comparison, the first occurrence of the word *book* in the New Testament is found in the following passage.

> The *book of the generation of Jesus Christ*, the son of David, the son of Abraham.
>
> —Matthew 1:1

It is rather interesting that the first occurrences in both Testaments carry the same theme. This seems to be very deliberate. In order to fully understand why, we must understand what the Bible says about Adam and Jesus. Adam is reckoned in many ways as a type of Christ.

> Which was the son of Enos, which was the son of Seth, which was the son of **Adam, which was the son of God.**
>
> —Luke 3:38

> Nevertheless death reigned from Adam to Moses, even over them that had not sinned after the similitude of Adam's transgression, who is the **figure of him that was to come.**
>
> —Romans 5:14

> For as in **Adam all die,** even so in Christ shall all be made alive. . . . And so it is written, The first man **Adam** was made a living soul; the last Adam was made a quickening spirit.
>
> —1 Corinthians 15:22,45

It is very important to note the correlation between Adam's death and the coming of Christ, the real Son of God. The Scriptures reveal that Adam died at the age of nine hundred thirty (Genesis 5:5). I will now show you what is the first verse of the **nine hundred thirtieth** chapter of the Bible.

> The book of the generation of Jesus Christ, the son of David, the
> son of Abraham.
>
> —Matthew 1:1

Truly, as in Adam and the words of the Old Testament, all die. But
with the coming of Christ in the New Testament, we all may have
eternal life!

We also see a relationship with the number *seven* in Matthew 1,
for we find that there are *forty-two* (*7 x 6*) generations listed in this
genealogy. However, still more amazing is the fact that you will find
the word **book** in the New Testament exactly *forty-two* (*7 x 6*) times!
This is further evidence that points to the inseparable relationship
between Jesus and the *book*. Also, looking at the precise phrase "the
book," we see that it is used exactly twenty-seven times in the New
Testament. Is it a mistake then that there are exactly twenty-seven
books in the New Testament? The importance of the lineage or *generation* of Jesus Christ is declared by the fact that we find the word
generation in the Old Testament exactly *seventy* times, showing us
more of the relationship between the number *seven*, the number for
perfection and completion, and the number *ten*, the number for divine authority as King. The very first time we find the exact words of
the *Ten* Commandments, the book of the Covenant, is in the *seventieth* chapter of the Bible, Exodus 20. The New Testament equivalent
to this is that we find the phrase **kingdom of God** in various forms
also mentioned *seventy* times. It is remarkable but no coincidence
that when the *seventh* trumpet sounds we find this being declared:

> And the seventh angel sounded; and there were great voices in heav-
> en, saying, **The kingdoms of this world are become the kingdoms of
> our Lord, and of his Christ; and he shall reign for ever and ever.**
>
> —Revelation 11:15

The act of receiving and then opening this little *book* was such an
important detail that Jesus Himself acted out this future event. Remember, many of the details of Christ's second coming can be found

by understanding the details of His first coming. Here is an amazing typological reference to the receiving of the little book.

> And *Jesus returned in the power of the Spirit* into Galilee: and there went out a fame of him through all the region round about. And he taught in their synagogues, *being glorified of all.* And he came to Nazareth, where he had been brought up: and, as his custom was, he went into the synagogue on the sabbath day, and stood up for to read. And *there was delivered unto him the book* of the prophet Esaias. And *when he had opened the book*, he found the place where it was written, The Spirit of the Lord is upon me, because he hath anointed me to preach the gospel to the poor; he hath sent me to heal the brokenhearted, to preach deliverance to the captives, and recovering of sight to the blind, to set at liberty them that are bruised, To preach the acceptable year of the Lord. *And he closed the book, and he gave it again to the minister*, and sat down. And the *eyes of all them that were in the synagogue were fastened on him*. And he began to say unto them, *This day is this scripture fulfilled in your ears.*
>
> —Luke 4:14–21

As you can plainly see, many of the elements of the second coming that we have seen so far are contained in this passage. Notice that the Scriptures say that the book was "delivered" to Him. Notice that He "opened the book." The text that he reads from is Isaiah 61. As Isaiah has *sixty-six* chapters, so the Bible has *sixty-six* books. Allow me to show you the exact text He was quoting from in order to show you a very important principle.

> The spirit of the Lord GOD is upon me; because the LORD hath anointed me to preach good tidings unto the meek; he hath sent me to bind up the brokenhearted, to proclaim liberty to the captives, and the opening of the prison to them that are bound; To proclaim the acceptable year of the LORD, and the day of vengeance of our God; to comfort all that mourn.
>
> —Isaiah 61:1–2

There is an important principle that those who wish to know God's revealed wisdom need to understand. Every time an Old Testament passage is quoted in the New Testament, the reader should find out where it was quoted from to get the full picture of what God is trying to say. One of the reasons for this is the fact that when it is pointed out in the New Testament that Jesus has fulfilled a prophecy of the Old Testament, almost without fail the Old Testament prophecy has not been completely and perfectly fulfilled at His first advent. Notice that Jesus only quoted half of verse two, leaving out the prophecy of the "day of vengeance of our God." This almost always indicates to us that Christ's first advent was only a partial fulfillment of everything God wants Him to accomplish. This does not apply to the death on the cross by Christ because the Scriptures are clear that Christ has already offered Himself as a sacrifice *once*. However, it is clear that this sacrifice was always intended for the original keepers of the law, Israel. When Christ returns, this one-time act of His sacrifice will be complete when Israel receives this sacrifice by accepting Christ as their Messiah. You will notice also that Christ "closed the book" and handed it back to the minister. This reveals to us as well that the Scriptures, which were spoken of as being fulfilled, were only partially fulfilled then, but will be completely fulfilled when Christ opens the *book* the second time, this time for all eternity.

As we have seen, this book does not just represent one single thing, but many things, yea, *all things*. All things are going to be accomplished, all things are going to be fulfilled, all things are going to be revealed, and it is Jesus, the King of Kings that is going to accomplish, fulfill and reveal. Look again at the passages we read earlier.

> *All things that the Father hath are mine*: therefore said I, that he shall take of mine, and shall shew it unto you. A little while, and ye shall not see me: and again, *a little while, and ye shall see me, because I go to the Father*.
>
> —John 16:15–16

The Father loveth the Son, and hath given *all things into his hand*.
—John 3:35

Labour not for the meat which perisheth, but for that meat which endureth unto everlasting life, which the *Son of man shall give unto you*: for *him hath God the Father sealed*. . . . *All that the Father giveth me shall come to me*; and him that cometh to me I will in no wise cast out. For *I came down from heaven*, not to do mine own will, but the will of him that sent me. And this is the Father's will which hath sent me, that of *all which he hath given me I should lose nothing*, but should raise it up again at the last day. And this is the will of him that sent me, that every one which seeth the Son, and believeth on him, may have everlasting life: and I will raise him up at the last day.

—John 6:27,37–40

Jesus knowing that the *Father had given all things into his hands*, and that he was come from God, and went to God.

—John 13:3

This book is the Book of All Things. It is presented to our Savior, placed in His nail-scarred hands, so that when He is revealed, all of these things will be revealed and accomplished. It is interesting to find that the exact phrase "all things" is mentioned exactly **forty-nine (7 x 7)** times in the Old Testament. Consider what our Savior said, just before He came to this earth the first time. These words are recorded for us in Hebrews 10.

Wherefore *when he cometh into the world*, he saith, Sacrifice and offering thou wouldest not, but *a body hast thou prepared me*: In burnt offerings and sacrifices for sin thou hast had no pleasure. Then said I, *Lo, I come* (in the *volume of the book it is written of me,) to do thy will, O God*. Above when he said, Sacrifice and offering and burnt offerings and offering for sin thou wouldest not, neither hadst pleasure therein; which are offered by the law; Then said he, Lo, I come to do thy will, O God. *He taketh away the first, that he may establish the second*. By the which will we are sanctified through the offering of the body of Jesus Christ once for all. And every priest

standeth daily ministering and offering oftentimes the same sacrifices, which can never take away sins: But this man, after he had
offered one sacrifice for sins for ever, *sat down on the right hand of
God.*

—Hebrews 10:5–12

This passage reveals several different things. First, that Jesus' coming
to the earth is for the sole purpose of doing the will of the Father.
This applies to His first and second coming. Many misunderstand-
ings about Christ's second advent come as a result of failing to understand that God's purpose for sending His Son was not completely
fulfilled at His first coming. Secondly, we see that God has prepared a
body for His Son. In the first advent, this body was the normal body of
flesh and blood that came as a result of being born of Mary. In His
second advent, this body will be the Gentile body of believers, who,
when He appears in the clouds, will be caught up, both alive and
dead, to be with Christ. This is the body of His second coming.

Also from Hebrews 10 we see still more of the connection of the
book and Jesus Himself. Let's look at the passage again.

Then said I, Lo, I come (in the **volume of the book** it is written of
me,) to do thy will, O God. . . . Then said he, Lo, I come to do thy
will, O God. He taketh away the first, that he may establish the
second. . . . But this man, after he had offered one sacrifice for sins
for ever, sat down on the right hand of God.

—Hebrews 10:7,9,12

Notice that in the volume of the book, the Word of God, is written
everything that Christ has come to do. God really has sent forth His
Word to accomplish His will (*"So shall my word be that goeth forth out of
my mouth: it shall not return unto me void, but it shall accomplish that which
I please, and it shall prosper in the thing whereto I sent it"* [Isaiah 55:11]),
and it will perform everything God has sent it to do. This was only
partially accomplished at Christ's first coming, but will be completely performed at His second coming.

In the teaching of Hebrews 10:9, I believe that what is going to be done, according to the Scriptures, is that this temporary Word of God, the Bible in its present form, is going to be done away with to make way for the real Word of God. Some discussion of this was presented in *By Divine Order*. It is the clear teaching behind what the apostle Paul said.

> For we know in part, and we prophesy in part. But when that *which is perfect is come, then that which is in part shall be done away.* When I was a child, I spake as a child, I understood as a child, I thought as a child: but when I became a man, I put away childish things. For now we see through a glass, darkly; but then face to face: now I know in part; but then shall I know even as also I am known.
>
> —1 Corinthians 13:11–12

Again, do not misunderstand my regard for the present Word of God. It is only as perfect as anything can be in the present world. But the Scriptures are clear on this teaching, and that is why Jesus and the Word of God are forever linked together. That is why they are both at the right hand of God. Jesus Himself told us that heaven and earth would pass away, but his Words would never pass away. Do we understand this to mean that in the New Heaven we will all be walking around with King James Bibles in our hands? Of course not. But we obviously and reasonably understand that the True Word will take the place of the temporary, type replaced by antitype, etc.

> The *words of the LORD are pure words*: as silver tried in a furnace of earth, purified *seven times. (This is the four hundred ninetieth chapter of the Bible!)*
>
> —Psalm 12:6

The Number Eight

As the number seven shows God's completion and perfection, re-vealed to us in the creation week, the number eight shows us God's eternal plan for a new beginning, a new creation. After the seven days of the week have expired, a new week begins, which would technical-ly be the eighth day after the beginning of the previous week. The Scriptures tell us that it was this eighth day, or "the first day of the week" that our Lord was resurrected. It is understandable that we would find the exact phrase "first day of the week" mentioned pre-cisely eight times in the Holy Bible.

In Genesis 5, we find that Adam, who has lost both sons by way of the crime of murder, is given a new son, Seth. This was his "new beginning" son. Accordingly, in Genesis 5:4, Adam lived eight hun-dred years after the birth of Seth. "Seth" is mentioned exactly eight times in the Scriptures.

Turning to Genesis 8, we see God's plan for the ages clearly spelled out. God has ended the world by a flood in Genesis 7, the number seven representing perfection and completion. Now, we look in Gen-esis 8 and find that the ark and its eight human inhabitants have found rest in a new world. It is in Genesis 8 that Noah, his family, and all the animals are allowed to leave the ark and begin in a brand new place, washed clean by water, a symbol of the Word of God. Interest-ingly, we find the name "Noah" a total of forty-eight (8 x 6) times in the Old Testament, and "Noe" and "Noah" a total of eight times in the New Testament, for a grand total of fifty-six times (8 x 7). Twice in the New Testament is Noah associated with the number eight.

> Which sometime were disobedient, when once the longsuffering of God waited in the days of Noah, while the ark was a preparing, wherein few, that is, eight souls were saved by water.
> —1 Peter 3:20

> And spared not the old world, but saved Noah the eighth person, a preacher of righteousness, bringing in the flood upon the world of the ungodly.
> —2 Peter 2:5

Also in Genesis 8 we find that God mentions eight things that will not cease in this new world that He has created for Noah and life on earth.

> While the earth remaineth, seedtime and harvest, and cold and heat, and summer and winter, and day and night shall not cease.
> —Genesis 8:22

In Revelation 21, John is allowed to see the vision of a New Heaven and a New Earth. I believe that the chronology of the seven-day week is a representation of God's plan for the world. At the conclusion of the sixth day (six thousand years after the creation) Christ will come to the earth to establish a kingdom that will last one thousand years. This kingdom is the Sabbath of rest for the entire world, and would fulfill the type of the seventh day. Immediately after this, the old universe and old earth will pass away, bringing in the new creation of God on the eighth day, or at the beginning of the eight thousandth year since the creation. From this point, the reckoning of time will pass away as well, for this new creation of God is everlasting, with no end. It is noteworthy at this point to see that at the conclusion of the millennial reign of Christ, Satan is loosed for a short time to, once again, wage a futile war against Christ the King. This will be covered later.

In John's vision of this new heaven and earth, he also describes a new city, Jerusalem. Here is how he describes this city.

> And I John saw the holy city, new Jerusalem, coming down from God out of heaven, prepared **as a bride adorned for her husband.**
>
> —Revelation 21:2

You might notice that this appears in verse two, corresponding with what we saw in Genesis 2, the union of Adam and Eve as husband and wife. The eighth verse that "man" is mentioned in the Scriptures tells us that, ". . . It is not good that the man should be alone; I will make him an help meet for him" (Genesis 2:18). In Adam and Eve we see the type, and in Revelation 21:2 we see the antitypical fulfillment in Christ and His beautifully adorned bride, the Church. In the Scriptures, the words "wedding" and "wedlock" are mentioned exactly eight times, and all the forms of the words "marry" and "marriage" are mentioned exactly eighty times.

This new creation of earth, heaven, and Jerusalem, will be the perfect fulfillment of everything God wanted to accomplish in His creation process. We believe that this is what Jesus referred to in the Scriptures as the "kingdom of heaven." This phrase is used only in the fortieth (8 x 5) book of the Bible, the gospel according to Matthew. It is mentioned there thirty-two (8 x 4) times.

This new creation will also be the fulfillment of the prophetic type of the Feast of Tabernacles.

> Speak unto the children of Israel, saying, The fifteenth day of this seventh month shall be the feast of tabernacles for seven days unto the LORD. On the first day shall be an holy convocation: ye shall do no servile work therein. Seven days ye shall offer an offering made by fire unto the LORD: on **the eighth day shall be an holy convocation unto you;** and ye shall offer an offering made by fire unto the LORD: it is a solemn assembly; and ye shall do no servile work therein.
>
> —Leviticus 23:34–36

This feast was to be a reminder to all Israel that the Lord their God would always dwell with His people. However, the literal definition of the word "tabernacle" is "tent" or a *temporary* dwelling place. The tabernacle that Moses built in the wilderness was never intended to be the true, permanent dwelling place of God, for God does not dwell in temples made with hands (Acts 7:48). It is interesting to observe that our English word "tavern" comes directly from the word "tabernacle" and in its classic sense, a tavern was a temporary resting place, never permanent. Even the more permanent Temple that Solomon built, which was finished in the **eighth** month (1 Kings 6:38), ended up being not so permanent. Now, according to verse forty-two of Leviticus 23, the children of Israel were to dwell in tabernacles, or "booths," for seven days, and come out of these on the eighth day for a holy convocation. This is reminiscent of what Paul revealed in the New Testament.

> For we know that if our **earthly house of this tabernacle** were dissolved, we have a building of God, an house not made with hands, eternal in the heavens. For in this we groan, earnestly desiring to be clothed upon with our house which is from heaven.
>
> —2 Corinthians 5:1–2

As Israel dwells in earthly tabernacles for seven days, so must all earth dwellers live in this temporary dwelling place called earth for seven thousand years. However, on the eighth day, the day of new beginnings, we will dwell in the permanent house of God for eternity. Here is how John described it in the book of Revelation.

> And I saw a new heaven and a new earth: for the first heaven and the first earth were passed away; and there was no more sea. And I John saw the holy city, new Jerusalem, coming down from God out of heaven, prepared as a bride adorned for her husband. And I heard a great voice out of heaven saying, Behold, the **tabernacle of God is with men, and he will dwell with them, and they shall be his people, and God himself shall be with them, and be their God.**
>
> —Revelation 21:1–3

By the way, the word "tabernacle" is mentioned three hundred twenty-eight (8 x 41) times in the King James Bible. This true tabernacle will be the eternal dwelling place of God Almighty, and in the phrase "and he will dwell with them" we find the perfect fulfillment of the prophecy of Isaiah concerning a child, born of a virgin, given the eight-letter name of "Immanuel." This name is mentioned three times in the Bible, once in Isaiah 8:8, and according to Matthew 1:23, literally means "God with us."

The number eight and salvation

The story of Noah and the eight inhabitants of the ark is a wonderful representation of God's salvation at work. While everyone, and everything else passes away, God, through the medium of water (a symbol of His Word) saves Noah and his family. As we make our way through the pages of the Bible, we can see other uses of the number eight and God's plan of salvation.

The eighth time "Abraham" is mentioned is in Genesis 17:24 when he was circumcised, which God commanded to be done to all of Abraham's seed on the eighth day. The thirty-second (8 x 4) time "Abraham" is mentioned is in Genesis 21:2 when Sarah gives birth to one of Abraham's eight sons, Isaac. Isaac is mentioned one hundred twenty-eight (8 x 8 x 2) times in the Scriptures. He was the first to be circumcised on the eighth day. This circumcision is a symbol of the work of God's salvation in a person's life (Colossians 2:11). The word "salvation" is mentioned one hundred and four times (8 x 13) in the Scriptures. The minister of this salvation is Immanuel, who is given the name of Jesus, who was also circumcised on the eighth day. The Scriptures call him "Saviour" twenty-four (8 x 3) times. He is called "Son of Man" eighty-eight times in the New Testament.

It was Jesus who came to proclaim salvation to the Jew first, then the Gentiles. It was His apostles who declared that His words were the "words of eternal life" (John 6:68). Jesus Himself referred to "my words" and "my word" sixteen (8 x 2) times in the Scriptures. His words are commonly found following the phrases "Jesus said" and "said Jesus," which are mentioned a total of eighty-eight times, and "Jesus answered," mentioned a total of sixty-four (8 x 8) times. Modern printing practices make it easy for us to find Jesus' blood-red words in exactly eight books of the Bible (Matthew, Mark, Luke, John, Acts, 1 Corinthians, 2 Corinthians, Revelation.) The entire King James Version of the New Testament contains a total of 180,392 words, a number divisible by eight.

Jesus was given the title of "Redeemer" exactly eight times in the Bible. This theme of redemption is found in the eighth book of the Bible, the book of Ruth. In the book of Ruth, you will find, not only the story of the redemption of Naomi through the possession of land, but you will also find the word "redeem" used exactly eight times. In the redemption process mentioned in Ruth 4, Ruth, a Gentile, is purchased along with the land in order to raise up the seed of Ruth's dead husband. Ruth is mentioned twelve times in this book, the number twelve being a number for the church, in this case, the Gentile church. As a result of this union, a man child is born whose name was Obed. In verses fourteen and fifteen it tells us that this man child will be famous in all Israel and that he will be a *restorer* of Naomi's life. This is indicative of Christ's second coming, when Israel learns the true identity of the Messiah and He restores them back to life. It is interesting to see a pattern of eights that is related to this story. In Ruth 4:18–22, a lineage is mentioned listing Pharez at the beginning. Obed is the eighth in the lineage of Pharez. Obed was born in Bethlehem. Obed is the grandfather of David, the eighth son of Jesse. David was also born in Bethlehem. Jesus, the Son of Man (mentioned eighty-eight times in the New Testament), is also born in Bethlehem. Bethlehem is mentioned exactly eight times in the New Testament.

The number eight and the Lake of Fire

Perhaps the most interesting aspect of the number eight is its relationship to God's eternal punishment, the Lake of Fire. After the thousand-year seventh-day reign of Christ over the earth, the book of Revelation describes the following events, events that take place at the beginning of the eighth prophetic day.

> And the devil that deceived them was cast into the lake of fire and
> brimstone, where the beast and the false prophet are, and shall be
> tormented day and night for ever and ever. . . . And death and hell
> were cast into the lake of fire. This is the second death. And whoso-
> ever was not found written in the book of life was cast into the lake
> of fire.
>
> —Revelation 20:10,14–15

After Satan is loosed from his prison in the bottomless pit, he is allowed to once again deceive the nations with his false gospel. He
again tries to muster an army big enough to destroy the kingdom of
Christ, and in Revelation 20:9 we see that he leads this army to encir-
cle the camp of the saints. At this time, God sends fire down from
heaven to consume them all. God then casts Satan into the Lake of
Fire, where the beast and false prophet already are. These are followed by the rest of the enemies of God, Death, Hell, and all those
whose names are not written in the Book of Life. All these events
take place at the beginning of the eighth millenium and are associated with the number eight.

We see an illustration of this in Genesis 8.

> And Noah builded an altar unto the LORD; and took of every clean
> beast, and of every clean fowl, and offered burnt offerings on the
> altar. And the LORD smelled a sweet savour; and the LORD said in
> his heart, I will not again curse the ground any more for man's sake;
> for the imagination of man's heart is evil from his youth; neither
> will I again smite any more every thing living, as I have done. While
> the earth remaineth, seedtime and harvest, and cold and heat, and
> summer and winter, and day and night shall not cease.
>
> —Genesis 8:20–22

Noah, who has just departed the ark with its eight human inhabitants, is now standing on a new earth that has been washed clean with
water. He then offers a sacrifice on an altar to the Lord, and the Lord
smelled the sweetness of the burnt offering. It is here that the Lord
promised that eight things would not cease, as we previously men-

tioned. It is interesting to add here that the altar of incense in the wilderness tabernacle was commanded to be built in the eightieth chapter of the Bible, Exodus 30. It is written in the eighth book of the New Testament, 2 Corinthians, that, ". . . we are unto God a sweet savour of Christ, in them that are saved, and in them that perish" (2 Corinthians 2:15).

That God will destroy His enemies with fire, thus ridding them for eternity, is evidenced throughout the Scriptures. In Lamentations 3, the eight hundredth chapter of the Bible, Jeremiah laments that his enemies have risen up and compassed against him, yet believes God that He will, ". . . Persecute and destroy them in anger from under the heavens of the LORD" (Lamentations 3:66). Notice, also how the following verses carry this same theme.

> They compassed me about; yea, they compassed me about: but in the name of the LORD I will destroy them. They compassed me about like bees; they are quenched as the fire of thorns: for in the name of the LORD I will destroy them."
>
> —Psalm 118:11–12

> Therefore wait ye upon me, saith the LORD, until the day that I rise up to the prey: for my determination is to **gather the nations**, that I may assemble the kingdoms, to pour upon them mine indignation, even all my fierce anger: for all the earth shall be **devoured with the fire of my jealousy**.
>
> —Zephaniah 3:8

In 2 Chronicles 7, the fire of God fell from heaven and consumed the sacrifice on the newly built altar of Solomon's temple. This was followed by an eight-day dedication of the altar. Later, in 2 Chronicles 29, Hezekiah and the priests cleanse and sanctify the altar of the Lord for eight days so that the sacrifices can resume. According to Luke 9:28, the eighth day is mentioned as the day in which Jesus is transfigured and He speaks of His sacrificial death to Moses and Elijah, both of whom witnessed the fire of God fall from heaven (Leviticus 9:24; 1 Kings 18:38).

Soon after the death of Solomon, king of Israel, his servant Jeroboam rises up and becomes king over the ten northern tribes of Israel. In 1 Kings 12 we are told that Jeroboam, fearing that through
worshipping in Jerusalem the nation would be united again, erected
two golden calves, one in Bethel, one in Dan. On the fifteenth day of
the **eighth** month, he has a dedication feast in honor of these two
idols. In chapter thirteen, God sends a prophet to Jeroboam to proclaim the following.

> And he cried against the altar in the word of the LORD, and said, O
> altar, altar, thus saith the LORD; Behold, a child shall be born unto
> the house of David, **Josiah** by name; and upon thee shall he offer
> the priests of the high places that burn incense upon thee, and **men's**
> **bones shall be burnt upon thee.**
>
> —1 Kings 13:2

This prophet declared that because of Jeroboam's idolatry, God would
raise up a man child (*type* of Christ) that would burn the priests of his
idolatry upon this same altar. This child's name was going to be Josiah. Years later, a child was born from the house of David whose name
was Josiah.

> Josiah was **eight** years old when he began to reign. . . .
>
> —2 Kings 22:1

Exactly eighteen years after Josiah became an eight-year-old king in
Jerusalem, he did all that the prophet had prophesied that he would
do, including burning the bones of the priests of Jeroboam on the
same altar he erected at Bethel. As for Jeroboam, he also met up with
God's judgment by way of the mighty army of Abijah and his four
hundred thousand (a gospel army) fighting men.

> And Abijah set the battle in array with an army of valiant men of
> war, even four hundred thousand chosen men: **Jeroboam also set**
> **the battle in array against him with eight hundred thousand**

chosen men, being mighty men of valour. . . . But Jeroboam caused an ambushment to come about behind them: so they were before Judah, and the ambushment was behind them. And when Judah looked back, behold, the battle was before and behind: and they cried unto the LORD, and the priests sounded with the trumpets. Then the men of Judah gave a shout: and as the men of Judah shouted, it came to pass, that God smote Jeroboam and all Israel before Abijah and Judah.

—2 Chronicles 13:3,13–15

You might take note that the details of this battle follow closely with the eighth day final battle that Satan and his hosts wage against God and His people, mentioned in Revelation 20. It is most reassuring to the true believer that although Satan and his army, even today, may seem a fearsome foe, there will come a time when the powers of darkness will meet a final and eternal destruction. Even the future Beast himself, with his war against the saints of God, will suffer God's burning vengeance for all of eternity.

And the beast that was, and is not, even he is the eighth, and is of the seven, and goeth into perdition.

—Revelation 17:11

And the beast was taken, and with him the false prophet that wrought miracles before him, with which he deceived them that had received the mark of the beast, and them that worshipped his image. These both were cast alive into a lake of fire burning with brimstone.

—Revelation 19:20

The Number Nine

As we continue to see in our wonderful study of the use of numbers in the Bible, these numbers all seem to point to various themes surrounding the second coming of our Savior. This divine plan is no less present when we look at the number nine.

The number nine and fruit bearing

In Genesis 9, God gives Noah the commandment to go forth over all the earth and "be fruitful" (vs. 1). In verse nine, God makes a reference to the "seed" of Noah, a symbol of the fruit of man. In the ninth book of the New Testament, the book of Galatians (nine letters), we find a list of the nine fruits of the Spirit.

1. Love	2. Joy
3. Peace	4. Longsuffering
5. Gentleness	6. Goodness
7. Faith	8. Meekness
9. Temperance	

Just prior to this list of fruits in Galatians 5:22–23, Paul gives a list of the works (fruit) of the flesh. They total eighteen (9 x 2) in all.

1. Adultery	2. Fornication
3. Uncleanness	4. Lasciviousness

5. Idolatry   6. Witchcraft

7. Hatred   8. Variance

9. Emulations   10. Wrath

11. Strife   12. Seditions

13. Heresies   14. Envyings

15. Murders   16. Drunkeness

17. Revellings   18. Such like

After these fruits of sin are mentioned, the Scriptures expressly reveal that they which do such things cannot inherit the kingdom of God. In light of this idea, let us look at an instance where this same number, eighteen, is used.

> And, behold, there was a woman which had a spirit of infirmity eighteen years, and was bowed together, and could in no wise lift up herself.
>
> —Luke 13:11

As we will see more fully in the chapter on the number twelve, women in the Bible seem to represent types of the Church in various ways. Here we have a woman who does not merely have an infirmity, but a *spirit of infirmity*, most obviously a demonic influence. It could well be understood that the eighteen years she endured this *spirit of infirmity* could directly correspond with the eighteen works of the flesh previously mentioned in Galatians. Many of the ailments that Jesus healed during His ministry were symbolic of various sins. Physical blindness is a type of Israel who has eyes to see, but cannot see, and is blinded until Christ comes again (Romans 11:25). Leprosy is indicative of spiritual uncleanness (Leviticus 13:44). It is noteworthy to see that Jesus, in healing and loosing this woman from her bondage, does so on the Sabbath (seventh) day, speaking exactly seven words.

> And when Jesus saw her, he called her to him, and said unto her, **Woman, thou art loosed from thine infirmity.**
>
> —Luke 13:12

The number nine and the birth pangs of the Messiah

In the temple of the human body, we see the design of God in the birth process, a woman's pregnancy generally lasting nine months. There seems to be a very important prophetic principle tied to this theme: *the birth of the manchild.*

In Revelation 12 we see a woman crowned with twelve stars, a type of Israel, who travails in preparation to give birth to a man child who is to rule all nations with a rod of iron. This man child is Jesus Christ. In the following verses, we will compare important scriptures that reveal to us this idea of a travailing woman, and the coming of Christ.

> And she being with child cried, **travailing in birth**, and pained to be delivered. . . . And she brought forth a **man child**, who was to rule all nations with a rod of iron: and her child was caught up unto God, and to his throne.
>
> —Revelation 12:2,5

> A woman when she is in **travail hath sorrow**, because her hour is come: but as soon as she is delivered of the child, she remembereth no more the anguish, for joy that **a man is born** into the world. And ye now therefore have sorrow: but I will see you again, and your heart shall rejoice, and your joy no man taketh from you.
>
> —John 16:21–22

The Scriptures seem to interweave the idea that, even though there may be troublesome times, most likely during the seven years of Jacob's trouble, this in itself will bring Christ back to the earth to be the Savior of Israel and ruler of the world. In light of this, it is interesting that we find the word *sorrow* exactly *seventy* times in the Bible. In the Old Testament, the word is mentioned exactly *fifty-four (9 x 6)* times. Notice the number six for preparation, and the number nine for sorrows and birth pangs. This is indicated by the first verse where we find the word *sorrow*.

Unto the woman he said, I will greatly multiply thy **sorrow and**
thy **conception; in sorrow thou shalt bring forth children;** and
thy desire shall be to thy husband, and he shall rule over thee.

—Genesis 3:16

The Scriptures in Isaiah 53:3 refer to Jesus as a "man of sorrows,"
referring to His suffering on the cross of Calvary. It was at the **ninth**
hour that His suffering was completed (Luke 23:44–46). It was at the
ninth hour that Jesus spoke nine words, "My God, my God, why has
thou forsaken me?" (Matthew 27:46). Also, the exact phrase "ninth
hour" is mentioned exactly **nine** times in the Scriptures. The very
sufferings of Christ seem to have a prophetic purpose to them, especially in the light of what Christ declares in Luke 23 to those *women*
who are weeping for his sorrows.

And there followed him a great company of people, and of women,
which also bewailed and lamented him. But Jesus turning unto them
said, Daughters of Jerusalem, **weep not for me, but weep for your-**
selves, and for your children. For, behold, the days are coming, in
the which they shall say, **Blessed are the barren, and the wombs**
that never bare, and the paps which never gave suck.

—Luke 23:27–29

It seems very likely that with this statement, Christ is prophesying
the coming *days of sorrow* that precede His second coming. He also
makes mention of an Old Testament prophecy concerning a barren
woman that is blessed by God and brings forth a child into the world.
Remembering that the word *sorrow* was mentioned *fifty-four (9 x 6)*
times in the Old Testament, we see the divine order of God's Word
once again when we find this prophecy in Isaiah *54*. Notice what the
Scriptures reveal.

Sing, O barren, thou that didst not bear; break forth into singing,
and cry aloud, thou that didst not travail with child: for more are
the children of the desolate than the children of the married wife,

saith the LORD. . . . Fear not; for thou shalt not be ashamed: neither be thou confounded; for thou shalt not be put to shame: for thou shalt forget the shame of thy youth, and shalt not remember the **reproach** of thy widowhood any more. For thy Maker is thine husband; the LORD of hosts is his name; and thy Redeemer the Holy One of Israel; The God of the whole earth shall he be called. For the LORD hath called thee **as a woman forsaken and grieved in spirit**, and a wife of youth, when thou wast refused, saith thy God. For a small moment have I forsaken thee; but with great mercies will I gather thee. In a little wrath I hid my face from thee for a moment; but with everlasting kindness will I have mercy on thee, saith the LORD thy Redeemer. **For this is as the waters of Noah unto me:** for as I have sworn that the waters of Noah should no more go over the earth; so have I sworn that I would not be wroth with thee, nor rebuke thee.

—Isaiah 54:1,4–9

Here once again, the Bible draws a connection between the events and themes of the second coming and the days of Noah. In accordance with the design of the woman's body temple, there is one particular incident that precedes the birth of any child: the breaking forth of waters.

The next thing we notice from Isaiah 54, is that, in giving conception to the forsaken woman, God takes away the *reproach* that she has. The word *reproach* is literally defined by Webster as an expression of censure or blame, a bad name. In the Scriptures, we find several women who have a reproach because of their inability to bring a man child into the world. Accordingly, we find the very word *reproach* in the Old Testament exactly *eighty-one* (*9 x 9*) times! Here is the first occurrence.

And God remembered **Rachel**, and God hearkened to her, and opened her womb. And she conceived, and bare a son; and said, **God hath taken away my reproach.**

—Genesis 30:22–23

As with each of these cases, the child she bears, Joseph, is a *type* of Christ, who became the savior of his brethren. We could also look at the stories of Hannah, Naomi, the unnamed mother of Sampson, Elizabeth, and Sarah and see clearly that each of these women had some sort of reproach or a contempt upon them because of their lack of producing a man child. In each case, God hears their plea and opens up their womb, giving each of them a man, who in their several ways, becomes a *type* of Christ. The exception is Naomi, where it is her daughter-in-law, Ruth, who produces the man child, Obed. However, this child is given over to Naomi (Ruth 4:14–17).

In the overall connection with the theme of the number nine, we see that each of these women are given *seed*. The Scriptures point out to us that *seed* is a symbol of the Word of God (Matthew 13:19–23; Luke 8:11; 1 Peter 1:23). The Bible is also clear that the Word of God is none other than Jesus Himself (John 1:1; 1 John 5:7). Therefore, it should come as no surprise to find the phrase "word of God" mentioned in the New Testament exactly *forty-five* (*9 x 5*) times!

The word "pangs" is mentioned exactly nine times in the Scriptures. In each case, we find their relationship to a woman that is about to give birth, and prophetic events that accompany the coming of Jesus Christ. In each case, the reader is encouraged to study the context of each passage in order to gain a broader understanding of prophetic events.

> And they shall be afraid: pangs and sorrows shall take hold of them; they shall be in pain as a woman that travaileth: they shall be amazed one at another; their faces shall be as flames.
>
> —Isaiah 13:8

> Therefore are my loins filled with pain: pangs have taken hold upon me, as the pangs of a woman that travaileth: I was bowed down at the hearing of it; I was dismayed at the seeing of it.
>
> —Isaiah 21:3

> Like as a woman with child, that draweth near the time of her deliv-

ery, is in pain, and crieth out in her pangs; so have we been in thy
sight, O LORD.

—Isaiah 26:17

O inhabitant of Lebanon, that makest thy nest in the cedars, how
gracious shalt thou be when pangs come upon thee, the pain as of a
woman in travail!

—Jeremiah 22:23

Kerioth is taken, and the strong holds are surprised, and the mighty
men's hearts in Moab at that day shall be as the heart of a woman in
her pangs.

—Jeremiah 48:41

Behold, he shall come up and fly as the eagle, and spread his wings
over Bozrah: and at that day shall the heart of the mighty men of
Edom be as the heart of a woman in her pangs.

—Jeremiah 49:22

The king of Babylon hath heard the report of them, and his hands
waxed feeble: anguish took hold of him, and pangs as of a woman
in travail.

—Jeremiah 50:43

Now why dost thou cry out aloud? is there no king in thee? is thy
counsellor perished? for pangs have taken thee as a woman in travail.

—Micah 4:9

It is also noted that the various forms of the word "travail" and the
word "child" are found in the same verse ten times, but only nine of
those verses carry the theme of childbirth. Notice again these various
verses.

And his daughter in law, Phinehas' wife, was with child, near to be
delivered: and when she heard the tidings that the ark of God was

taken, and that her father in law and her husband were dead, she bowed herself and travailed; for her pains came upon her.

—1 Samuel 4:19

Sing, O barren, thou that didst not bear; break forth into singing, and cry aloud, thou that didst not travail with child: for more are the children of the desolate than the children of the married wife, saith the LORD.

—Isaiah 54:1

Before she travailed, she brought forth; before her pain came, she was delivered of a man child.

—Isaiah 66:7

For I have heard a voice as of a woman in travail, and the anguish as of her that bringeth forth her first child, the voice of the daughter of Zion, that bewaileth herself, that spreadeth her hands, saying, Woe is me now! for my soul is wearied because of murderers.

—Jeremiah 4:31

Ask ye now, and see whether a man doth travail with child? wherefore do I see every man with his hands on his loins, as a woman in travail, and all faces are turned into paleness?

—Jeremiah 30:6

Behold, I will bring them from the north country, and gather them from the coasts of the earth, and with them the blind and the lame, the woman with child and her that travaileth with child together: a great company shall return thither.

—Jeremiah 31:8

A woman when she is in travail hath sorrow, because her hour is come: but as soon as she is delivered of the child, she remembereth no more the anguish, for joy that a man is born into the world.

—John 16:21

For when they shall say, Peace and safety; then sudden destruction cometh upon them, as travail upon a woman with child; and they shall not escape.

—1 Thessalonians 5:3

And she being with child cried, travailing in birth, and pained to be delivered.

—Revelation 12:2

Once again the student of the Word of God is encouraged to study the prophetic contexts of these passages. It is quite clear that all of these point us to the days that precede the second coming of the Lord Jesus Christ, the so-called "birth pangs of the Messiah." Many of these same events were prophesied in the Olivet Discourse, contained in Matthew 24, Mark 13, and Luke 21. Jesus called these days ". . . the beginning of sorrows" (Matthew 24:8).

The number nine and the day of clouds

Behold, he cometh with clouds; and every eye shall see him, and they also which pierced him: and all kindreds of the earth shall wail because of him. Even so, Amen.

—Revelation 1:7

There is a very common, very important symbol that is often associated with the visible appearing of Jesus Christ. From the above verse we see it is the symbol of *clouds*. In 1 Thessalonians 4:17, the *clouds* are where we are joined together with the dead in Christ at the Rapture to meet Jesus, who appears in the clouds. Let's look at a few other verses that indicate this very important principle.

And then shall appear the sign of the Son of man in heaven: and then shall all the tribes of the earth mourn, and they shall see the Son of man **coming in the clouds** of heaven with power and great glory.

—Matthew 24:30

Jesus saith unto him, Thou hast said: nevertheless I say unto you, Hereafter shall ye see the Son of man sitting on the right hand of power, and **coming in the clouds** of heaven.

—Matthew 26:64

And then shall they see the Son of man **coming in the clouds** with great power and glory.

—Mark 13:26

And Jesus said, I am: and ye shall see the Son of man sitting on the right hand of power, and **coming in the clouds** of heaven.

—Mark 14:62

And when he had spoken these things, while they beheld, he was taken up; and **a cloud received him** out of their sight. And while they looked stedfastly toward heaven as he went up, behold, two men stood by them in white apparel; Which also said, Ye men of Galilee, why stand ye gazing up into heaven? this same Jesus, which is taken up from you into heaven, **shall so come in like manner** as ye have seen him go into heaven.

—Acts 1:9–11

As we can clearly see from these verses, the symbol of Christ coming in the clouds is a uniquely unmistakable sign. In fact, it seems that this sign was so important, our heavenly Father, the Author of order, incorporated this symbol into the story of the first coming of Jesus Christ.

And she brought forth her firstborn son, and wrapped him **in swaddling clothes**, and laid him in a manger; because there was no room for them in the inn. . . . And this shall be a sign unto you; Ye shall find the **babe wrapped in swaddling clothes**, lying in a manger.

—Luke 2:7,12

Notice that the angel mentions that the *swaddling clothes* are given as a sign of the coming of the Savior. That is exactly what the disciples were asking for in the Matthew 24 discourse on the second coming.

> And as he sat upon the mount of Olives, the disciples came unto him privately, saying, Tell us, when shall these things be? **and what shall be the sign of thy coming**, and of the end of the world? . . . And then shall appear **the sign of the Son of man in heaven**: and then shall all the tribes of the earth mourn, and they shall see the Son of man **coming in the clouds** of heaven with power and great glory.
>
> —Matthew 24:3,30

The Bible is its own best dictionary. The very symbols that are seemingly cryptically given us in the Scriptures, are themselves, revealed by these same Scriptures. Mary wrapped Jesus in *swaddling* clothes. It was the very first thing she did to Him after He was born. Does the Bible give the interpretation of what it was Mary performed? Notice the verse placement of the following passage, and the very words that are used.

> When I made the **cloud the garment thereof, and thick darkness a swaddlingband** for it.
>
> —Job 38:9

The swaddling clothes that Mary wrapped Jesus in at His first coming are the symbol of the clouds and thick darkness that accompany His second coming! As we look at the very phrase "thick darkness," we find that it is often associated with *clouds* and always has a prophetic theme associated with it. Accordingly, you will find the phrase "thick darkness" mentioned exactly nine times in the Authorized Version of the Bible. Its first usage in the Scriptures is found in the book of Exodus.

> And Moses stretched forth his hand toward heaven; and there was a **thick darkness** in all the land of Egypt three days.
>
> —Exodus 10:22

This was the ninth plague that God sent to Egypt. It stands to reason
then that the very next plague fell upon the first born. Let's look at
some of the other uses of this phrase and try to gain some biblical
understanding.

> And ye came near and stood under the mountain; and the moun-
> tain burned with fire unto the midst of heaven, with darkness, *clouds,*
> *and thick darkness.*
>
> —Deuteronomy 4:11

> These words the LORD spake unto all your assembly in the mount
> out of the midst of the fire, of the *cloud, and of the thick darkness,*
> with a great voice: and he added no more. And he wrote them in
> two tables of stone, and delivered them unto me.
>
> —Deuteronomy 5:22

> Blow ye the *trumpet* in Zion, and sound an alarm in my holy moun-
> tain: let all the inhabitants of the land tremble: for the *day of the*
> *LORD* cometh, for it is nigh at hand; A day of darkness and of gloom-
> iness, a *day of clouds and of thick darkness*, as the morning spread
> upon the mountains: a great people and a strong; there hath not
> been ever the like, neither shall be any more after it, even to the
> years of many generations.
>
> —Joel 2:1–2

> The great *day of the LORD* is near, it is near, and hasteth greatly,
> even the voice of the day of the LORD: the mighty man shall cry
> there bitterly. That day is a day of wrath, a day of trouble and dis-
> tress, a day of wasteness and desolation, a day of darkness and gloom-
> iness, *a day of clouds and thick darkness*, A day of the *trumpet* and
> alarm against the fenced cities, and against the high towers.
>
> —Zepheniah 1:14–16

In the above passage from Zephaniah's prophecy, we see the dreadful
nature of the *day of the Lord,* similar to the time of sorrows that we

have examined in this chapter. One of the greatest messages that the Bible has to offer is that even though dreadful times and tribulation come, there is always hope. To see this hope, we once again turn the pages of our Bibles back to Genesis 9. This is God's love manifested for His people.

> And God said, This is the **token** of the covenant which I make be-tween me and you and every living creature that is with you, for perpetual generations: I do set my **bow in the cloud**, and it shall be for a token of a covenant between me and the earth. And it shall come to pass, **when I bring a cloud over the earth, that the bow shall be seen in the cloud:** And I will remember my covenant, which is between me and you and every living creature of all flesh; and the waters shall no more become a flood to destroy all flesh. And **the bow shall be in the cloud;** and I will look upon it, that I may remember the everlasting covenant between God and every living creature of all flesh that is upon the earth.
>
> —Genesis 9:12–16

Truly we can see the majesty of God in the very language of the King James Version. God said that He is going to bring the cloud over the earth, and when He does, we can look at the cloud and see *the Bow!* The Bow is Jesus. He is the ultimate token of God's covenant. In Him is fulfilled all the promise of salvation instead of destruction. And as we examine this passage in the light of all of the others that we have seen so far, we can clearly see why God is using these symbols, and how He is revealing His wonderful plan for the ages. The Day of the Lord is a day of clouds. In that day, God is going to initiate His plan of judgments, wrath, and redemption upon the earth. When He brings this cloud over the earth, He will look in it and see the Bow that He put there, and remember His covenant with the earth. To further un-derstand the connection between the bow in Genesis 9 and its identi-ty as Jesus, we look to the book of Ezekiel.

> As the appearance of the **bow that is in the cloud in the day of rain,** so was the appearance of the brightness round about. This

was the appearance of the likeness of the glory of the LORD. And
when I saw it, I fell upon my face, and I heard a voice of one that
spake.

—Ezekiel 1:28

In this passage, Ezekiel is given a glimpse of the throne that God sits
upon. Notice that he describes the *glory of the* LORD as a *bow that is in
the cloud in the day of rain*. This is almost exactly what is described for
us in Genesis 9. In Revelation 4, John also sees the throne of God also
surrounded by a rainbow (vs. 3). With the understanding that the
Glory of the Lord is none other than Jesus himself, a familiar verse
comes immediately to mind.

And the glory of the LORD shall be revealed, and all flesh shall see it
together: for the mouth of the LORD hath spoken it.

—Isaiah 40:5

This verse most definitely speaks of the person of Jesus Christ being
the Glory of the Lord that will be revealed in the last days. Study this
chapter and you will see this doctrine very plainly. One final note
concerning the Glory of the Lord in a cloud is taken from Exodus 40.
This is the **ninetieth** chapter of the Bible.

Then a **cloud** covered the tent of the congregation, **and the glory
of the** LORD **filled the tabernacle.** And Moses was not able to
enter into the tent of the congregation, because the cloud abode
thereon, and the glory of the LORD filled the tabernacle. And when
the cloud was taken up from over the tabernacle, the children of
Israel went onward in all their journeys: But if the cloud were not
taken up, then they journeyed not till the day that it was taken up.
For the cloud of the LORD was upon the tabernacle by day, and fire
was on it by night, in the sight of all the house of Israel, throughout
all their journeys.

—Exodus 40:34–38

Moses' purpose in erecting the tabernacle was so that God could travel with them and lead them to the Promised Land. God is very interested in dwelling with His people and communing with them, so long as they serve Him. The true fulfillment of this is when Christ appears in the clouds in the last days, and pitches His own tabernacle in order to dwell in the midst of His people.

The Number Ten

The number ten and its various factors (one hundred, one thousand, ten thousand, etc.) will always represent the theme of authority and dominion in the Bible. Whether this authority or dominion is in God's hands or man's, we can look at the scriptural use of this number and clearly understand its meaning and use. Let us examine this fascinating and extremely important number.

Again, the first place we look is in the corresponding Genesis chapter. As we look at Genesis 10, several key items are easily apparent. First, we have mention of the first king ever named since the creation. His name is Nimrod. We know that he is a king because Genesis 10:10 reveals to us that he had a *kingdom*. This is the first time this word is used in the Scriptures. This seems to set the tone for understanding this number.

Secondly, we notice that there is an extensive genealogy given to us concerning the descendants of the three sons of Noah: Shem, Ham, and Japheth. We will not list the entire genealogy in this chapter, suffice it to say that there are precisely **seventy** descendants that are listed here in Genesis 10. Verse thirty-two tells us that ". . . by these were the nations divided in the earth after the flood." These seventy nations represent the kingdoms of the earth that are still in existence to this day. It is interesting to note that there were seven continents that the earth was divided into in the days of Peleg (Genesis 10:25).

Revelation 11 tells us that these seventy kingdoms from the seven continents will come under the direct authority of Jesus Christ. ". . . The kingdoms of this world are become the kingdoms of our Lord, and of his Christ; and he shall reign for ever and ever" (Revelation 11:15). The prophets even reveal an amazingly clear time prophecy concerning when the kingdoms of the world become the thousand-year kingdom of Christ. It is at the Feast of Tabernacles, as declared to God's servants the prophets.

> And it shall come to pass, that every one that is left of all the nations which came against Jerusalem shall even go up from year to year to worship the King, the LORD of hosts, and to keep the feast of tabernacles.
>
> —Zechariah 14:16

It is important to note that the phrase "feast of tabernacles" is mentioned exactly ten times in the Bible.

At this point, it is important to understand that one of the most serious themes in the Bible is that of biblical authority. The large amount of verses and Bible illustrations that teach this cannot be mentioned here, yet even those who only begin to read the Scriptures should understand this concept. Rebellion is *NEVER* tolerated in the Scriptures. It is even given the abominable equivalence to witchcraft in 1 Samuel 15:23. The only biblical exception to this is when man's law or authority supercedes God's. The true Christian is wise when he/she understands that when God places a person under the authority of another person, that authority must be respected, and never rebelled against. We are taught in the scriptures that men are subject even to wicked kings, wives are subject to their husbands, servants are subject to their masters, children are subject to their parents, local congregations are subject to the biblical authority of the pastor, and all must be subject to the final authority of God through His holy Word. It goes without saying then that for a man to override the authority of God's Word by way of changing, adding, or omitting from it, is an act of rebellion.

Even God's respect for authority is manifest in the story of the exodus of the children of Israel from Egypt. Nowhere in the Scriptures does it indicate that God gave Moses and the Israelites His permission to rebel against the authority of Pharaoh. Remember, it was God who placed Israel under Pharaoh's dominion in the days of Jacob in the latter half of the book of Genesis. God's instructions to Moses were to go to Pharaoh and say, ". . . Let my people go, that they may serve me" (Exodus 8:1). This was done repeatedly by Moses, and each time was followed by a plague sent by God to coax Pharaoh into changing his mind. The last time this is spoken is in Exodus 10. This was the last time that Pharaoh was to see Moses' face. It was after this that God sent the **tenth** plague upon Egypt, the death of the firstborn. It was through ten plagues that the authority over Israel was transferred from Pharaoh to God.

Immediately after the death of Pharaoh and his armies in the Red Sea, God led Israel to Mount Sinai, where he gave them His "fiery law." The exact phrase "the law" is mentioned three hundred twenty times in the Bible. Here we see this number as 10 x 4 x 4 x 2. We will see more of this connection between the number ten and the number four. They were the first version of the Holy Book of God, written on tables of stone with the very right hand of God, and they represented God's ultimate authority over His people by way of His written Word. They are the **Ten** Commandments. It should come as no surprise that we find these Ten Commandments in Exodus 20, the seventieth (10 x 7) chapter of the Bible. It is interesting yet understandable why God's law would be placed in such a fashion. Accordingly, we find the phrase "kingdom of God" in various forms mentioned exactly seventy times in the Bible. Since we are dealing with this theme of God ruling over the nations of the earth, we will also add that the title "King" with a capital K is mentioned exactly seventy times in the Scriptures.

In Genesis 24 we see a revealing story concerning the securing of a *bride* for the *only begotten son* of Abraham. In this chapter Abraham sends his servant to search for a bride for his son, Isaac. This servant takes with him ten camels (Genesis 24:10). It is interesting to see that when Rebekah is brought to Isaac, it is these ten camels that bring her. God revealed to Isaiah the reason for this. "So shall my word be that goeth forth out of my mouth: it shall not return unto me void, but it shall accomplish that which I please, and it shall prosper in the thing whereto I sent it" (Isaiah 55:11). In this story we also see an interesting image of the Rapture. In verse sixty-seven, the Scriptures reveal, "And Isaac brought her into his **mother Sarah's** tent, and took Rebekah, and she became his wife; and he loved her . . ." (Genesis 24:67). The Lord also revealed this imagery to Paul who said in Galatians, "But Jerusalem which is above is free, which is the mother of us all" (Galatians 4:26). This is in reference to the two sons of Abraham, Ishmael, born of the bondwoman Hagar, which represented those under the law of Mt. Sinai, and Isaac, born of the free woman, Sarah. This scripture reveals to us that Sarah was a type of heaven from which those who are *born again* come. As Isaac took his bride into his mother Sarah's tent for their union, so Christ will come and gather His bride and take her to heaven, and so shall we ever be with the Lord.

God instructed Moses to take the two tablets of stone that contained the Ten Commandments, and place them inside a specially designed chest, referred to as the Ark of the Covenant. This Ark represented the throne of God on earth, where God would dwell and reign over His people. This Ark was placed in a very sacred and holy part of the tabernacle, referred to as the "Most Holy Place." The walls of the tabernacle were ten cubits high. The most holy place was exactly ten cubits wide by ten cubits long. This makes the dimensions of the Most Holy Place where God sits on the throne and reigns over His people 10 x 10 x 10, or, one thousand square cubits.

> Blessed and holy is he that hath part in the first resurrection: on such the second death hath no power, but they shall be priests of God and of Christ, and shall reign with him a **thousand years.**
> —Revelation 20:6

Those who study eschatology are generally divided into three camps. There are those who do not believe that the thousand-year reign of

Christ is a literal time frame, but give it a symbolic interpretation. They say that it represents an uncertain length of time whereby Christ will reign in the hearts of mankind, until the time of the final judgment. This theory is held by many, especially in the world of theological academia, despite the fact that there is no biblical evidence to support the premise that "a thousand years" is *only* symbolic. Are we not limited to believing *only* what the Bible tells us to believe?

Of this theory, I will say this. As we have obviously seen in this book, the numbers in the Bible are all connected to a symbolic spiritual theme. There seems to be no exception to this so far. Yet when we examined their plain usage in the text of Scripture, did they not have a very literal interpretation? When Naaman is instructed to dip in the river Jordan seven times, would it suffice him to see the symbolic significance of what he was told to do, and believe in faith that he would be healed? No. He must do exactly what Elisha demanded him, by the Word of God. We have seen the symbolic significance of David picking up five stones to defeat Goliath, but did he not indeed pick up five stones? Are there not really three that bear record in heaven? Surely these numbers have symbolic meaning, but all of them are as literal as the resurrection itself, and are meant to be interpreted that way. There is no exception to this. As displayed in the Most Holy Place itself, being 10 x 10 x 10 cubits where God sits on the throne to reign over His people, so will Christ reign 10 x 10 x 10 years over all the earth.

Might I add at this point that the exact phrase "thousand years" is mentioned exactly **ten** times in the Scriptures. I think this speaks for itself.

It is nothing short of the mighty, providential hand of God that we find a very fitting message in the thousandth chapter of the Bible. It is a message that not only speaks of the kingdom of God and Christ's reign on the earth, but it also reveals to all mankind exactly what is required of anyone who wishes to be part of this wonderful kingdom. Notice this verse in the thousandth chapter of the Bible.

Jesus answered and said unto him, Verily, verily, I say unto thee,

Except a man be **born again**, he cannot see the **kingdom of God.**

—John 3:3

In the four gospels of the New Testament, "the kingdom" is mentioned exactly one hundred (10 x 10) times. These four gospels tell the story of Jesus, the King of the Jews, who came four hundred (10 x 10 x 4) years after the prophet Malachi, the last book of the Old Testament. Malachi was the thirty-ninth book of the Bible, making the book of Matthew, the beginning of the four gospels about the King of the Jews, the fortieth (10 x 4) book of the Bible. Matthew 3 tells us of John the Baptist, the voice of one crying in the wilderness who prepares the way for the coming of Christ. He and his words are prophesied in the book of Isaiah 40.

In Genesis 41 the Scriptures tell us that Joseph is released from his prison and given the position of great authority over all of the land of Egypt. It is in verse forty (10 x 4) that Pharaoh gives him this authority and says, "Thou shalt be over my house, and **according unto thy word** shall all my people be ruled: only in the throne will I be greater than thou." It is understood that, in this, Joseph is a type of Christ who will reign over both Jew and Gentile. At this time, Joseph is thirty (10 x 3) years old. In the framework of the book of Genesis, Joseph reigns from chapter forty-one to chapter fifty, a total of **ten** chapters. He reigns a total of eighty (10 x 8) years and dies when he is one hundred ten (10 x 11) years old. You can say that this is by an act of chance (much like evolution), but I believe it shows the nature and order of God and His Word.

In Genesis 49, Jacob prophesies concerning his sons in the last days. In verse **ten** he says, "The **sceptre** shall not depart from Judah, nor a **lawgiver** from between his feet, until Shiloh come; and unto him shall the gathering of the people be." This reveals to us that the King of God's people would come from the tribe of Judah. However, when Israel began to cry out for a king in the book of 1 Samuel, God told Samuel to anoint Saul, of the tribe of Benjamin, as the first king (1 Samuel 9:17). Although his beginning was humble, the majority of 1 Samuel tells us that Saul became a wicked king, who ruled the people with tyranny. God raised up a mighty man by the name of David, who was of the tribe of Judah, to be king in Saul's stead. The book of Ruth traces the lineage of David from the tribe of Judah through Pharez. Notice the numerical placement of David in this lineage, found in Ruth 4:18–22.

1. Pharez	2. Hezron
3. Ram	4. Amminadab
5. Nahshon	6. Salmon
7. Boaz	8. Obed
9. Jesse	10. David

It was according to the Word of the Lord given through Jacob in a verse numbered "ten" that the tenth generation through Judah's son Pharez would become the king of God's people. As we continue to look further at God's divine order, we see that it was in the tenth book of the Bible, 2 Samuel, that David replaced Saul as king of Israel. It was declared to us in 2 Samuel 3:10!

> To translate the kingdom from the house of Saul, and to set up the throne of David over Israel and over Judah, from Dan even to Beersheba.
>
> —2 Samuel 3:10

The Scriptures reveal to us that David reigned as king of Israel for exactly forty years, telling us also that this reign was divided into two time frames, thirty-three years and seven years (2 Samuel 5:5; 1 Kings 2:11; 1 Chronicles 3:4, 29:27). The Scriptures also reveal to us that Jesus reigned as King of the Jews from his birth to his death (Matthew 2:2, 27:37) a period of thirty-three years. It is expected that during the final seven-year Tribulation, Christ will once again begin to reign over his people during these seven years. It is also interesting to note that, according to the chronology of the Bible, Jesus' appearance as King of the Jews occurred some one thousand years after the reign of David.

When "feet" are mentioned in the Bible, it usually carries the idea of dominion or authority, probably because the feet have ten toes. God told Israel that everywhere the soles of their feet traveled in the land of Canaan would be theirs (Deuteronomy 11:24). In Joshua 10, Joshua told the captains of the guard to place their feet on the backs of the necks of the kings of the Philistines. Ruth laid herself down at the feet of Boaz, a symbol of his dominion as the husband and redeemer, a type of Christ. The only surviving heir to what would be Saul's kingdom, Mephibosheth, was lame in both his feet (2 Samuel 9:13). He had his dominion and his feet taken from him. In 2 Samuel 22 and Psalm 18, David declares that God has made his enemies to fall under his feet. Notice the use of the words "tread" or "trodden" as you study the Scriptures, and you will see this act of dominion.

Luke 7 tells us of a sinful woman who came to Jesus. The Bible tells us that she washed his feet with her tears, and dried them with her hair. To do so, she must place the feet of Christ on her own head. In this symbolic act, she is placing her life under the total authority of the Word of God made flesh, Jesus. The demon-possessed man in the country of the Gadarenes (Luke 8), after he was delivered of his "legion," was found clothed, in his right mind, at Jesus feet. In Romans 16:20, Paul reveals that God will bruise Satan under our feet shortly. And 1 Corinthians 15:25 tells us that Jesus must reign until He has put all His enemies *under his feet*! This is why the Scriptures tell us, "The LORD said unto my Lord, Sit thou at my right hand, until I make thine enemies **thy footstool**" (Psalm 110:1).

In Genesis 1, God gave man dominion over everything that was in the earth. Man lost this dominion to Satan, who became the "god of this world." Christ will claim this dominion for His own in the last days. In Revelation 10, Christ, the mighty angel, ". . . set his right foot upon the sea, and his left foot on the earth." By doing so, He is reclaiming the world which He created with ten words (Genesis 1:1), for His own, and beginning the process of placing His enemies under His feet.

The gospel of Matthew tells us of the parable of the ten virgins.

The first verse in chapter twenty-five specifically states, "Then shall the kingdom of heaven be likened unto ten virgins, which took their lamps, and went forth to meet the bridegroom." You will notice however, that these ten virgins are divided into two groups: those who are ready, and those who are not. The use of the number five here seems to indicate their acceptance or rejection of God's grace. Those virgins who have received the grace of God that bringeth salvation have the oil of the Holy Spirit and the lamps of the Word of God to lighten their path. When the midnight cry rang out, those five wise virgins entered the feast of the Bridegroom, Jesus, and the door was shut. Those five foolish virgins were those who had a form of godliness, but denied the power of God and His grace. They are convincing Christian "lookalikes" but there is no Spirit and no true Word to lighten their path. They are caught on the wrong side of a shut door, and now must suffer the wrath of God.

As was mentioned earlier, the word "King" with a capital K is mentioned precisely seventy times in the Scriptures. When we look at the word "king" or "kings," without paying attention to capitalization, we find them mentioned exactly two thousand, five hundred forty times, a multiple of ten. The phrase "book of the kings of Israel" is mentioned ten times in the Bible. The word "throne" or "thrones" is mentioned one hundred thirty (10 x 13) times in the Old Testament. The word "prince" is mentioned ten times in the New Testament. The tenth occurrence of this word is found in Revelation 1:5 when it declares Jesus as ". . . the prince of the kings of the earth. . . ." And in the entire Bible, all forms of the word "prince" are mentioned exactly three hundred eighty times, a multiple of ten.

The next phrase we look at in the Bible is "kingdom." This comes in three forms in the Scriptures. The words "kingdom" and "kingdoms" are mentioned exactly three hundred ninety-nine times in the Bible, not a multiple of ten. However, there is one other form that this word comes in. It is mentioned as "kingly throne" and is found in Daniel 5:20. This two-word phrase actually has as its root the same Hebrew word for "kingdom." This gives us a total of four hundred occurrences, or 10 x 10 x 4. Notice the inclusion of the number four, for the four gospels. The following verse reveals for us the connection between the gospels and the kingdom of God.

> And this **gospel of the kingdom** shall be preached in all the world for a witness unto all nations; and then shall the end come.
>
> —Matthew 24:14

I will point out to you that this exact phrase, "gospel of the kingdom," is mentioned four times in the Bible. Also, as we saw earlier, the thousandth chapter of the Bible is found in the fourth gospel, the Gospel of John, chapter three.

The Bible gives the symbol of a "mountain" to represent kingdoms. The words "mount" and "mountain" are used exactly **four hundred** times in the Scriptures. From Daniel 2, we learned the following.

> Then was the iron, the clay, the brass, the silver, and the gold, broken to pieces together, and became like the chaff of the summer threshingfloors; and the wind carried them away, that no place was found for them: and **the stone** that smote the image became **a great mountain**, and filled the whole earth. . . . And in the days of these kings shall the God of heaven set up **a kingdom**, which shall never be destroyed: and the kingdom shall not be left to other people, but it shall break in pieces and consume all these kingdoms, and it shall stand for ever.
>
> —Daniel 2:35,44

In the Old Testament, Mount Edom, or Seir, always represented the kingdom of the Edomites, the descendants of Esau. Mount Sinai, or Horeb, was referred to as the mountain of God where the Ten Commandments were given. In Exodus 19, God instructed the Israelites to come near the mountain, but not on it, because the true kingdom of God had not come upon them as yet. In Exodus 19, this mount is mentioned precisely ten times. However, the New Testament, in referencing this story, reveals to us that those who are born again, may come boldly to this mountain, the kingdom of God.

For ye are not come unto the mount that might be touched, and
that burned with fire, nor unto blackness, and darkness, and tempest, And the sound of a trumpet, and the voice of words; which
voice they that heard intreated that the word should not be spoken
to them any more: (For they could not endure that which was commanded, And if so much as a beast touch the mountain, it shall be
stoned, or thrust through with a dart: And so terrible was the sight,
that Moses said, I exceedingly fear and quake:) But ye are come
unto mount Sion, and unto the city of the living God, the heavenly Jerusalem, and to an innumerable company of angels.

—Hebrews 12:18–22

This passage reveals to us that the holy city, heavenly Jerusalem, where
God sits on the throne, is the true kingdom of God. The "holy city" is
mentioned precisely ten times in the Scriptures. As you study the
Scriptures, take note of any story or prophecy that mentions a mount
or mountain. In many of these, the symbol of God's kingdom will
become plain to you.

And it shall come to pass in the last days, that the mountain of the
Lord's house shall be established in the top of the mountains, and
shall be exalted above the hills; and all nations shall flow unto it.

—Isaiah 2:2

One thousand shall flee at the rebuke of one; at the rebuke of five
shall ye flee: till ye be left as a beacon upon the top of a mountain,
and as an ensign on an hill.

—Isaiah 30:17

For in mine holy mountain, in the mountain of the height of Israel,
saith the Lord GOD, there shall all the house of Israel, all of them in
the land, serve me: there will I accept them, and there will I require
your offerings, and the firstfruits of your oblations, with all your
holy things.

—Ezekiel 20:40

Again, the devil taketh him up into an exceeding high mountain, and showeth him all the kingdoms of the world, and the glory of them.

—Matthew 4:8

And seeing the multitudes, he went up into a mountain: and when he was set, his disciples came unto him.

—Matthew 5:1

And here is the mind which hath wisdom. The **seven heads** are seven mountains, on which the woman sitteth. And there are seven kings: five are fallen, and one is, and the other is not yet come; and when he cometh, he must continue a short space.

—Revelation 17:9–10

The number ten and tithing

It should come as no real surprise to the reader that the words "tithe," "tithes," and "tithing" are mentioned a total of forty (10 x 4) times in the Bible. Here again we see a perfect combination of two important Bible numbers: ten for God's dominion, and four for the gospels. It should also be easily understood by the reader that the literal meaning of the word *tithe* is "tenth" or ten percent. I will also note to the reader that there are those who do not see any sort of consistent significance in the numbers given to us in the Scriptures. Yet, we have an entire Bible doctrine whose sole significance is attached to the meaning of the number ten.

There has of late been a steady peppering of preachers, theologians and the like, who have come along over the years with a "god-given" calling to set the captives of the church free from what they claim is the false doctrine of paying ten percent of your earnings to a church. They insist that this is an Old Testament law that was done away with in the new age of grace. This author recalls hearing a local radio broadcast featuring a woman preacher who spent several broadcasts discussing the subject of how she thought tithing was no longer a scriptural mandate. It was followed several weeks later by her desperate plea for offerings because financial support for her program had dropped severely. Before long she was off the air completely.

There have been many good men over the years preach and write outstanding sermons and books on the subject of biblical tithing. I do not wish to transcend these great works, but merely to add a little more light to what they have already covered.

First, lets look at the first occurrence of the word "tithe."

> And Melchizedek king of Salem brought forth bread and wine: and he was the priest of the most high God. And he blessed him, and said, Blessed be Abram of the **most high God, possessor of heaven and earth**: And blessed be the most high God, which hath delivered thine enemies into thy hand. And he gave him **tithes** of all.
>
> —Genesis 14:18–20

We will look more closely at the New Testament revelation concerning this passage, but for now we find a couple of interesting points. First, this action of Abram was performed voluntarily. Secondly, we note that this tithing pre-dates the law given to Moses. But most importantly, it was given to the "most high God, possessor of heaven and earth" as a token of His dominion and total authority, hence we see the importance that the number ten plays in this doctrine. It is interesting that we see given here the description of God as the "possessor of heaven and earth." This takes us back to Genesis 1 where we see that God is the "possessor" because He is the "Creator." In the very first verse of Genesis 1, the initial act of creation was carried out by exactly **ten** words, "In the beginning, God created the heaven and the earth." Throughout the creation process, given in its entirety in Genesis 1, the phrase "God said" is used precisely **ten** times! Truly God's dominion extends over all the heavens and the earth.

In Malachi 3:**10**, God encourages His people to tithe.

> Bring ye all the tithes into the storehouse, that there may be meat in mine house, and prove me now herewith, saith the LORD of hosts, if I will not open you the windows of heaven, and pour you out a blessing, that there shall not be room enough to receive it.
>
> —Malachi 3:10

This command comes more in the form of an encouragement to will-fully give and see the mighty results of obedience to God and His law. With the several other instances of tithing mentioned in the Old Testament, there seems to be a pattern of joyful giving by God's people who, even though they are under royal command, are gladly paying tithes in honor of their King of Kings.

In Hebrews 7, we have a New Testament reference to Abram's Old Testament offering. Verses one and two seem to plainly reveal the connection between tithing and the royal number ten.

> For this Melchisedec, **king of Salem**, priest of the most high God, who met Abraham returning from the slaughter of the kings, and blessed him; To whom also Abraham gave a tenth part of all; first being by interpretation **King of righteousness**, and after that also **King of Salem**, which is, **King of peace**.
>
> —Hebrews 7:1–2

We now see that Melchisedec is an Old Testament *type* of Jesus the King. The question then of whether or not the doctrine of giving a tenth of our substance is valid for the New Testament church has a simple answer. Since Christ is indeed our King, it is clearly biblical that we should honor Him so with a tenth of our substance.

Tithing and the salvation of Israel

As with so many other things in the Bible, God uses the theme of tithing to point to a restored Israel in the last days. In the gospel of Luke, we find the following story.

> And as he entered into a certain village, there met him **ten men** that were lepers, which stood afar off: And they lifted up their voic-es, and said, Jesus, Master, have mercy on us. And when he saw them, he said unto them, Go shew yourselves unto the priests. And it came to pass, that, as they went, they were cleansed. And **one of them**, when he saw that he was healed, turned back, and with a loud voice glorified God, And fell down on his face at **his feet**, giv-

ing him thanks: and he was a Samaritan. And Jesus answering said, Were there not ten cleansed? but where are the nine? There are not found that returned to give glory to God, save this stranger. And he said unto him, **Arise, go thy way: thy faith hath made thee whole.**

—Luke 17:12–19

Although there were originally ten men who were healed, the precise tithing formula, a tenth or one in ten, returns to Jesus and falls at His feet, a sign of dominion. Jesus' blessing on this man is given in ten words. In this story, we see a picture of the promise given to Isaiah. In Isaiah 6, the prophet sees the glory of God, high and lifted up. The message that God has for Isaiah is that the land will be wasted and desolate, and His people will be given confusion and spiritual blindness. However, God is always the God of hope and salvation. He promises in verse thirteen that even though He has caused this desolation, ". . . yet in it shall be **a tenth, and it shall return**, and shall be eaten: as a teil tree, and as an oak, whose substance is in them, when they cast their leaves: so the holy seed shall be the substance thereof."

The "tenth" here may be seen as the dispersed of Israel that will come again to the land in the last days. They are characterized by the ten northern tribes of Israel that, through their continued rebellion, were captured by the Assyrians and dispersed all over the world, as declared in the following verses.

And he shall set up an ensign for the nations, and shall assemble the outcasts of Israel, and gather together the dispersed of Judah from the four corners of the earth.

—Isaiah 11:12

For a small moment have I forsaken thee; but with great mercies will I gather thee.

—Isaiah 54:7

The Lord GOD which gathereth the outcasts of Israel saith, Yet will I gather others to him, beside those that are gathered unto him.

—Isaiah 56:8

And I will gather the remnant of my flock out of all countries whither
I have driven them, and will bring them again to their folds; and
they shall be fruitful and increase.

—Jeremiah 23:3

And I will be found of you, saith the LORD: and I will turn away
your captivity, and I will gather you from all the nations, and from
all the places whither I have driven you, saith the LORD; and I will
bring you again into the place whence I caused you to be carried
away captive.

—Jeremiah 29:14

Hear the word of the LORD, O ye nations, and declare it in the isles
afar off, and say, He that scattered Israel will gather him, and keep
him, as a shepherd doth his flock.

—Jeremiah 31:10

Many, many more similar verses from the prophets of God could have
been quoted here, but the idea is clear. When Christ makes His glorious return to earth to establish his thousand-year kingdom on the
earth, He will gather the dispersed ten tribes of Israel, as a Shepherd
gathers his sheep. That this process is a seven-year process can be
seen in such things as the sixty-six who with Jacob descend to the
land of Goshen to meet up with four (gospels) of the house of Joseph
to become the seventy (Exodus 1:5); seventy elders of Israel who had
the spirit of Moses placed in them (Numbers 11:16–17); the seventy
years of Babylonian captivity through which a remnant was saved and
allowed to once again enter the land; the seventy weeks determined
on Israel to forgive her sins (Daniel 9:24); the seventy times seven
times that the sins of Jesus' brethren are to be forgiven (Matthew
18:22).

There are many other numerical indications in the Bible that reveal that Christ will spend seven years defeating his enemies in preparation for a thousand-year reign. Notice the use of seven, seventy
(7 x 10), one thousand, ten thousand, etc. in the following Bible types.

And Ehud escaped while they tarried, and passed beyond the quar-
ries, and escaped unto Seirath. And it came to pass, when he was
come, that he blew a trumpet in the mountain of Ephraim, and
the children of Israel went down with him from the mount, and he
before them. And he said unto them, Follow after me: for the LORD
hath delivered your enemies the Moabites into your hand. And
they went down after him, and took the fords of Jordan toward Moab,
and suffered not a man to pass over. And they slew of Moab at that
time about ten thousand men, all lusty, and all men of valour; and
there escaped not a man.

—Judges 3:26–29

And Judah went up; and the LORD delivered the Canaanites and the
Perizzites into their hand: and they slew of them in Bezek ten thousand men. And they found Adonibezek in Bezek: and they fought
against him, and they slew the Canaanites and the Perizzites. But
Adonibezek fled; and they pursued after him, and caught him, and
cut off his thumbs and his great toes. And Adonibezek said, Three-
score and ten kings, having their thumbs and their great toes cut
off, gathered their meat under my table: as I have done, so God hath
requited me. And they brought him to Jerusalem, and there he died.

—Judges 1:4–7

And Ahab had seventy sons in Samaria. And Jehu wrote letters,
and sent to Samaria, unto the rulers of Jezreel, to the elders, and to
them that brought up Ahab's children, . . . Then he wrote a letter
the second time to them, saying, If ye be mine, and if ye will hearken unto my voice, take ye the heads of the men your master's
sons, and come to me to Jezreel by to morrow this time. Now the
king's sons, being seventy persons, were with the great men of the
city, which brought them up. And it came to pass, when the letter
came to them, that they took the king's sons, and slew seventy persons, and put their heads in baskets, and sent him them to Jezreel.

—2 Kings 10:1,6–7

At the end of this seven-year period, there comes a triumphal, glorious act of Christ's dominion, detailed for us in Revelation 19. This final act has been prophesied since before the days of the flood of Noah. For it was Enoch, the seventh from Adam, who prophesied according to Jude:

> . . . Behold, the Lord cometh with **ten thousands** of his saints, To execute judgment upon all, and to convince all that are ungodly among them of all their ungodly deeds which they have ungodly committed, and of all their hard speeches which ungodly sinners have spoken against him.
>
> —Jude 1:14–15

The number ten and the kingdom of the Antichrist

Here, once again, we see the work of the great imitator, Satan. It should be readily apparent to the sincere student of the Word of God, that Satan only mimics what he sees and what he knows. He sees Christ associated with grace and the number five, therefore his Antichrist is associated with this number as well. He sees the perfection of the Word of God in the number seven, he imitates by proclaiming, "I will be like the most High," seven words. He even has seven heads, according to Revelation 12. Now we see his response to the number ten and God's divine authority.

> And as the **toes of the feet** were part of iron, and part of clay, so **the kingdom** shall be partly strong, and partly broken.
>
> —Daniel 2:42

> After this I saw in the night visions, and behold a fourth beast, dreadful and terrible, and strong exceedingly; and it had great iron teeth: it devoured and brake in pieces, and stamped the residue with the feet of it: and it was diverse from all the beasts that were before it; and it **had ten horns**. . . . And the **ten horns out of this kingdom are ten kings** that shall arise: and another shall rise after

them; and he shall be diverse from the first, and he shall subdue
three kings.

—Daniel 7:7,24

And there appeared another wonder in heaven; and behold a great
red dragon, having seven heads and **ten horns**, and seven crowns
upon his heads.

—Revelation 12:3

And I stood upon the sand of the sea, and saw a beast rise up out of
the sea, having seven heads and **ten horns**, and upon his horns ten
crowns, and upon his heads the name of blasphemy.

—Revelation 13:1

And the ten **horns which thou sawest** are **ten kings**, which have
received no kingdom as yet; but receive power as kings one hour
with the beast.

—Revelation 17:12

The Numbers Eleven, Twenty-Two, and Thirty-Three

In this chapter, we will focus on the numbers eleven, twenty-two, and thirty-three. The number eleven is recognized as the number for confusion and disorder. The number twenty-two is recognized as the number for light and revelation. The number thirty-three as the number for divine wisdom. You will notice that the number eleven is the base number of these three. The transition from confusion, eleven, to revelation and wisdom, twenty-two and thirty-three, seems to be directly related to the number of required witnesses needed to establish a principle from the Scriptures: "This is the third time I am coming to you. In the mouth of two or three witnesses shall every word be established" (2 Corinthians 13:1). The two witnesses here represent the books of the Old and New Testament. When they stand alone, one witness, they are misunderstood, confusion. When they stand together and are interpreted together, they reveal the mysteries of God, revelation knowledge. The three witnesses are represented by the Father, the Word, and the Holy Ghost, or the Spirit, the water, and the blood (1 John 5:7–8). These three testify of the Son of God, Jesus Christ, who was thirty-three years old when He died and rose again.

The Old Testament contains thirty-nine books, and the New Testament twenty-seven, neither of which, when viewed alone, are numbers of revelation. But when placed together, their sum becomes sixty-six, seen as 22 x 3, or 33 x 2. Truly the Holy Bible is a book of both revelation and wisdom. The Scriptures reveal that currently Israel is partially blind, but not totally. "For I would not, brethren, that ye should be ignorant of this mystery, lest ye should be wise in your own conceits; that blindness in part is happened to Israel, until the fulness of the Gentiles be come in" (Romans 11:25). The reason why they are partially blinded and not totally is because they only read the Old Testament, which currently has the veil of Moses on it (2 Corinthians 3:15).

In the gospel of Mark this principle is typologically portrayed.

> And he cometh to Bethsaida; and they bring a blind man unto him, and besought him to touch him. And he took the blind man by the hand, and led him out of the town; and when he had spit on his eyes, and put his hands upon him, he asked him if he saw ought. And he looked up, and said, I see men as trees, walking. After that he put his hands again upon his eyes, and made him look up: and he was restored, and saw every man clearly.
>
> —Mark 8:22–25

You will notice that Jesus spit in his eyes. The biblical explanation for this is found in the book of Proverbs.

> The mouth of a righteous man is a well of life: but violence covereth the mouth of the wicked.
>
> —Proverbs 10:11

> The words of a man's mouth are as deep waters, and the wellspring of wisdom as a flowing brook.
>
> —Proverbs 18:4

The spit of Jesus represents every word that proceeds out of His mouth, literally the Word of God. You will notice that this process takes place twice. The first time, corresponding to the reading of one witness, the Old Testament, the man only receives partial sight. The second time it happens, corresponding to the reading of the Old and New Testaments, he now has clear sight.

The number eleven and confusion

The number eleven is easily recognizable as the number for confusion, disorder, and chaos. And of course, the first place we look is the eleventh chapter of the book of Genesis.

> And the whole earth was of one language, and of one speech.
>
> —Genesis 11:1

Please take note of the order of God in this passage. We see that there are three separate things that are expressed in terms of unity: whole earth, one language, one speech. Up until this time, the dwellers of the earth were speaking the original language of the garden of Eden, most likely Hebrew. The Hebrew language contains its own special numerical pattern that will be examined later in this chapter. The order and structure of verse one reveals the divine order of the Godhead, who is three yet one. As is well known, the men of the earth at this time set about to unite themselves by way of a city and a tower to reach the heavens. This method of reaching heaven is man's method and not God's, for He has provided His Son Jesus as the ladder to the presence of God (Genesis 28:12; John 1:51).

As a result of man's choosing his own way rather than God's, God judges them by confusing their languages, thus we see disorder and confusion.

> Go to, let us go down, and there confound their language, that they may not understand one another's speech. So the LORD scattered them abroad from thence upon the face of all the earth: and they left off to build the city.
>
> —Genesis 11:7–8

When we examine the plain use of the number eleven in the text of the Scriptures, we can clearly see its association with confusion. During Jesus' ministry, He selected twelve men to be his apostles, similar to the twelve tribes of Israel. However, one of those, Judas Iscariot, whose name is mentioned eleven times, was removed from his office by his betrayal of Christ. This leaves eleven disciples. Notice how the Scriptures reveal the theme of confusion associated with these eleven disciples.

> Then the eleven disciples went away into Galilee, into a mountain where Jesus had appointed them. And when they saw him, they worshipped him: but **some doubted**.
>
> —Matthew 28:16–17

> Afterward he appeared unto the **eleven** as they sat at meat, and upbraided them with their **unbelief** and hardness of heart, because they **believed** not them which had seen him after he was risen.
>
> —Mark 16:14

> And returned from the sepulchre, and told all these things unto the **eleven**, and to all the rest. It was Mary Magdalene, and Joanna, and Mary the mother of James, and other women that were with them, which told these things unto the apostles. And their **words seemed to them as idle tales, and they believed them not**.
>
> —Luke 24:9–11

So long as there were only eleven disciples, there was confusion in the ranks of the disciples who had a hard time believing that Jesus was risen from the dead. It wasn't until the addition of a new disciple, Mathias, who became number twelve, that the Holy Spirit poured out on them, giving them the understanding to interpret the event as the one prophesied by Joel. There is, however, one last mention of the eleven disciples even after Mathias had been added.

> But Peter, standing up with **the eleven**, lifted up his voice, and said unto them, Ye men of Judaea, and all ye that dwell at Jerusalem, be this known unto you, and hearken to my words.
>
> —Acts 2:14

The event mentioned here is referred to as Pentecost. The spirit was poured out on those men, and they began to speak in tongues on that day. First, it is important to note that these tongues were human languages. The word "language" is mentioned exactly thirty-three times in the Old Testament. It is also interesting to note that these languages were primarily *Gentile* languages. You will find the word "Gentiles" mentioned exactly ninety-nine (11 x 9) times in the New Testament. If looked upon as 33 x 3, we can see how the Gentiles, who have been the recipients of this Holy Ghost outpouring, walk in the wisdom of Holy Scriptures. We can also see how the Gentile age is the age of confusion for Israel. God warned the prophet Isaiah of this event when He said, "For with stammering lips and another **tongue** will he speak to this people" (Isaiah 28:11). Accordingly, you will find the word "tongue" in the New Testament exactly thirty-three times. God used the events at Pentecost to reveal that He was now placing His kingdom in the hands of the Gentiles, and sending confusion to Israel for choosing a murderer, Barabbas, over the Messiah, Jesus.

It was Jesus Himself who signaled this confusion to Israel by way of the following statement.

> And about the ninth hour Jesus cried with a loud voice, saying, Eli, Eli, lama sabachthani? that is to say, My God, my God, why hast thou forsaken me?
>
> —Matthew 27:46

The language spoken by Jesus was Syriac, a Gentile language. This statement is recorded for us twice (Mark 15:34), indicating the span of the Gentile age, two thousand years (see chapter on the number two). The interpretation is given to us Gentiles in plain English as "My God, My God, why hast thou forsaken me?" This is a direct, word for word quotation from Psalm 22. In this prophecy, many of the things that took place while Jesus was on the cross were foretold. However, no one at the base of the cross understood what Jesus said.

Some of them that stood there, when they heard that, said, This
man calleth for Elias.

—Matthew 27:47

And some of them that stood by, when they heard it, said, Behold,
he calleth Elias. [The two forms of Elijah's name, "Elias" and "Elijah," are mentioned ninety-nine (11 x 9) times, the English interpretation of Jesus' statement contains nine words.]

—Mark 15:35

Had the Jews understood that Jesus was quoting Psalm 22, they would
have recognized the things that took place on the cross. They would
have known that their very own Messiah was dying for them as a
sacrifice. They would have known, and repented and believed. But
they didn't know, they didn't understand. "And he said, Go, and tell
this people, Hear ye indeed, but understand not; and see ye indeed,
but perceive not" (Isaiah 6:9).

As God confused the languages at Babel, so He confused Israel
with languages on the day of Pentecost, the apostles speaking in Gentile tongues, and the sign of the *cloven tongue* on each of them. A
cloven tongue is a breached tongue, indicating the number two, also
indicative of the two thousand-year Gentile age. When the Holy Spirit is poured the second time on Israel, God will once again use the
sign of a language, only this time, it will be their mother tongue. "For
then will I turn to the people a **pure language**, that they may all call
upon the name of the LORD, to serve him with one consent" (Zephaniah 3:9).

That Israel will be saved in the last days is no mystery to those
who believe every word of the Scriptures. But the Scriptures are clear
in revealing that Israel must be born again the same way the Gentiles
have been for some two thousand years. They must not only believe
the Old Testament, but also the New Testament. To the Jew now, the
New Testament is a corruption and a contemptible essay that was
manufactured by the Gentiles, whom they refer to as the *goyim*, or
heathens. However, in time, the Jews will recognize a very familiar

pattern in the New Testament that may help them understand that it was written for them and for their salvation. Let me explain.

Every learned Jew recognizes that the Hebrew alphabet contains precisely twenty-two letters, the number twenty-two being the number for revelation. Incidentally, the word "letter(s)" is mentioned exactly twenty-two times in the New Testament. However, there are also five extra letters, called *final forms* that are slight variations of the originals. These final forms are placed at the end of a Hebrew word to indicate to the reader that a word has ended and the very next letter forms a new word. This is done because the written Hebrew of the Bible manuscripts contains no spaces between words. It was done to eliminate any confusion as to what the Scriptures were saying. This makes a total of twenty-seven Hebrew letters, twenty-two primary forms, and five final forms at the end.

There is a word in the Bible that follows this exact same pattern. It is the word "mystery." This word is mentioned exactly twenty-two times, all of them in the New Testament. The only other form of this word is the word "mysteries," mentioned five times, all in the New Testament. The plain use of this word reveals its nature and connection to the number twenty-two and the number five.

> He answered and said unto them, Because it is given unto you to know the mysteries of the kingdom of heaven, but to them it is not given.
>
> —Matthew 13:11

> And he said unto them, Unto you it is given to know the mystery of the kingdom of God: but unto them that are without, all these things are done in parables.
>
> —Mark 4:11

> And he said, Unto you it is given to know the mysteries of the kingdom of God: but to others in parables; that seeing they might not see, and hearing they might not understand.
>
> —Luke 8:10

> For I would not, brethren, that ye should be ignorant of this mystery, lest ye should be wise in your own conceits; that blindness in part is happened to Israel, until the fulness of the Gentiles be come in.
>
> —Romans 11:25

> To whom God would make known what is the riches of the glory of this mystery among the Gentiles; which is Christ in you, the hope of glory.
>
> —Colossians 1:27

The explanation that the Bible gives is that the mystery, which has been kept secret, is now revealed to the Gentiles during the age of grace. This mystery is being hidden from Israel until the Gentile age is over with. The mystery is that Jesus Christ is the Son of God, the Savior of mankind, and the Redemption of Israel. This mystery will be revealed to them at the second coming of Christ. However, this mystery can only be revealed to them through the pages of the New Testament.

As we have seen, the Hebrew alphabet contains twenty-two letters and five final forms. The word "mystery" is mentioned twenty-two times, with five occurrences of its other form "mysteries." This gives us a total of twenty-seven. This is the exact number of books in the New Testament. And notice that there are twenty-two books, Romans through Revelation, that are epistles, or *letters*, revealing the true doctrine of Christ, and five books that deal with the story of Christ and the beginning of the church, Matthew through Acts. It would appear, though, that the pattern of books seems to be backward, with the five grace books appearing first from left to right, followed by the twenty-two letter books. However, it is well known by many that the Hebrew letters are arranged in a perfect order, from right to left. This perfectly corresponds to the twenty-two letter books of the New Testament being placed on the right side of the New Testament, with the five grace books being on the left side. God really does know what He is doing!

They do err . . .

Because Israel's heart was hard, God sent them a delusion, just enough for them to not recognize their Messiah when He came to them some two thousand years ago. Now, as we stand at the threshold of the return of our Lord, it is the Gentile church who must take heed to doctrine and biblical understanding. A strong delusion will once again be sent to the world for all those who choose not to believe in the real Jesus, the real Spirit, and the real gospel (2 Thessalonians 2:11). Although virtually unnoticed by many, those who call themselves *believers*, today's generation of New Age Christian, are being set up to believe the greatest lie that has ever been told: the replacement of the true Jesus by a fake one.

As churches all over the world, but especially in America, begin trading pure doctrine for the lie of ecumenism, they themselves become part of that great whore known as BABYLON, THE GREAT. As true believers, should we not recognize that our beliefs and doctrines should ONLY come from the Holy Scriptures? Instead, we readily accept the words of so-called "learned theologians" and "doctors of the law," or the latest modern day "prophet" or dreamer of dreams, even when they contradict the clear teaching of the preserved Word of God. The single worst mistake that any believer can make is to believe or teach anything that does not come from the Word of God. When we step out of the Bible that God has given us for our understanding, and begin interpreting scripture by all sorts of unbiblical methods, we begin a journey toward a misunderstanding of Scripture and God's ways, then eventually, walk in the paths of *false doctrine*.

Again, we turn to the scriptures for our understanding.

> But they also have *erred through wine*, and through *strong drink are out of the way*; the priest and the prophet have erred through strong drink, they are swallowed up of wine, they are out of the way through strong drink; *they err in vision, they stumble in judgment*.
>
> —Isaiah 28:7

There are some important symbols that must be understood before we move on. The most important of which is the symbol of *"wine and strong drink.*" As we look at how God used these two phrases in the Word, we find that they are symbolic of false doctrine and lack of spiritual knowledge. Let's look at some other scriptures that testify of this idea.

Do not drink *wine nor strong drink,* thou, nor thy sons with thee, when ye go into the tabernacle of the congregation, lest ye die: it shall be a statute for ever throughout your generations: And that ye *may put difference between holy and unholy, and between unclean and clean.*

—Leviticus 10:9–10

Ye have not eaten bread, neither have ye *drunk wine or strong drink*: that ye might *know that I am the LORD your God.*

—Deuteronomy 29:6

Thou hast shewed thy people hard things: thou hast made us to drink the *wine of astonishment.*

—Psalm 60:3

Wine is a mocker, *strong drink* is raging: and whosoever is *deceived thereby is not wise.*

—Proverbs 20:1

They that tarry long at the *wine*; they that go to seek *mixed wine.* Look not thou upon the wine when it is red, when it giveth his colour in the cup, when it moveth itself aright. At the last it *biteth like a serpent, and stingeth like an adder.* Thine *eyes shall behold strange women, and thine heart shall utter perverse things.*

—Proverbs 23:30–33

It is not for kings, O Lemuel, it is not for kings to drink *wine*; nor for princes *strong drink*: Lest they drink, and *forget the law,* and *pervert the judgment of any of the afflicted.*

—Proverbs 31:4–5

Woe unto them that rise up early in the morning, that they may follow *strong drink*; that continue until night, till *wine* inflame them! And the harp, and the viol, the tabret, and pipe, and wine, are in their feasts: but they regard not the work of the Lord, neither consider the operation of his hands. Therefore my people are gone into captivity, *because they have no knowledge*: and their honourable men are famished, and their multitude *dried up with thirst*.

—Isaiah 5:11–13

Yea, they are greedy dogs which can never have enough, and they are *shepherds that cannot understand: they all look to their own way, every one for his gain,* from his quarter. Come ye, say they, I will fetch *wine*, and we will fill ourselves with *strong drink*; and to-morrow shall be as this day, and much more abundant.

—Isaiah 56:11–12

For thus saith the Lord God of Israel unto me; Take the *wine* cup of this fury at my hand, and cause all the nations, to whom I send thee, to drink it. And they shall drink, and be moved, *and be mad*, because of the sword that I will send among them.

—Jeremiah 25:15–16

Babylon hath been a golden cup in the Lord's hand, that made all the earth drunken: the nations have *drunken of her wine; therefore the nations are mad.*

—Jeremiah 51:7

Neither shall any priest *drink wine*, when they enter into the inner court. Neither shall they take for their wives a widow, nor her that is put away: but they shall take maidens of the seed of the house of Israel, or a widow that had a priest before. *And they shall teach my people the difference between the holy and profane, and cause them to discern between the unclean and the clean.*

—Ezekiel 44:21–23

Ye are all the children of light, and the children of the day: we are not of the night, nor of darkness. Therefore let us not sleep, as do others; but let us watch and be sober. For they that sleep sleep in the night; and they that be *drunken are drunken in the night. But let us, who are of the day, be sober*, putting on the breastplate of faith and love; and for an helmet, the hope of salvation.

—1 Thessalonians 5:5–8

As you can see, God has dealt over and over with His people not having the spiritual knowledge that they must have. In a world where Bibles are almost commonplace, there seems to be in many cases less understanding than ever before. As with so many other things in the King James Version of the Bible, there are some very revealing numerical patterns that are associated with wine, strong drink, and the Holy Spirit. First, *wine* is mentioned two hundred thirty-one times in the Bible. This breaks down to *33 x 7*. The Bible has *sixty-six* books in it, which is the product of both twenty-two and thirty-three. The Scriptures plainly reveal to us the close relationship between *wine* and the *Holy Spirit*.

And be not drunk with *wine*, wherein is excess; but be *filled with the Spirit*.

—Ephesians 5:18

There is a definite and obvious contrast between those who are drunken with intoxicating wine, the earthly wine, who cannot discern things properly, and those who are filled with the Spirit of Christ, the heavenly Wine, and are being filled with the knowledge of God. I will also point out to you that the phrase *strong drink* is mentioned *twenty-two* times. Twenty-two is the number associated with light and revelation, and when we examine how *strong drink* is used in the Bible, we, once again, see the contrast between it and the Holy Spirit.

Wine is a mocker, strong drink is raging: and whosoever is *deceived* thereby *is not wise*.

—Proverbs 20:1

For he shall be great in the sight of the Lord, and shall drink *neither wine nor strong drink; and he shall be filled with the Holy Ghost*, even from his mother's womb.

—Luke 1:15

So the Scriptures are clear to us that we should not be full of the strong drink of false doctrines and misinterpretation, but, as Jesus taught us, be filled with the *new wine* from heaven, the Holy Spirit of truth.

And no man putteth new wine into old bottles: else the new wine doth burst the bottles, and the wine is spilled, and the bottles will be marred: but *new wine* must be put into *new bottles*.

—Mark 2:22

Only those who are born again can receive of this *new wine*, the wisdom of the Spirit of God. Those who are only acting "spiritual" will stumble in doctrine, and will be set up to believe the great lie that is about to come. Consistent with the biblical patterns, the phrase *new wine* is found *twenty-two* times in the Scriptures. The Scriptures clearly indicate that new wine is wine that comes fresh from the cluster of grapes before the fermentation process takes place. Notice this very revealing verse.

Thus saith the LORD, As the new wine is found in the cluster, and one saith, Destroy it not; for a blessing is in it: so will I do for my servants' sakes, that I may not destroy them all.

—Isaiah 65:8

Please notice the exact wording of this verse. Do you remember what was found and subsequently brought unto the children of Israel from the land of Canaan?

And they came unto the brook of Eshcol, and cut down from thence a branch with one cluster of grapes, and they bare it between two upon a staff; and they brought of the pomegranates, and of the figs.

—Numbers 13:23

Using the Scriptures as our guide, we can see the *branch* as none other than Jesus Christ (Zechariah 6:12). It truly is the Branch of Jesus Christ that contains the new wine of the Holy Spirit, found in the clusters. Do you remember what was said of the disciples when the Holy Spirit was poured out on the day of Pentecost? Here is the *twenty-second* occurrence of the phrase *new wine*.

> Others mocking said, *These men are full of new wine*. But Peter, standing up with the eleven, lifted up his voice, and said unto them, Ye men of Judaea, and all ye that dwell at Jerusalem, be this known unto you, and hearken to my words: For *these are not drunken*, as ye suppose, seeing it is but the third hour of the day. But this is that which was spoken by the prophet Joel; And it shall come to pass in the last days, saith God, *I will pour out of my Spirit* upon all flesh: and your sons and your daughters shall prophesy, and your young men shall see visions, and your old men shall dream dreams.
>
> —Acts 2:13–17

When we look back at the passages mentioned in Jeremiah 51 as well as Revelation 18, we see that God calls those who will not adhere to sound doctrine, "Babylon" (remember Babel?). As God delivered the two tribes of Judah and Benjamin to this land of confusion for seventy years, so He will deliver the pseudo-believing Gentiles to be part of the Babylonian system during the final seven years. The church today desperately needs spiritual wisdom and understanding in order to correctly identify the great lies that are about to be told on this earth.

In a later part of Isaiah, God reveals to those who can understand sound doctrine, exactly how to interpret scripture.

> Whom shall he teach knowledge? and whom shall he make to understand doctrine? them that are weaned from the milk, and drawn from the breasts. For precept must be upon precept, precept upon precept; line upon line, line upon line; here a little, and there a little.
>
> —Isaiah 28:9–10

Notice first that the symbol of milk is given. We understand that *milk* is a symbol of the Word of God, but is also a symbol of the *childish* understanding of the Word of God. Here is what the New Testament says.

> I have fed you with *milk*, and not with meat: for *hitherto ye were not able to bear it*, neither yet now are ye able.
>
> —1 Corinthians 3:2

> For when for the time ye ought to be teachers, ye have need that one teach you again which be *the first principles* of the oracles of God; and are become such as *have need of milk*, and not of strong meat. For every one that useth *milk is unskilful in the word of righteousness: for he is a babe*.
>
> —Hebrews 5:12–13

> As *newborn babes, desire the sincere milk of the word*, that ye may grow thereby.
>
> —1 Peter 2:2

There is absolutely nothing wrong with having a childish understanding of the Word of God and His precepts. Jesus Himself commanded that we are to come to him as little children. The Bible is so perfect in all its ways that it is understood in its basic principles by those who have little or no understanding at all of God and His ways. That is how someone comes to repentance: by understanding the very basics of the gospel message. One simple verse, John 3:16 for instance, can be given to a lost soul who is hungry for new life, and can be believed enough to accept Jesus' death on the cross for our sins.

However, when it comes to understanding doctrine, including prophetic doctrine, this is where the real work begins. Principle must be laid upon principle, line of scripture added to line of scripture, prophetic precept must be added to prophetic precept, and so on. As you have already seen in this study, every clue to each prophetic event is contained in the Scriptures, but not all in the same place. That would make it too easy. Jesus told His followers to search the Scriptures, the law and the prophets, and see that they all testified of Him. As you become more familiar with the language, numbers, typology, and doctrines of the Bible, you gain a wonderful understanding of God and His plan for the ages. The bottom line is that you must stick with the Bible, and it alone will be your guide.

As I speak to normal, average Americans, I find that most of the ones I have encountered have a belief that we are near the second coming of Jesus Christ. I usually bring the issue up to those I wish to witness to as a means of presenting the gospel message to them. However, because most people who believe Christ is coming back do not know from the Scriptures who Jesus really is, they will believe that Satan's counterfeit christ is the real thing. Remember, the devil's greatest strategy is subtlety. In everything he does, he mirrors and mocks the one and true Christ, so that he can deceive the nations with false Christianity. Satan will convince the world that he is God.

> How art thou fallen from heaven, O *Lucifer*, son of the morning! how art thou cut down to the ground, which didst weaken the nations! For thou hast said in thine heart, I will ascend into heaven, I will exalt my throne above the stars of God: I will sit also upon the mount of the congregation, in the sides of the north: I will ascend above the heights of the clouds; *I will be like the most High*.
>
> —Isaiah 14:12–14

> And no marvel; for Satan himself is transformed into an *angel of light*.
>
> —2 Corinthians 11:14

May the world beware!

The Revelation of Jesus Christ

In the book of Revelation we find that Christ begins the events surrounding His second coming by taking a seven-sealed book from the Father's right hand. For more on this sealed book, see the chapter on the number seven. When He receives this book, He begins to break the seals and open the book, revealing its contents to the entire world. Although this book has been interpreted as being many different things, the Scriptures clearly indicate that it represents everything that the Father wants the Son to accomplish here on earth. "Then said I, Lo, I come (in the volume of the book it is written of me,) to do thy will, O God" (Hebrews 10:7).

It may be said then, that this book is the book of *all things*, representing all things that the Father wishes to accomplish through His Son. Notice what John said concerning this.

> **All things** that the Father hath are mine: therefore said I, that he shall take of mine, and shall **shew it unto you.**
>
> —John 16:15

> The Father loveth the Son, and hath given **all things into his hand.**
>
> —John 3:35

> Labour not for the meat which perisheth, but for that meat which endureth unto everlasting life, which the Son of man shall give unto you: for **him hath God the Father sealed.**
>
> —John 6:27

> Jesus knowing that the Father had given **all things into his hands,** and that he was come from God, and went to God.
>
> —John 13:3

We can see the close relationship between the above passages and the description given in Revelation 5. Truly the Father has given all things into the hand of His Son, and the Son, through the Spirit will reveal these things to His people. In John 6:27 we saw a fascinating correlation between the sealed book and Jesus Himself, whom God has sealed. Is not the Son of God and the Word of God the same? Are they not equal? Does not now the Son of God sit on the same right hand in which the book is found? This is why only Jesus is worthy to take the book from the Father and open its seals. It is understandable then that we would find the exact phrase "all things" mentioned exactly two hundred twenty (22 x 10) times in the Bible. Seeing its association with the theme of revelation (twenty-two), we find the following verses to be themselves, revealing.

And I said, What shall I do, Lord? And the Lord said unto me, Arise, and go into Damascus; and there it shall be told thee of all things which are appointed for thee to do.

—Acts 22:10

But God hath revealed them unto us by his Spirit: for the Spirit searcheth all things, yea, the deep things of God.

—1 Corinthians 2:10

But though I be rude in speech, yet not in knowledge; but we have been thoroughly made manifest among you in all things.

—2 Corinthians 11:6

But that ye also may know my affairs, and how I do, Tychicus, a beloved brother and faithful minister in the Lord, shall make known to you all things.

—Ephesians 6:21

Consider what I say; and the Lord give thee understanding in all things.

—2 Timothy 2:7

According as his divine power hath given unto us all things that pertain unto life and godliness, through the knowledge of him that hath called us to glory and virtue.

—2 Peter 1:3

But ye have an unction from the Holy One, and ye know all things.

—1 John 2:20

The **Revelation of Jesus Christ**, which God gave unto him, to shew unto his servants things which must shortly come to pass; and he sent and signified it by his angel unto his servant John: Who bare record of the word of God, and of the testimony of Jesus Christ, and of all things that he saw.

—Revelation 1:1–2

In Luke 10:22 the Scriptures tell us, "All things are delivered to me of my Father: and no man knoweth who the Son is, but the Father; and who the Father is, but the Son, and he to whom the Son will reveal him." It is the Son that will share with the world who the Father is. Those who wish to know God the Father, must do so through the Son of God, Jesus. The Son has the ability to reveal the Father because *all things* have been delivered to the Son by the Father. It is by no means an accident that we find the phrase *all things* mentioned two hundred twenty times, but also Jesus' title of *Son*, with a capital S exactly two hundred twenty times in the revealed New Testament.

Despite Satan's best efforts, the true Son of God, Jesus Christ will be revealed in the last days and all eyes will see Him on that day, including those that pierced Him (Revelation 1:7). It was Israel that pierced Christ, so it will also be Israel to whom Jesus will reveal Himself in the last days. This event is typologically portrayed in the story of Joseph.

In Genesis 37:9, we find that Joseph dreamed a dream in which the sun, moon, and eleven stars bowed down to him. This seems to set the theme for what we are about to see. If you remember, God sent Israel confusion when Christ came the first time for two reasons. First, it was because of the hardness of their hearts. Second, it was done so that salvation could be offered to the Gentiles (Romans 11). These same themes are given in the story of Joseph. Because Joseph told the dream to his brethren, they hardened their hearts against him, and out of jealousy, conspired his murder, sold him for money, took his garment from him and rent it, and dipped it in blood, his father foretelling that an *evil beast* had done this. All these are components of the crucifixion of Jesus Christ by the Jews.

It is at this time that God brings Joseph through a series of events whereby he becomes the savior of the Gentiles, the Egyptians. We pick up the story in Genesis 41.

> Behold, there come seven years of great plenty throughout all the land of Egypt: And there shall arise after them seven years of famine; and all the plenty shall be forgotten in the land of Egypt; and the famine shall consume the land.
>
> —Genesis 41:29–30

Pharaoh has dreamed a dream that he can find no interpretation for. He is told of a Hebrew slave, Joseph, who can interpret his dream. Because of the inspiration of the Holy Spirit, Joseph is allowed to interpret Pharaoh's dream. Because of this, Pharaoh places Joseph as an authority, second only to himself. During the seven years of plenty, Joseph is to be steward of all the food of the land. Now, the Scriptures seem to be going out of their way to mention a very interesting fact.

> And Joseph was **thirty years old** when he stood before Pharaoh king of Egypt. And Joseph went out from the presence of Pharaoh, and went throughout all the land of Egypt.
>
> —Genesis 41:46

It was at thirty years of age that Joseph became the minister of Pharaoh. It was at thirty years of age that Jesus became the Minister of God, according to the Law of Moses. The revealing of Joseph's age at this point may not seem very important until you take notice of the events that follow. The Scriptures tell us that Joseph was seventeen years old when he dreamed his dreams and was sold by his brothers (Genesis 37:9). His age at the beginning of the seven years of plenty was thirty, making his age at the end of the seven years of plenty to be thirty-seven. Then the seven years of famine begin. It is important to remember that Joseph dreamed that his eleven brethren would bow to him. It is also important to remember that because the number eleven is present, there must then be some sort of confusion involved in this. Please take note of what the Scriptures reveal as we see Joseph's brethren present themselves to Joseph in search of food.

> And Joseph was the governor over the land, and he it was that sold to all the people of the land: and Joseph's brethren came, and **bowed down themselves before him** with their faces to the earth. And Joseph saw his brethren, and he knew them, **but made himself strange unto them**, and spake roughly unto them; and he said unto them, Whence come ye? And they said, From the land of Canaan to buy food. And Joseph knew his brethren, **but they knew not him.**
> —Genesis 42:6–8

As Joseph purposely hid his true identity from his brothers, so did Jesus from His brethren, Israel. However, we find later on that Joseph does indeed reveal himself to his brothers.

> And Joseph said unto his brethren, Come near to me, I pray you. And they came near. And he said, **I am Joseph your brother,** whom ye sold into Egypt. Now therefore be not grieved, nor angry with yourselves, that ye sold me hither: **for God did send me before you to preserve life.** For these **two years** hath the famine been in the land: and yet there are five years, in the which there shall neither be earing nor harvest.
> —Genesis 45:4–6

Joseph finally reveals that he is not only their brother, but their savior as well. He does so after two years of the famine has expired. There are five years (grace) in which he will save them. If you have been keeping count, you will notice that Joseph is now thirty-nine years old when he reveals himself to his brothers. This is precisely **twenty-two** years after he was sold to the Gentiles! Surely there is an order to everything in the Bible. The fortieth year of Joseph's life begins the five years of saving grace given to the children of Israel. You may now understand why there are exactly thirty-nine books in the Old Testament. It is right after these thirty-nine books that Jesus reveals Himself in the fortieth book of the Bible, Matthew, culminating in the sixty-sixth book of the Bible, which begins with the following statement: "The Revelation of Jesus Christ . . ." (Revelation 1:1).

The Number Twelve

Now the LORD had said unto Abram, Get thee out of thy country,
and from thy kindred, and from thy father's house, unto a land that
I will shew thee: And I will make of thee a great nation, and I will
bless thee, and make thy name great; and thou shalt be a blessing:
And I will bless them that bless thee, and curse him that curseth
thee: and in thee shall all families of the earth be blessed.

—Genesis 12:1–3

These verses, found in the twelfth chapter of the Bible, seem to set
the theme for the number twelve. As we look at how this number is
used throughout the Scriptures, we will see that it represents God's
promise to the inhabitants of the earth. In the Scriptures we find the
word "covenant" in all its forms mentioned exactly three hundred
(12 x 25) times. It is no mistake that we find by counting that Genesis 12:1 is the three hundredth verse of the Bible! In the New Testament alone, all the forms of the word "promise" are mentioned sev-
enty-two (12 x 6) times. When this number is seen in the text of the
Scriptures, it is a token to all that His promise is still intact and valid.

In Genesis 6 we find that, even in the face of God's pending destruction of the earth and its inhabitants, God makes the following
promise to mankind.

And the LORD said, My spirit shall not always strive with man, for that he also is flesh: yet his days shall be an hundred and twenty years.

—Genesis 6:3

God kept His one hundred twenty-year promise, hoping that through the Spirit's striving with mankind they would repent of their deeds, but this did not happen. The Scriptures indicate that only Noah found grace in God's sight during this time, so God made a covenant with Noah, that He would spare them when He poured out His wrath on the earth.

But with thee will I establish my covenant; and thou shalt come into the ark, thou, and thy sons, and thy wife, and thy sons' wives with thee.

—Genesis 6:18

The token of God's covenant with Noah at this point is the ark of safety that God told Noah to build. God instructed Noah to build this ark three hundred cubits long, fifty cubits wide, and thirty cubits high. The particular significance of these numbers can be seen in other places in this book. The total volume of the ark was $450,000^3$ cubits. This breaks down to 12 x 12 x 5 x 5 x 5 x 5 x 5. In these numbers we can clearly see God's covenant with Noah and His grace on Noah's life. It was noted in the verse above that God promised Noah that he would come into the ark of salvation as a token of God's promise. Notice the twelfth time Noah's name is mentioned in the Scriptures.

And the LORD said unto Noah, Come thou and all thy house into the ark; for thee have I seen righteous before me in this generation.

—Genesis 7:1

Moving ahead to Genesis 12, we see God making a covenant with Abram that He would bless him and that a great nation would come from him. He further promised that all the families of the earth would be blessed. This covenant points us directly to Jesus Christ, who came from the seed of Abraham, to be God's gift to all mankind. God confirmed this covenant with Abraham, gave it to his son Isaac, and to Isaac's son Jacob, these three. It was through Jacob and his four (gospel) wives that the evidence of God's covenant was seen in the twelve sons of Jacob. These are the twelve tribes of Israel with whom God has made and will fulfill a perpetual covenant.

As a sign to the tribes of Israel who were led out of the land of bondage that God was still going to fulfill his promise to them, the Lord did many notable things associated with the number twelve. In Exodus 15:27 we see that after the Israelites made it through the baptism of the Red Sea, God led them to Elim where there were twelve wells of water. These wells of water represent the refreshing salvation of God, as Jesus revealed to the woman at the well (John 4). He also revealed this as the Angel of the Lord to Hagar when she was banished to the wilderness (Genesis 21). The promise was made to Hagar that God would make of her son a great nation (see Genesis 12:1–3) who also produced twelve sons. I believe that this is a type of a restored nation of Israel in the last days (see Galatians 4).

Once in the wilderness, God instructed Moses to build a tabernacle so that He could dwell with His people wherever they went. The tabernacle was erected first, and then the twelve tribes in their order were to camp around the tabernacle. This reveals God's true desire to dwell in the midst of His people, and is the meaning behind the name Immanuel (God with us.) In the tabernacle were symbols of the Godhead: the table of shewbread, the menorah with seven candles, and the Ark of the Covenant. It was the table of shewbread that represented Christ. This table symbolizes the communion and fellowship of Jesus Christ. It was spoken of by David in the Twenty-third Psalm, "Thou preparest a table before me . . ." and was promised by Christ Himself to His disciples. "That ye may eat and drink at my **table** in my kingdom, and sit on thrones judging the **twelve tribes** of Israel" (Luke 22:30). On this table of shewbread sat twelve loaves of bread, one for each tribe. It is interesting to note that the twelve loaves of shewbread rest on top of the table. This reveals Christ as not only the foundation of the church, but also the resting place of His saints.

In Exodus 28, God instructs Moses to appoint Aaron as the high priest. Placed upon Aaron's chest as part of his priestly attire was a breastplate, foursquare, made of two stones, placed upon his two shoulders, with four rows of three stones, one for each of the twelve tribes, with their names written on it. Here is what God intends to reveal through this breastplate.

> And Aaron shall bear the names of the children of Israel in the breast-plate of judgment upon his heart, when he goeth in unto the holy place, for a memorial before the LORD continually.
>
> —Exodus 28:29

As Aaron went into the most holy place with the blood of a lamb to be sprinkled on the mercy seat seven times for the atonement of Israel, the twelve-stoned breastplate was to be a memorial before the Lord. This was a token of the promise to the twelve tribes of Israel that a Lamb would be slain for the salvation of the seed of Abraham. According to the law, Aaron was supposed to perform this prophetic act once a year, or every twelve months. Concerning these twelve months, it can be mentioned here that during the course of the year, according to known astronomical facts, the sun passes through twelve different constellation groups, one each month. The Scriptures refer to this as the *mazzaroth* (Job 38:32), and historically they are called the *zodiac*. Other Christian writers have written on the true biblical witness of the stars. Suffice it to say here that this sheds some light on the promise that God made to Abraham concerning his seed. "And he brought him forth abroad, and said, Look now toward heaven, and tell the stars, if thou be able to number them: and he said unto him, So shall thy seed be" (Genesis 15:5).

In the book of Deuteronomy, Moses prophesied of Christ by saying, "The LORD thy God will raise up unto thee a Prophet from the midst of thee, of thy brethren, like unto me; unto him ye shall hearken" (Deuteronomy 18:15). We see the fulfillment of this associated with the number twelve when we see this familiar passage from the New Testament.

> And when he was **twelve years old**, they went up to Jerusalem after the custom of the feast. . . . And it came to pass, that after three days they found him in the temple, sitting **in the midst of the doctors**, both hearing them, and asking them questions. And all that heard him were astonished at his understanding and answers.
>
> —Luke 2:42,46–47

This was the token that God had not forgotten His promise to Israel that He would both save them and deliver them to the land of promise. This was also symbolized in the very life of Moses, the Old Testament deliverer who, when he was one hundred twenty years old, was shown all the land that would be inherited, as He swore to Abraham, Isaac, and Jacob (Deuteronomy 34).

As we move ahead through the Scriptures, we see that God's covenant with twelve tribes of Israel is breached in the twelfth book of the Bible, 2 Kings. The kingdom of David had been divided, ten tribes to the north, Judah and Benjamin to the south. The ten northern tribes were taken captive by the Assyrians, and Judah and Benjamin were taken to Babylon by Nebuchadnezzar. Although the covenant had been breached, it was not completely broken forever. God would raise up a "repairer of the breach" (Isaiah 58:12), Jesus of Nazareth.

When Jesus came the first time, he was followed about by twelve men whom He had specially chosen to be His disciples called apostles, the word "apostles" being mentioned exactly sixty (12 x 5) times in the Bible. These men followed Jesus in His three and one-half–year ministry that led to the cross of Calvary. These men were symbolized in the Old Testament as David's one hundred twenty-thousand–man army that fought to make David the king in Jerusalem (1 Chronicles 12:37–38). These twelve apostles symbolize the one hundred forty-four thousand—twelve thousand men from each of the twelve tribes of Israel—who follow Christ the Lamb wherever He goes (Revelation

7, 14:1–5). These twelve apostles also symbolize the very foundation
of the church of the living God, as mentioned in Ephesians.

> And are built upon the foundation of the apostles and prophets,
> Jesus Christ himself being the chief corner stone.
>
> —Ephesians 2:20

It is the foundation that the twelve apostles laid with their pure doctrine that becomes the foundation of the true realization and fulfillment of God's covenant with Abraham, New Jerusalem. In Revelation 21 John describes this holy city as the Bride of Christ himself.
She has twelve foundations, the foundations of the apostles, she has
twelve gates, each with one of the twelve tribes names written on it.
She has walls that are one hundred forty-four cubits; the width,
breadth, and height of the city is twelve thousand furlongs. It is understandable that "Jerusalem" would be mentioned one hundred forty-four (12 x 12) times in the New Testament. She is the eternal hab-
itation of both the Old Testament wilderness church, symbolized in
the twelve tribes, and the New Testament Gentile church, symbolized by the twelve apostles. New Jerusalem indeed is the perfect fulfillment of God's promise to all mankind that have been saved by the
blood of the Lamb.

At this point I will ask the reader to take a close look at your right
or left hand. Notice that there are lines in the palm of your hand that
appear as canyons carved on the face of it. The devil has a religion
that teaches that a man's future can be discerned by reading the lines
in the palm of the hand. This is only Satan's futile attempt at mimick-
ing something that God said in the book of Isaiah; something that
does have to do with a token of God's future promise to His covenant
people. Look closely at the palm of your hand and see that your thumb
is separate from the other four fingers. Take a close look at those four
fingers. Imagine that each finger represents one of the walls of New
Jerusalem. On each of these fingers is three lines, showing the three
segments of each finger. On each wall of New Jerusalem is three gates,
each one with a tribe of Israel written on it. Of course, the total num-

ber of finger segments seen on these four fingers is twelve. This same finger pattern can also be seen on the breastplate worn by the high priest referred to earlier in this chapter. In case you think that this is just a fanciful imagination, please notice what God said to His holy city in Isaiah 49.

> Behold, I have graven thee upon the palms of my hands; thy walls are continually before me.
>
> —Isaiah 49:16

Every time God sees His hand, He remembers His covenant with His people, Israel.

law and authority that sin entered into the world, thus the mark of thirteen on Adam's life and Seth's birth.

The next place we see the number thirteen used in significance is in Genesis 13:13 where it says, "But the men of Sodom were wicked and sinners before the LORD exceedingly." The total number of words in this verse is thirteen. Sodom is a type of a wicked city called Babylon the Great. We will see more of the connection later. For now, let us look at other places in the Scriptures and see the theme of rebellion and wickedness associated with the number thirteen.

And Samuel said to Saul, Thou hast done foolishly: thou hast not kept the commandment of the LORD thy God, which he commanded thee: for now would the LORD have established thy kingdom upon Israel for ever.

—1 Samuel 13:13

Therefore I will shake the heavens, and the earth shall remove out of her place, in the wrath of the LORD of hosts, and in the day of his fierce anger [this is a prophecy concerning Babylon].

—Isaiah 13:13

Then shalt thou say unto them, Thus saith the LORD, Behold, I will fill all the inhabitants of this land, even the kings that sit upon David's throne, and the priests, and the prophets, and all the inhabitants of Jerusalem, **with drunkenness**.

—Jeremiah 13:13

Certain men, the **children of Belial**, are gone out from among you, and have withdrawn the inhabitants of their city, saying, Let us go and serve other gods, which ye have not known.

—Deuteronomy 13:13

And **ye shall be hated** of all men for my name's sake: but he that shall endure unto the end, the same shall be saved.

—Mark 13:13

The Number Thirteen

The number thirteen is one of the most interesting of all biblical numbers. It is clearly associated with rebellion and depravity. It is a number that most often points to the person the Beast, the false prophet, and Babylon the Great.

We see this number appear in the form of the age of Adam when Eve produced Seth. Here is the thirteenth occurrence of Adam's name in the Bible.

> And **Adam** knew his wife again; and she bare a son, and called his name Seth: For God, said she, hath appointed me another seed instead of Abel, whom Cain slew.
>
> —Genesis 4:25

In Genesis 5, it tells us Adam's age when this occurred.

> And Adam lived an **hundred and thirty years** [13 x 10], and begat a son in his own likeness, after his image; and called his name Seth.
>
> —Genesis 5:3

Since Abel died, and the lineage of Cain was cursed and destroyed in the flood, the lineage from which all men come is through the lineage of Seth. It is because of Adam's disobedience and rebellion to God's

Displayed in these verses are various types of evil things that men do, defying the laws of a holy God. In Mark 7 there is a list of thirteen evil things that reside in the heart of all men.

> For from within, out of the heart of men, proceed evil thoughts, adulteries, fornications, murders, Thefts, covetousness, wickedness, deceit, lasciviousness, an evil eye, blasphemy, pride, foolishness: All these evil things come from within, and defile the man.
>
> —Mark 7:21–23

Notice that one of these mentioned is the evil eye. It is the evil eye that sits atop thirteen rows of stones on a pyramid, which is the great seal of the United States seen on the back of a one dollar bill. All the forms of the word "evil," including "evildoer," "evildoers," "evil-favouredness," and "evils" are mentioned a total of six hundred thirty-seven (13 x 49) in the Authorized Version of the Bible.

Now let us look at how this number relates to the Beast, false prophet, and Mystery Babylon. First we find in Revelation 13 the appearance of two beasts.

> And I stood upon the sand of the sea, and saw a **beast rise up out** of the sea, having seven heads and ten horns, and upon his horns ten crowns, and upon his heads the name of blasphemy. And the beast which I saw was like unto a leopard, and his feet were as the feet of a bear, and his mouth as the mouth of a lion: and the **dragon gave him his power,** and his seat, and great authority. . . . And I beheld **another beast coming up out of the earth**; and he had two horns like a lamb, and **he spake as a dragon.**
>
> —Revelation 13:1–2,11

Notice that the dragon, Satan, is closely connected to both of these beasts. This dragon is mentioned exactly thirteen times in the book of Revelation. This dragon is the same serpent found in Genesis 3. Job 26:13 (13 x 2) reveals that it was the spirit of God who "formed the crooked serpent." God signified this by placing a thirteen-star

CROOKED SERPENT between the Big Dipper and the Little Dipper. It is Satan's true desire to rebel against the authority of God and sit on His throne of power. This we see from two sources in the Old Testament—Isaiah 14 and Ezekiel 28.

> How art thou fallen from heaven, O Lucifer, son of the morning! how art thou cut down to the ground, which didst weaken the nations! For thou hast said in thine heart, I will ascend into heaven, I will exalt my throne above the stars of God: I will sit also upon the mount of the congregation, in the sides of the north: I will ascend above the heights of the clouds; I will be like the most High.
>
> —Isaiah 14:12–14

> Son of man, say unto the prince of Tyrus, Thus saith the Lord GOD; Because thine heart is lifted up, and thou hast said, I am a God, I sit in the seat of God, in the midst of the seas; yet thou art a man, and not God, though thou set thine heart as the heart of God.
>
> —Ezekiel 28:2

You will notice from these verses that we not only see the revealing of Satan's plan to sit on God's throne, but recorded for us are his exact words. In Job 1–2, Satan's words are recorded for us as well when he tries to convince God that Job will curse God to His face, as Satan has done. The total number of words spoken by Satan in these three passages is one hundred ninety-five (13 x 15). Contained in these words are his rebellion and contempt for God and His people.

His plan to confiscate and dominate the throne of God will be given to a man the Scriptures refer to as "the Beast." We see the appearance of this beast in Revelation 13. This beast is described as a lion, a leopard, and a bear. Disregarding any extrabiblical explanations for these symbols, we turn in our Bibles to Hosea 13 for the clues as to why this beast appears this way.

> When Ephraim spake trembling, he exalted himself in Israel; but when he offended in **Baal**, he died. And now they sin more and

more, and have made them molten images of their silver, and idols according to their own understanding, all of it the work of the craftsmen: they say of them, **Let the men that sacrifice kiss the calves.**
. . . Therefore **I will be unto them as a lion:** as a **leopard** by the way will I observe them: I will meet them as a **bear** that is bereaved of her whelps, and will rend the caul of their heart, and there will I devour them like a **lion: the wild beast shall tear them.**

—Hosea 13:1–2,7–8

The first thing to notice from this text is that God is angry at Ephraim for worshipping Baal. According to *Unger's Bible Dictionary,* Baal is the son of Dagon, a half-man, half-sea creature mentioned thirteen times in the Scriptures. You will remember that the beast of Revelation 13 comes from the sea. It is also interesting to note that Baal, and various forms of his name are mentioned one hundred thirty times in the Scriptures. Furthermore, Baal was usually depicted in idolatry as a bull or a calf. It is the religious ceremony of kissing a calf that God is angry about. You will remember that it was a molten calf that was made by Aaron at the base of Mt. Sinai. Because of this sin, God turned Ephraim over to a reprobate mind, and sent them a strong delusion that they should believe a lie. Notice in verse seven that God says "I will be unto them as. . . ." They will think they are worshipping God, but they will be worshipping God's counterfeit, the Beast.

Because of the continued wickedness of God's people and their refusal to heed the prophet's warnings of God's pending judgment, God turned Jerusalem over to the evil king of Babylon, Nebuchadnezzar. This Nebuchadnezzar comes from a long line of kings of Babylon, starting with Nimrod, first mentioned in Genesis 10. Nimrod was the thirteenth descendant from Adam. It was he who actually built the city of confusion, Babel, later to become Babylon. History charges Nimrod with being the father of all the mystery religions of the world. It is the revival of these mystery religions that will make up a one-world church of the last days.

In looking at the details of Nebuchadnezzar and his association with the Beast of Revelation 13, we find that Nebuchadnezzar is mentioned exactly ninety-one (13 x 7) times in the Scriptures. One of the most notable resemblances between him and the Beast is found in Daniel 2. In this chapter, Nebuchadnezzar has a dream of a golden image with four parts. Daniel gives the interpretation of the dream as follows.

> Thou, O king, art a **king of kings**: for the God of heaven hath given thee a kingdom, power, and strength, and glory. And wheresoever the children of men dwell, the beasts of the field and the fowls of the heaven hath he given into thine hand, and hath made thee ruler over them all. **Thou art this head of gold.**
>
> —Daniel 2:37–38

Daniel reveals to Nebuchadnezzar that he is a king of kings, not the king of kings; a type of the false christ in the last days whom God will turn the world over to. In Daniel 3, we find that Nebuchadnezzar has a golden image made, the same image that he saw in his dream. In verse seven, the Scriptures tell us that Nebuchadnezzar caused all nations, people, and languages to fall down and worship his image of gold. This is precisely the scenario set for us in Revelation 13.

> And deceiveth them that dwell on the earth by the means of those miracles which he had power to do in the sight of the beast; saying to them that dwell on the earth, that they should make an image to the beast, which had the wound by a sword, and did live. And he had power to give life unto the image of the beast, that the image of the beast should both speak, and cause that as many as would not worship the image of the beast should be killed.
>
> —Revelation 13:14–15

The relationship that the Beast has to Satan is indicated in the Scriptures as that of father and son. Various times in the Scriptures you will find phrases such as "children of Belial," "son of Belial," "ye are of your father the devil," "child of the devil," etc. The first time any of these phrases appear in the Scriptures is "children of Belial" mentioned in Deuteronomy 13:13. First Thessalonians 2 warns us of the man of sin who wishes to sit on God's throne showing everyone that he is God. The Scriptures here call him "son of perdition." This phrase is found only one other time in the Bible.

> While I was with them in the world, I kept them in thy name: those that thou gavest me I have kept, and none of them is lost, but the son of perdition; that the scripture might be fulfilled.
>
> —John 17:12

This is in reference to a man who officially has thirteen letters in his name: Judas Iscariot. The scripture that might be fulfilled would be Psalm 55:13. This verse contains thirteen words.

> But it was thou, a man mine equal, my guide, and mine acquaintance.
>
> —Psalm 55:13

In John 13, Jesus announces to His disciples that one of His very own is this son of perdition. He does so by speaking exactly thirteen words.

> When Jesus had thus said, he was troubled in spirit, and testified, and said, Verily, verily, I say unto you, that one of you shall betray me.
>
> —John 13:21

The second beast that we see in Revelation 13 is a beast called "false prophet." This title is found exactly four times (four for the false gospel) in the Scriptures, three times in the book of Revelation including Revelation 16:13, and one time in Acts 13. In Acts 13 he is characterized as a sorcerer, full of subtlety, given the name of Barjesus, and called a child of the devil. He is stricken with blindness, as the beast and false prophet will be in Revelation 16:10.

This false prophet performs signs and wonders in Revelation 13:13. God warned His people of a false prophet doing signs and wonders in Deuteronomy 13.

If there arise among you a prophet, or a dreamer of dreams, and giveth thee a sign or a wonder, And the sign or the wonder come to pass, whereof he spake unto thee, saying, Let us go after other gods, which thou hast not known, and let us serve them; Thou shalt not hearken unto the words of that prophet, or that dreamer of dreams: for the LORD your God proveth you, to know whether ye love the LORD your God with all your heart and with all your soul. Ye shall walk after the LORD your God, and fear him, and keep his commandments, and obey his voice, and ye shall serve him, and cleave unto him.

—Deuteronomy 13:1–4

Since Deuteronomy 13 and Revelation 13 deal with the same subject matter, and both contain exactly eighteen verses, Deuteronomy can be seen as a key to understanding exactly what Revelation speaks of.

In 1 Kings 13, we find another story of a prophet who prophesies falsely. It is in verse twenty-six (13 x 2) that we find that this false prophet was slain because of his rebellion and refusal to obey the word of the Lord.

It can be said that as the prophets go, so go the religion. When prophets spoke according to the Word of God, the religion was pure and undefiled. When they refused to speak according to God's Word, the religion and the people became corrupt. This was evident in Bible times and is blatant in today's so-called Christian church. Wherever there is a false doctrine there is a blatant disregard for "every word of God." God sent the true prophet Ezekiel to warn the people and the false prophets of the error of their ways. We find this in Ezekiel 13.

And mine hand shall be upon the prophets that see vanity, and that divine lies: they shall not be in the assembly of my people, neither shall they be written in the writing of the house of Israel, neither shall they enter into the land of Israel; and ye shall know that I am the Lord GOD. Because, even because they have seduced my people, saying, Peace; and there was no peace; and **one built up a wall**, and, lo, others daubed it with **untempered morter**: Say unto them which daub it with untempered morter, that it shall fall: there shall be an overflowing shower; and ye, O great hailstones, shall fall; and a stormy wind shall rend it. Lo, **when the wall is fallen,** shall it not be said unto you, Where is the daubing wherewith ye have daubed it? Therefore thus saith the Lord GOD; I will even rend it with a stormy wind in my fury; and there shall be an overflowing shower in mine anger, and great hailstones in my fury to consume it. So will **I break down the wall that ye have daubed with untempered morter, and bring it down to the ground,** so that the foundation thereof shall be discovered, and it shall fall, and ye shall be consumed in the midst thereof: and ye shall know that I am the LORD. Thus will I accomplish my wrath upon **the wall,** and upon them that have daubed it with **untempered morter,** and will say unto you, The wall is no more, neither they that daubed it; To wit, the prophets of Israel which prophesy concerning Jerusalem, and which see visions of peace for her, and there is no peace, saith the Lord GOD.

—Ezekiel 13:9–16

Woe to the preacher that strays away from the pure words of God! These prophets of prosperity and peace are speaking soothing words to a generation that needs to hear the message of John the Baptist, "Repent, for the kingdom of heaven is at hand." God describes their doings as building a wall, but using untempered mortar. This untempered mortar is described in Ezekiel 22:28 as the prophets saying' ". . . Thus saith the Lord GOD, when the LORD hath not spoken." In this case, God's wrath is directed specifically to the wall that was built by the false prophets with their lies. Many churches are being built today upon a wide assortment of false doctrines. Their numbers are staggering, their offerings enormous, and their media influence is extensive, but the doctrines are still false and not according to the whole truth of God's Word. When God pours out His judgments upon this earth as described in the book of Revelation, these walls will fall, and their false doctrines and secret sins will be discovered and brought to light by He whose face shines as the sun.

In case you haven't made a connection with this prophecy and another passage of Scripture, we will direct your attention to Joshua 6. The city is the walled city of Jericho. God proclaims that Joshua, the priests, and the Ark of the Covenant must circle the walls of Jericho once a day for six days, a total of six times. On the seventh day, they are to march around Jericho seven times, a grand total of thirteen. When this is accomplished, there is heard the sound of trumpets, and shouting. It is at this time that the walls of Jericho fall to the ground.

Also, in case you haven't put these pieces of the puzzle together, Jericho is a *type* of a wicked adulteress city of the last days. Jericho is a type of the church who has committed spiritual adultery against God, as God describes in Ezekiel 14. This famous city is mentioned two hundred ninety-nine (13 x 23) times in the Scriptures. She is given a very notable thirteen-word title in Revelation 17: "MYSTERY, BABYLON THE GREAT, THE MOTHER OF HARLOTS AND ABOMINATIONS OF THE EARTH."

The Number Seventeen

And God said unto Noah, The end of all flesh is come before me; for
the earth is filled with violence through them; and, behold, I will
destroy them with the earth.

—Genesis 6:13

In the Scriptures, beginning with the first verse of Genesis, we find
that this is the seventeenth occurrence of the phrase "God said." Of
particular interest is what God said after this statement was made.
The context, of course, is the great deluge that God is about to send
to the earth. As we have already seen from previous chapters, the
flood of Noah plays an extremely important typological role in last
days events. This statement, ". . . the end of all flesh is come before
me . . ." seems to set the stage for the overall theme of the number
seventeen.

It was noted by Bullinger and Vallowe that the number seventeen
was the seventh prime number. This gives the number seventeen an
association with the theme of the number seven, that of completion
and perfection. As we will see in the following analysis, the number
seventeen overwhelmingly represents *the completion of time* and *change*
or *transformation*. Simply put, it represents the change that will take
place at the end of time.

The number seventeen and Abraham

As with many of the primary numbers in the Scriptures, our theme behind a given number can usually be located in the corresponding Genesis chapter. It is in Genesis 17 that we will begin our journey of discovery. Let's see what the Scriptures reveal to us.

> And Abram fell on his face: and God talked with him, saying, As for me, behold, my covenant is with thee, and thou shalt be a father of many nations. Neither shall **thy name any more** be called Abram, but thy name shall be Abraham; for a father of many nations have I made thee.
>
> —Genesis 17:3–5

In this chapter, three main ideas are given. The first, the renaming (changing) of Abram. There is ample biblical evidence to clearly see that this renaming of Abram is a symbol that is closely associated with the salvation of Israel. Notice what God declares in the book of Isaiah.

> For Zion's sake will I not hold my peace, and for Jerusalem's sake I will not rest, until the righteousness thereof go forth as brightness, and **the salvation thereof as a lamp that burneth.** And the Gentiles shall see thy righteousness, and all kings thy glory: and thou shalt be called by a new name, which the mouth of the LORD shall name.
>
> —Isaiah 62:1–2

This end-time prophecy foretells of a time when Christ's gift of salvation is given for the sake of Zion, and God promises that He will not *rest* until the day when this is accomplished. Of course, this most definitely reveals to us a time prophecy of the seventh millennium, for it was on the **seventh** day that God rested from His creation work (Genesis 2:3).

Please notice also what the Scriptures reveal in verse one of this passage. God declares that the salvation of Israel will go forth as a burning lamp. Does this remind us of another passage involving Abram and the covenant of salvation that God made with him? Please notice not only what is revealed, but in what verse it is revealed as well.

> And it came to pass, that, when the sun went down, and it was dark, behold a smoking furnace, and a **burning lamp** that passed between those pieces.
>
> —Genesis 15:17

In the book of Revelation, this new name/salvation promise is given to all those who overcome. Notice also the verse placement of this promise.

> He that hath an ear, let him hear what the Spirit saith unto the churches; To him that overcometh will I give to eat of the hidden manna, and will give him a white stone, and in the stone **a new name** written, which no man knoweth saving he that receiveth it.
>
> —Revelation 2:17

It is by the grace of our wonderful Savior that we receive this new name that accompanies our salvation. Let's take a closer look at Genesis 17 when God changes the name of Abram, and see the mighty grace of God.

> Neither shall thy name any more be called Abram, but thy name shall be Abraham; for a father of many nations have I made thee.
>
> —Genesis 17:5

Of immediate note is the fact that this name change takes place in verse five. The number five, as we have seen, overwhelmingly speaks of grace and redemption. When we examine this name change in the original Hebrew, we find that God included in Abram's new name the fifth letter, *hey*, in the inspired Hebrew aleph-bet. Corresponding with this idea, we also see, secondly, that God did the same thing with Abraham's wife, Sarai.

> And God said unto Abraham, As for Sarai thy wife, thou shalt not
> call her name Sarai, but **Sarah** shall her name be.
>
> —Genesis 17:15

Here again, we see that God simply added this same letter *hey* to
Sarai's old name, representing His grace on her, giving her a new
name. It is also interesting to see that this passage appears in verse
fifteen (5 x 3).

The third idea we find as we study Genesis 17 is that in this chapter God institutes the practice of circumcision (vss. 10–14). This also,
as revealed to us in the New Testament (cf. Romans 2:29, 4:11, 15:8;
Philippians 3:3; Colossians 2:11), is a symbol of the grace of God and
the salvation of all who will receive. As this practice was given to
Abraham, the father of Israel, so shall its perfect fulfillment be in the
nation of Israel in the last days, after the time of the Gentile church is
fulfilled (the Rapture).

Time no longer

The next place we look in relation to the number seventeen and its
theme of the *end of time* is found in Revelation 10.

> And the angel which I saw stand upon the sea and upon the earth
> lifted up his hand to heaven, And sware by him that liveth for ever
> and ever, who created heaven, and the things that therein are, and
> the earth, and the things that therein are, and the sea, and the things
> which are therein, that there should be **time no longer**: But in the
> days of the voice of the seventh angel, when he shall begin to sound,
> **the mystery of God should be finished**, as he hath declared to his
> servants the prophets.
>
> —Revelation 10:5–7

While much could be said about the many fascinating details that are
given us in Revelation 10, we will focus our attention on the phrase
"time no longer." In many King James Bibles that contain marginal
notes, one will usually find a note pertaining to verse six that gives an
alternate reading of this phrase, *"no more delay,"* supposedly based

upon the original Greek. With all due respect to my friends who are Greek scholars, don't pay any attention to that. It is this author's opinion that the Bible can be taken and understood at face value, especially in light of the following numerical patterns.

Although you will not find this phrase mentioned in the Bible seventeen times or any multiple of seventeen, it is very interesting to note that you will find the word "time" mentioned in the New Testament exactly **one hundred seventy** (17 x 10) times. A comprehensive look at the use of this one simple word will not be made here. What we will look at are several of the verses that are either associated with the number seventeen, or the *end of time* second coming of Jesus Christ.

> Then Herod, when he had privily called the wise men, enquired of them diligently what time the star appeared. [*Notice that Herod draws attention to the exact time that the star, which accompanied Christ's first coming, appeared.*]
>
> —Matthew 2:7

> From that time Jesus began to preach, and to say, Repent: for the kingdom of heaven is at hand.
>
> —Matthew 4:17

> And, behold, they cried out, saying, What have we to do with thee, Jesus, thou Son of God? art thou come hither to torment us before the time?
>
> —Matthew 8:29

> Let both grow together until the harvest: and in the time of harvest I will say to the reapers, Gather ye together first the tares, and bind them in bundles to burn them: but gather the wheat into my barn.
>
> —Matthew 13:30

> For then shall be great tribulation, such as was not since the beginning of the world to this time, no, nor ever shall be.
>
> —Matthew 24:21

And he said, Go into the city to such a man, and say unto him, The Master saith, **My time is at hand**; I will keep the passover at thy house with my disciples.

—Matthew 26:18

And saying, **The time is fulfilled**, and the kingdom of God is at hand: repent ye, and believe the gospel.

—Mark 1:15

And seeing a fig tree afar off having leaves, he came, if haply he might find any thing thereon: and when he came to it, he found nothing but leaves; for the time of figs was not yet. [*In Matthew 24, Christ referenced this time of figs as a sign of His coming.*]

—Mark 11:13

For in those days shall be affliction, such as was not from the beginning of the creation which God created unto this time, neither shall be.

—Mark 13:19

Behold, your house is left unto you desolate: and verily I say unto you, Ye shall not see me, until **the time come** when ye shall say, Blessed is he that cometh in the name of the Lord.

—Luke 13:35

Then Jesus said unto them, **My time** is not yet come: but your time is alway ready. . . . Go ye up unto this feast: I go not up yet unto this feast: for **my time** is not yet full come.

—John 7:6,8

When they therefore were come together, they asked of him, saying, Lord, wilt thou at **this time** restore again the kingdom to Israel?

—Acts 1:6

But when the time of the promise drew nigh, which God had sworn to Abraham, the people grew and multiplied in Egypt.

—Acts 7:17

Therefore judge nothing before the time, until the Lord come, who both will bring to light the hidden things of darkness, and will make manifest the counsels of the hearts: and then shall every man have praise of God.

—1 Corinthians 4:5

For the time is come that judgment must begin at the house of God: and if it first begin at us, what shall the end be of them that obey not the gospel of God?

—1 Peter 4:17

Many, many more scriptural illustrations could be given from the Old and New Testaments using this one simple word called *time*. There will indeed come a time when all things will be fulfilled and this world will be done away with, including the elimination of time, making way for the new heavens and earth where time no longer exists. In our reference from Revelation 10 concerning "time no longer," we do not find the phrase "no longer" mentioned seventeen times, or associated with the number seventeen. However, we do find a similar phrase, "no more," associated with this number. In the Old Testament it is mentioned exactly one hundred seventy-one times, but contained in exactly **one hundred seventy** verses. In the New Testament, this same pattern is present as well, for we find this phrase mentioned fifty-seven times, but limited to **fifty-one** (17 x 3) verses. We will see this number fifty-one appear in a very interesting place shortly. For now, we once again look at *how* this phrase is used in the pages of God's perfect book. As with the word "time" this is not a comprehensive look. I encourage the reader to examine the many scriptures for themselves.

Wherefore they are **no more** twain, but one flesh. What therefore God hath joined together, let not man put asunder. [*The marriage* *union of a man and a woman is a typological picture of the joining of Christ and His Church, Ephesians 5.]*

—Matthew 19:6

Verily I say unto you, I will drink **no more** of the fruit of the vine, until **that day** that I drink it new in the kingdom of God.

—Mark 14:25

From that **time** many of his disciples went back, and walked no **more** with him. [*It is interesting to see the number 666 here and the concept of a great falling away that is associated with the coming of the antichrist, II Thessalonians 2:2-3.*]

—John 6:66

And when they were come up out of the water, the Spirit of the Lord **caught away Philip**, that the eunuch saw him **no more**: and he went on his way rejoicing.

—Acts 8:39

From Mark 14:25, we find yet another bread crumb that God has used to mark the trail of biblical knowledge and understanding. Jesus is obviously referring to "that day" when He establishes His throne over all the earth. It is understandable then, that we find the very phrase "that day" mentioned two hundred and four (17 x 12) times in the Old Testament. It is mentioned twenty-two times (the number for revelation) in the New Testament. Of the many references to "that day" in the Old Testament, it seems that they all point to the day of the consummation of all that God will accomplish on the earth, including the salvation of Israel, as in this verse.

But I will deliver thee in **that day**, saith the LORD: and thou shalt not be given into the hand of the men of whom thou art afraid.

—Jeremiah 39:17

In the New Testament, likewise, we have the overwhelming association of the phrase "that day" with the time Christ returns to perform all that He has been sent to do.

But ye, brethren, are not in darkness, that **that day** should overtake you as a thief.

—1 Thessalonians 5:4

For the which cause I also suffer these things: nevertheless I am not ashamed: for I know whom I have believed, and am persuaded that he is able to keep that which I have committed unto him against that day.

—2 Timothy 1:12

Henceforth there is laid up for me a crown of righteousness, which the Lord, the righteous judge, shall give me at **that day**: and not to me only, but unto all them also that love his appearing.

—2 Timothy 4:8

One final note concerning the passage in Revelation 10. You will notice that in verse seven we see that the mystery of God is going to come to a complete end "as he hath declared to *his servants the prophets*." This exact phrase, "servants the prophets," is mentioned exactly seventeen times in the Scriptures. This pattern is bolstered by the fact there are exactly seventeen books, Isaiah to Malachi, that record precisely what God has declared to His servants the prophets. It is these and other prophetic utterances from the Scriptures that Christ will perfectly fulfill at the end of time (Hebrews 10:7).

As with so many other numbers in the Scripture, once we gain a firm grasp on what a number means, we can easily follow the patterns and passages that God has left for us and see His divine plan for mankind. For instance, it is interesting to see that the seventeenth time we find the word "God" is in Genesis 1:17. The seventeenth time we find Jesus' name in the Scriptures is in Matthew 7:28, ". . . when Jesus had **ended** these sayings. . . ." The eighty-fifth (17 x 5) chapter of the New Testament "just happens" to be John 17. In this beloved chapter we find Jesus praying for His disciples shortly before He lays down His life for their sins. He begins this prayer by saying, ". . . Father, **the hour is come**; glorify thy Son, that thy Son also may

glorify thee. . . ." Surely, when Jesus comes, He will not only be glorified by His Father, but also by His church as well (2 Thessalonians
1:10). Christ also asks His Holy Father, ". . . I will that they also,
whom thou hast given me, be with me where I am . . ." (vs. 24). This
is reminiscent of the statement that Christ made in John 14:3: "And if
I go and prepare a place for you, I will come again, and receive you
unto myself; that where I am, there ye may be also." Here again we
can clearly see the immediate connection between the things that
Christ will perform at His second coming, including the Rapture of
the church, and the number seventeen.

When we count to the seventeenth chapter of the New Testament, we come to Matthew 17. You may wish to read this chapter
before continuing with this book. You will notice that the most prominent portion of this chapter deals with an interesting thing that Christ
performed.

> And after **six days** [*six thousand years*] Jesus taketh Peter, James, and
> John his brother, and bringeth them up into an **high mountain**
> apart, And was **transfigured** before them: and **his face did shine**
> **as the sun**, and his raiment was white as the light.
>
> —Matthew 17:1–2

It is immediately noticed that the action that Jesus performed represents a change in the body of Christ, much like the change that took
place with Abraham in Genesis 17, and points us to the time when
"we shall not all sleep, but we shall all be changed." The description
of His face shining as the sun is precisely the way John described
Jesus in Revelation 1:16. It is believed by many that this transfiguration is a picture of the future translation of the church. This idea is
given further credence by the following verse.

> That ye may be blameless and harmless, the sons of God, without
> rebuke, in the midst of a crooked and perverse nation, among whom
> **ye shine as lights** in the world.
>
> —Philippians 2:15

In Matthew 2:11 we find that the wise men from the east brought Jesus, the King of Jews, gifts of gold, frankincense, and myrrh. Aside from other possible symbolic meanings behind these gifts, it is interesting to note the Scriptures mention frankincense exactly seventeen times, myrrh exactly seventeen times, and you will find gold mentioned three hundred ninety-one (17 x 23) times in the Old Testament. What fitting gifts to offer to the King who has come to give salvation to His people, Israel.

In the Old Testament we find that there was a change in the form of government that ruled over God's people, Israel. God instituted His divine authority over Israel by first taking them out from the dominion of Pharaoh. It was then that He gave them His Ten Commandments, symbolizing His rule over them. The law of God was administered by a series of judges. These judges, beginning with Moses, are listed and numbered below.

1. Moses	2. Joshua
3. Othniel	4. Ehud
5. Shamgar	6. Deborah
7. Gideon	8. Abimelech
9. Tola	10. Jair
11. Jephthah	12. Ibzan
13. Elon	14. Abdon
15. Samson	16. Eli
17. Samuel	

You will notice that there were precisely seventeen judges who judged the people under this form of government. The true believer should understand that God truly and consistently does *everything* by His divine order, and never changes. It was Samuel, the seventeenth judge of Israel, that was commanded by God to change the government of Israel from the office of judge to that of a monarchy. This is precisely why God allowed the government to change despite Samuel's displeasure (1 Samuel 8:6). It fit precisely into God's plan not only for that day, but **that day** to come.

God allowed Samuel to anoint a person to be king over all Israel. In this is a foreshadowing of Christ who becomes the true and rightful King of the Jews. This was His title when He came to the earth the first time. However, the Jews rejected Him as their King, and the kingdom was given over to the Gentiles. When the time of the Gentiles is complete, Christ will come again to fulfill His reign as King of the Jews. There is an interesting connection with this theme and the number seventeen. Using the formula of seventeen, being the number for this transition, and the number ten for divine authority as king, we look to the one hundred seventieth chapter of the Bible. Interestingly enough, this chapter is Deuteronomy 17. From our look at the number seven and the seven-sealed book that is in God's right hand, we see the importance of this passage.

> And it shall be, when **he sitteth upon the throne of his kingdom,** that he shall write him a copy of this law in a **book** out of that which is before the priests the Levites: And it shall be with him, and he shall read therein all the days of his life: that he may learn to fear the LORD his God, **to keep all the words** of this law and these statutes, to do them: That his heart be not lifted up above his brethren, and that he turn not aside from the commandment, to the right hand, or to the left: to the end that he may prolong his days in his kingdom, he, and his children, in the midst of Israel.
>
> —Deuteronomy 17:18–20

This being the one hundred seventieth (17 x 10) chapter of the Bible, it is understandable why we would find the word "seventeen" exactly ten times in the Bible.

From earlier places in this book, we saw the significance and the relationship between Jesus and the *book* that is in God's right. We saw that as Jesus began the works of His first coming by taking the *book* and opening it in Luke 4, He also begins the works associated with His second coming by taking the *book* from the right hand of the Father and opening it. Of interest, again, is the exact verse placement in Luke 4 when Jesus performs this typological act.

And there was delivered unto him **the book** of the prophet Esaias.
And when he had **opened the book,** he found the place where it
was written.

—Luke 4:17

Seeing that the number seventeen is a number of transition, the ending of the old and bringing in of the new, we can see that the last
section of the Old Testament, that of the prophets, contains seventeen books. It is at this point that we turn the page from the Old
Testament to the New Testament. This transition is also displayed in
Hebrews 12:18–24. Notice how the Scriptures here are arranged to
follow this exact pattern of seventeen.

1. "For ye are not come unto the mount that might be touched,
2. and that burned with fire,
3. nor unto blackness,
4. and darkness,
5. and tempest,
6. And the sound of a trumpet,
7. and the voice of words...
8. But ye are come unto mount Sion,
9. and unto the city of the living God,
10. the heavenly Jerusalem,
11. and to an innumerable company of angels,
12. To the general assembly
13. and church of the firstborn, which are written in heaven,
14. and to God the Judge of all,
15. and to the spirits of just men made perfect,
16. And to Jesus the mediator of the new covenant,
17. and to the blood of sprinkling, that speaketh better things than
    that of Abel."

Notice that there is a natural transition between the seventh and eight
thing mentioned in this passage, showing the change that takes place
between the old covenant and the new. The first seven things that are

mentioned come to us from Exodus 19. In this chapter, Moses is instructed to purify the people and prepare for the *third day*. When he hears the *trumpet* and the sound of thunder and sees the smoke on the mountain, he is to gather the people in order to meet God there. This is a revealing illustration of not only the gathering of Christ's church at the Rapture, but also the gathering of the lost sheep of Israel. In Deuteronomy 4, God wanted it made plain to Israel that they were to never forget *that day* when Moses gathered the people for this occasion.

> Only take heed to thyself, and keep thy soul diligently, lest thou forget the things which thine eyes have seen, and lest they depart from thy heart all the days of thy life: but teach them thy sons, and thy sons' sons; **Specially the day** that thou stoodest before the LORD thy God in Horeb, when the LORD said unto me, Gather me the people together, and I will make them hear my words, that they may learn to fear me all the days that they shall live upon the earth, and that they may teach their children.
>
> —Deuteronomy 4:9–10

Here again the patterns of God never fail. When we look at Exodus 19 for the very verse in which Moses gathered the people together to meet with God, here is what we find.

> And Moses brought forth the people out of the camp to meet with God; and they stood at the nether part of the mount.
>
> —Exodus 19:17

It was at this point that God officially transferred the children of Israel from the authority of Pharaoh to the authority of God by first sending ten plagues to Pharaoh and the Egyptians, then by giving them His Ten Commandments in Exodus 20.

At the beginning of this chapter, we noted that the seventeenth time the phrase "God said" is used was found in Genesis 6:13 when God said, ". . . The end of all flesh is before me. . . ." From that point forward we can see that God intended to bring flood waters on the earth, bringing an end to all flesh. However, in Genesis 8, we see that this was part of the transition between the old world and the new world. It certainly does not imply that God did not really mean *"all"* flesh, but when we view this story in its correct typological frame, we can truly look to the day when God will in fact do away with *all flesh* when this world is done away with and the New Earth is established. Remember that "flesh and blood cannot inherit the kingdom of God" (1 Corinthians 15:50).

Therefore, according to the divine order of God, it is very interesting and revealing to see that the exact dates for the prevailing flood waters are associated with the number seventeen.

> In the six hundredth year of Noah's life, in the second month, the **seventeenth day** of the month, the same day were all the fountains of the great deep broken up, and the windows of heaven were opened.
> —Genesis 7:11

> And the waters returned from off the earth continually: and after the end of the hundred and fifty days the waters were abated. And the ark rested in the seventh month, on the **seventeenth** day of the month, upon the mountains of Ararat.
> —Genesis 8:3–4

It was on the seventeenth day of the seventh month that the transition between the old world and the new world took place. There are literally hundreds of references in the Scriptures to the typological significance of the flood waters in Noah's day. Of course the one that sticks out the most is found in Luke *17.*

> And as it was in the days of Noe, so shall it be also in the days of the Son of man. They did eat, they drank, they married wives, they were given in marriage, until the day that Noe entered into the ark, and the flood came, and destroyed them all.
> —Luke 17:26–27

The number seventeen and the salvation of Israel

There is a portion of the story of Noah's ark that this author believes deals with the future salvation of Israel.

> Also he sent forth a dove from him, to see if the waters were abated from off the face of the ground; But the dove found no rest for the sole of her foot, and she returned unto him into the ark, for the waters were on the face of the whole earth: then he put forth his hand, and took her, and pulled her in unto him into the ark. And he stayed yet other seven days; and again he sent forth the dove out of the ark; And the dove came in to him in the evening; and, lo, in her mouth was an olive leaf pluckt off: so Noah knew that the waters were abated from off the earth.
>
> —Genesis 8:8–11

The two key symbols in this passage are the dove and the olive leaf. In order to understand what is being depicted here, we must understand these symbols fully. You may already recognize the symbol of the dove. It represents the Holy Spirit.

> And Jesus, when he was baptized, went up straightway out of the water: and, lo, the heavens were opened unto him, and he saw the Spirit of God descending like a dove, and lighting upon him.
>
> —Matthew 3:16 (cf. Mark 1:10; Luke 3:22; John 1:32)

The next symbol is that of the olive leaf. For this we look to Romans 11.

> What then? **Israel** hath not obtained that which he seeketh for; but the election hath obtained it, and the rest were blinded. . . . And if some of the branches be broken off, and thou, being a wild olive tree, wert graffed in among them, and with them partakest of the root and fatness of the **olive tree**.
>
> —Romans 11:7,17

> I will be as the dew unto **Israel**: he shall grow as the lily, and cast
> forth his roots as Lebanon. His branches shall spread, and his beau-
> ty shall be as the **olive tree**, and his smell as Lebanon.
>
> —Hosea 14:5–6

The natural branches on the olive tree are the children of Israel, who by their refusal to accept their Messiah have had their branches removed temporarily by the Gentiles, the wild branches. Notice in the story of Noah, he sends the dove out the first time, but it returns to him with nothing. God sent His Holy Spirit on Pentecost to save Israel first, but Israel would not be saved. God will send His Holy Spirit again (Ezekiel 37:8–9), and this Spirit will gather the remnant of Israel, as the olive leaf, and establish the throne of Jesus in Jerusalem.

In another amazing connection with this idea, we examine the details of the first Holy Spirit outpouring mentioned in Acts 2. In verse *seventeen* Peter quotes Joel 2, saying, "And it shall come to pass in the last days, saith God, I will pour out of my Spirit upon all flesh. . . ." Accordingly, there are exactly *seventeen* groups in verses nine through eleven that hear the wonderful works of God as preached to them in their own tongues by the disciples.

In 2 Kings 13, the Scriptures tell us that Jehoahaz the son of Jehu reigned for seventeen years. He was an evil king and during his reign, God delivered Israel into the hand of Hazael, the king of Syria. This caused Jehoahaz to call unto the Lord. In verse five, we see the connection between the salvation of Israel and the number seventeen when it says, ". . . And the LORD gave Israel a saviour. . . ."

You may remember that from the chapter on the number seven and the amazing details of the seven-sealed book, we referenced Jeremiah 32. In Jeremiah 32, the prophet is told to purchase a piece of land, write the evidence of the purchase in an open book and a sealed book, and place them in earthen vessels. The idea was that God was going to give His people back their rightful inheritance, and the proof of this was in the *book*. Do you remember how much money the land was purchased for?

And I bought the field of Hanameel my uncle's son, that was in

Anathoth, and weighed him the money, even **seventeen** shekels of silver.

—Jeremiah 32:9

Finally, in relation to the salvation of Israel, we turn to John 21. In this passage we have what has amounted to a very enigmatic number. Many scholars over the years have introduced various ideas concerning this number and its meaning. This author's attempt, understandably, may not be the final effort, but it will be my best effort according to my incomplete understanding. Let's see what the Scriptures reveal.

But when the morning was now come, Jesus stood on the shore: but the disciples knew not that it was Jesus. Then Jesus saith unto them, Children, have ye any meat? They answered him, No. And he said unto them, Cast the net on the right side of the ship, and ye shall find. They cast therefore, and now they were not able to draw it for the multitude of fishes. Therefore that disciple whom Jesus loved saith unto Peter, It is the Lord. Now when Simon Peter heard that it was the Lord, he girt his fisher's coat unto him, (for he was naked,) and did cast himself into the sea. And the other disciples came in a little ship; (for they were not far from land, but as it were two hundred cubits,) dragging the net with fishes. As soon then as they were come to land, they saw a fire of coals there, and fish laid thereon, and bread. Jesus saith unto them, Bring of the fish which ye have now caught. Simon Peter went up, and drew the net to land full of great fishes, **an hundred and fifty and three**: and for all there were so many, yet was not the net broken.

—John 21:4–11

A million good sermons and lessons could be taught from this passage, but for brevity's sake, we shall only look at a few of the clues given us. First we see the familiar idea of Jesus' disciples acting out their role as "fishers of men" (Mark 1:*17*). There is an interesting passage in the Old Testament that seems to shed a considerable light on this idea.

But, The LORD liveth, that brought up the children of Israel from the land of the north, and from all the lands whither he had driven them: and I will **bring them again into their land** that I gave unto their fathers. Behold, I will send for many **fishers**, saith the LORD, and they shall **fish** them; and after will I send for many hunters, and they shall hunt them from every mountain, and from every hill, and out of the holes of the rocks.

—Jeremiah 16:15–16

It could very well be that this was precisely what Christ was referring to in giving His disciples this title. Another interesting thing about fish that seems to shed more light on this idea is that fish, unlike all land animals, *have no breath.* It is obviously apparent to the student of the Word of God the relationship the Bible makes between *breath* or *wind* and the Holy Spirit of God (cf. Genesis 2:7; Ezekiel 37:10; John 20:22; Acts 2:2). It would appear then, that these fish (the remnant of Israel) are brought out of the water onto dry land so that they may receive the Holy Spirit.

Now we deal with the number one hundred fifty-three. It has been pointed out by Bullinger that when all of the integers from one to seventeen are added together, the sum is one hundred fifty-three. It would look like this:

$$1+2+3+4+5+6+7+8+9+10+11+12+13+14+15+16+17=153$$

This is our first association with the number seventeen. The second we find by multiplying. From the chapter on the number nine, we learned that the number nine represents fruitbearing, and prophetically seems to point to the birth pangs of the coming of the Messiah, the time of Jacob's trouble. When you multiply nine by seventeen you reach one hundred fifty-three. The idea seems to be that the remnant of Israel, by way of the time of "great sorrows" is changed by salvation and the mighty wind of the Holy Spirit, hence the association with both nine and seventeen. To add to these miraculous numerical patterns, we find that "Zion" is mentioned exactly one hundred fifty-two times and "Zion's" is mentioned one time, a total of one hundred fifty-three occurrences of this very important word. Notice what the Scriptures say about the salvation of Israel and Zion.

> For God will save Zion, and will build the cities of Judah: that they may dwell there, and have it in possession.
>
> —Psalm 69:35

The Rapture and the number seventeen

The future Rapture of the Gentile church is one of the most eagerly awaited events among many believers, especially those who live in various parts of the world where Christians suffer severe persecution. For those believers who do not currently live under the constant threat of persecution, they see the Rapture as the time when they can shed off their current body of sin and temptation. To either group, the Rapture represents a much-needed and sought after change from mortal to immortal. It truly is the "blessed hope" of all believers. The day that Christ appears in the clouds to remove from the earth all believers, both dead and alive, is referred to in the book of Titus, the seventeenth book of the New Testament.

> Looking for that blessed hope, and the glorious appearing of the great God and our Saviour Jesus Christ; Who gave himself for us, that he might redeem us from all iniquity, and purify unto himself a peculiar people, zealous of good works.
>
> —Titus 2:13–14

The resurrection of the saints at Christ's coming and the instantaneous changing of those believers who are alive at His coming were both typified by Christ during His life here on earth. As we have already seen in this chapter, the transfiguration of Christ in Matthew 17 was a type of the change that will take place to those who are alive and remain. Christ did not have to die in order for this to take place, but He was changed nonetheless. Christ's third-day resurrection was a type of the resurrection of those believers who are asleep in the grave at His glorious appearing. In support of this idea, we see from the gospel of Matthew that there were others who were brought out of their graves at His resurrection.

> And the graves were opened; and many bodies of the saints which slept arose, And came out of the graves after his resurrection, and went into the holy city, and appeared unto many.
>
> —Matthew 27:52–53

Although it is never specifically mentioned in the Scriptures, the number seventeen is obviously present at the resurrection of Christ. According to the law, the Passover feast began on the evening of the fourteenth day of the first month (Leviticus 23:5). On the evening of the fourteenth, Christ sat down with His disciples and explained to them the mystery of the Passover and what it truly represented. The next day, on the fifteenth of the month, He was led up Golgatha's hill, crucified, and buried. On the third day from this point, the third day of the Passover, the **seventeenth** day of the month, Jesus rose from the dead, becoming the firstfruits of those that sleep (1 Corinthians 15:20). It is interesting to note that the flood dates given previously were also on the **seventeenth** day of the month.

As we saw from the chapter on the number five, 1 Corinthians 15 gives us some very crucial teachings concerning the change that will take place to those who are dead and alive at Christ's coming. There are those who do not believe in the Rapture. Some say that it was an invented doctrine and question its alleged clandestine roots. However, you cannot detract from what the Bible literally says.

> Behold, I shew you a mystery; We shall not all sleep, but we shall all be changed.
>
> —1 Corinthians 15:51

The literal interpretation of this verse tells us that there will be those who are alive, but will be changed anyway. This is not the resurrection of the dead in their case. It is precisely what happened to Enoch, and to Elijah. Seeing that this is such an important verse, teaching us the doctrine of the change that will take place at the end of the Gentile age, then it should also be associated with the number seventeen. Notice that this verse is the number fiftyone. This is 17 x 3!

You may have already taken the next step in our journey by now. But just in case you haven't, please take a look at the final verse in our study of the number seventeen. It's been right in front of our eyes all this time.

> Then we which are alive and remain shall be caught up together with them in the clouds, to meet the Lord in the air: and so shall we ever be with the Lord.
>
> —1 Thessalonians 4:17

The Number Twenty-Three

Similar to the number twenty-two, the number twenty-three is a number that is not often mentioned in the Scriptures, and yet has a significant scriptural meaning. In this case, we will see that the number twenty-three is the number for death, in particularly, sacrificial death.

In Genesis 23, we have the story of the death of Sarah, Abraham's wife.

First Corinthians 10:8 tells us that there were twenty-three thousand Israelites that died in one day because of fornication. In Romans 1:29–31, there is a list of twenty-three abominations that are committed by evil men. They are as follows.

1. unrighteousness	2. fornication
3. wickedness	4. covetousness
5. maliciousness	6. full of envy
7. murder	8. debate
9. deceit	10. malignity
11. whisperers	12. backbiters
13. haters of God	14. despiteful
15. proud	16. boasters
17. inventors of evil things	18. disobedient to parents
19. without understanding	20. covenantbreakers
21. without natural affection	22. implacable
23. unmerciful	

The very next verse in this chapter associates these deeds with death.

> Who knowing the judgment of God, that **they which commit** such things are **worthy of death**, not only do the same, but have pleasure in them that do them.
>
> —Romans 1:32

The word "killeth" is mentioned exactly twenty-three times in the Bible. The word "abominable" is mentioned twenty-three times in the Bible. Revelation 21:8 tells us that the abominable will have their place in the lake of fire, the second **death**. The phrase "sabbath day" is mentioned twenty-three times in the Old Testament. In Exodus 31:15 the law declares that anyone who works on the sabbath day will be put to **death**. The word "leaven" is also mentioned exactly twenty-three times in the Scriptures. Here again, the law of the Passover given in Exodus 12:15 reveals that anyone guilty of having leaven in their Passover bread would be cut off, put to death, in Israel.

The word "desolation" is mentioned forty-six (23 x 2) times in the Bible. In its many uses in the verse of the King James Bible, you can clearly see its connection with the theme of death, including the "abomination of desolation" mentioned in Luke 21:20. More will be mentioned about this later on in this chapter.

The Bible tells us in Romans 5:12 that through one man, Adam, sin entered into the world, and through sin, death entered into the world. This refers us to the story found in Genesis 3. In this chapter we find that the devil appears in the form of a serpent.

> Now the serpent was more subtle than any beast of the field which the LORD God had made. And he said unto the woman, **Yea, hath God said, Ye shall not eat of every tree of the garden?** And the woman said unto the serpent, We may eat of the fruit of the trees of the garden: But of the fruit of the tree which is in the midst of the garden, God hath said, Ye shall not eat of it, neither shall ye touch it, lest ye die. And the serpent said unto the woman, **Ye shall not**

surely die: For God doth know that in the day ye eat thereof, then your eyes shall be opened, and ye shall be as gods, knowing good and evil.

—Genesis 3:1–5

God made a promise to Adam that death would enter into the world if he broke the law that God gave him. The devil tells Eve his subtle, deceitful version of God's Word and convinces her to violate God's immutable law. The serpent's words were truly the words of death. If you will count the highlighted words in the above passage, which represent all the words that Satan spoke to Eve on that day, you will note that he spoke exactly **forty-six (23 x 2)** words to her!

The number twenty-three and sacrifice

As we have seen, the number twenty-three represents death, it has the very special connotation of sacrificial death. Obviously, this theme would point us to the sacrificial death of Jesus as He was crucified on Golgotha's hill. The word "crucified" is used exactly twenty-three times in the four gospel accounts. The twenty-third time either the word "crucify" or "crucified" is used in the Bible is in Luke 23:23. Christ died on the cross to pay the penalty for sin. His last words on the cross are recorded for us in John 19:30.

When Jesus therefore had received the vinegar, he said, **It is finished**: and he bowed his head, and **gave up the ghost**.

—John 19:30

Please take careful note that when Christ said this, He died. This author is firm in his belief that God's Word is perfect and without any error, and that every word in the pages of the Authorized Version have a very perfect place and order to them. It may surprise the reader to know that the exact words that Jesus spoke from the cross, "It is finished," only appear one other time in the whole of the Bible. Here is where they are recorded for us.

> Then when lust hath conceived, it bringeth forth sin: and sin, when
> it is finished, bringeth forth death.
>
> —James 1:15

The Bible is truly an amazing book! The connection between these
two verses is both obvious and stunning. Christ, who knew no sin,
became sin while on the cross (2 Corinthians 5:21). By his death,
which sin brought to pass, He has put an end to sin. Oh, what a
Savior!

In the twenty-third book of the Bible, the book of Isaiah, the sacrificial death of Jesus is prophesied in the most famous of messianic
prophecies, Isaiah 53. Although somewhat difficult to count, it appears that there are forty-six (23 x 2) different things that character-
ize the Messiah in this chapter. Notice what it says in numerical order.

> Who hath believed our report? and to whom is the arm of the LORD
> revealed? For . . .

1. he shall grow up before him as a tender plant,
2. and as a root out of a dry ground:
3. he hath no form nor
4. comeliness;
5. and when we shall see him, there is no beauty that we should
   desire him.
6. He is despised and
7. rejected of men;
8. a man of sorrows,
9. and acquainted with grief:
10. he was despised,
11. Surely he hath borne our griefs,
12. and carried our sorrows:
13. yet we did esteem him stricken,
14. smitten of God,
15. and afflicted.
16. But he was wounded for our transgressions,

17. he was bruised for our iniquities:
18. the chastisement of our peace was upon him;
19. and with his stripes we are healed. All we like sheep have gone astray; we have turned every one to his own way; and the
20. LORD hath laid on him the iniquity of us all.
21. He was oppressed,
22. and he was afflicted,
23. yet he opened not his mouth:
24. he is brought as a lamb to the slaughter,
25. and as a sheep before her shearers is dumb, so he openeth not his mouth.
26. He was taken from prison
27. and from judgment: and who shall declare his generation?
28. for he was cut off out of the land of the living:
29. for the transgression of my people was he stricken.
30. And he made his grave with the wicked,
31. and with the rich in his death; because
32. he had done no violence,
33. neither was any deceit in his mouth.
34. Yet it pleased the LORD to bruise him;
35. he hath put him to grief: when thou shalt make
36. his soul an offering for sin,
37. he shall prolong his days, and the pleasure of the LORD
38. shall prosper in his hand. He shall see of the
39. travail of his soul, and shall be satisfied: by his knowledge shall my righteous
40. servant justify many;
41. for he shall bear their iniquities. Therefore will I divide him a portion with the great, and
42. he shall divide the spoil with the strong; because
43. he hath poured out his soul unto death: and
44. he was numbered with the transgressors; and he
45. bare the sin of many, and
46. made intercession for the transgressors."

—Isaiah 53:1–12

The word "altar" is mentioned exactly twenty-three times in the New Testament. The altar is where the sacrifice was performed in the tabernacle. It was in the book of Exodus that the law of the sacrifice was given to Moses. The word "sacrifice" is mentioned twenty-three times in the book of Exodus. In the book of Leviticus, the book in which the Levites are instructed on carrying out their various duties, all the forms of the word "sacrifice" are mentioned exactly forty-six times. In Numbers 26:62, these Levites were numbered. There were exactly twenty-three thousand of them in this census.

There seems to be an amazing similarity between the wilderness tabernacle and the human blood cell. Specific information about this is contained in Dr. Chuck Thurstons's book, *Aleph-Bet Soup*, published by Hearthstone Publishing. It is noteworthy to see that the human blood contains exactly twenty-three pairs of chromosomes! This knowledge adds an awesome reality to Paul's words in the book of Romans. "I beseech you therefore, brethren, by the mercies of God, that ye present your **bodies a living sacrifice**, holy, acceptable unto God, which is your reasonable service" (Romans 12:1).

As was mentioned earlier in this chapter, the words "abominable" and "desolation" are each mentioned twenty-three times in the Scriptures. The Bible warns of an event that is called the "abomination of desolation" (Daniel 11:31, 12:11; Matthew 24:15; Mark 13:14). Many scholars believe that this is in reference to some sort of last-days desecration of the temple or tabernacle in Jerusalem by the Antichrist. There is also much speculation concerning the Ark of the Covenant, the replica of the throne of God in heaven on which the high priest would sprinkle lamb's blood in order to atone for the sins of Israel. Many theories abound as to its current location; however, it is possible that it may be discovered in the end times. Seeing the connection between the theme of sacrifice and the abomination of desolation, it is possible that the Antichrist might perform some sort of satanic sacrifice on this newly discovered Ark, truly an abomination before a Holy God. It also may well be the reason that it takes twenty-three hundred days for the sanctuary to be cleansed (Daniel 8:14), presumably after this takes place.

ACKNOWLEDGEMENTS

As I stated at the beginning of the book, God has taken me a long way from the worldly Christianity that I lived several years ago. Since then, He has led me in the path of some good men that have helped me in my walk with Christ. The order of their listing here does not indicate importance, for from each of them I have gained God's exact amount of wisdom and guidance.

In the spring of 2000 God led my wife and I across the path of Noah Hutchings and the wonderful people at Southwest Radio Church in Oklahoma City. It was at that time that I first read "Hutch's" book *God, The Master Mathematician*. Some of the material in his book has crept into mine. I encourage those who are interested in more Scripture numerics to purchase a copy of Dr. Hutchings' book for further understanding. "Out of the mouth of two or three witnesses . . . shall every word be established."

In October of 1999 I met evangelist and pastor Mike Hutsell. I gave him a copy of my first book, which was then called *The King James Code*. Mike was apparently so thrilled after reading it that he began to share it with every pastor he came in contact with. Soon, my phone began to ring as several of these pastors called either to share their appreciation for our ministry or to invite us to speak at their church. It was through Brother Mike that Lisa and I have been privileged to meet many pastors and congregations over the past three years. I heard Brother Mike in a tape recorded sermon say that he prayed for me and my ministry daily. Mike, you don't know how much that means to me. Thank you.

It was through Mike Hutsell that I met Pastor Reggie Kelly. Before 1997, I would have almost hated men like Brother Kelly. I have heard him over the years preach hard on the King James Bible, holy living, biblical separation, and so on, topics that are seldom heard in today's Laodicean church environment. He has taught me how to take a stand and yet do it in love. I thank God for him and his wonderful church.

And a sincere "thank you" goes to my "uncle" in the ministry, Brother Lonnie Burks and his wife Connie. They both have been a great source of leadership and help to Lisa and me. Thank you for "walking in Zion" when you preach.

ATALOGUE ·

"Every word of God is pure:"
— Proverbs 30:5

King James Bibles

We have searched for King James Bibles that avoid the misleading marginal notes and careless spelling seen in some.

Cambridge Large Print	**$67.95**
French Morocco Leather, gilt edge, ribbon, black or burgundy	
Hardback	**$32.95**
Holy Bible	**$19.95**
Black imitation leather, gilt edge	
120 page concordance-index, maps, smyth-sewn.	
New Testament	**$1.95**
Black vinyl with gold foil stamped title	
Paperback	**$1.65**
Case of 40 Paperbacks (includes shipping)	**$80.00**
Holy Bible	**$6.50**
Black vinyl with gold foil stamped title	
Paperback	**$5.95**
Case of 20 Paperbacks (includes shipping)	**$135.00**
Photographic Reproduction of KJV 1611	
New Testament *Vinyl cover*	**$25.00**
CD-ROM Photographic Reproduction of	
entire 1611 King James Bible	**$9.95**

THE LANGUAGE OF THE KING JAMES BIBLE
by Gail Riplinger

Ｔhis book helps you discover the KJV's built-in dictionary. It also proves that, unlike new versions, the vocabulary of the KJV is precise, internationally recognizable, and contains powerful sound symbolism to communicate meaning. It reveals the discovery of the world's oldest New Testament fragment which proves the KJV is correct and the new versions are wrong. Also exposed are the corrupt Dead Sea scrolls and lexicons used to create the NIV, ESV, NKJV, HCSB and NASB.

THE BOOK $12.95
Demonstrates the precision and power of the KJV

30% discount off 5 or more ($9.07)
40% discount off 14 or more ($7.77)

THE VIDEO (or DVD) $19.95
Many charts shown and included in Xerox format   2 Hrs

30% discount off 5 or more   ($14.00)

Transparencies $35.95

THE AUDIOS (CD or cassette lectures)
The Language of the KJV $5.95

More Language of the KJV $9.95

Language & Corrupt Lexicons: Roots of the New Versions $5.95

Shows how to answer those who say, 'But the Greek says.' Answers the toughest critics.

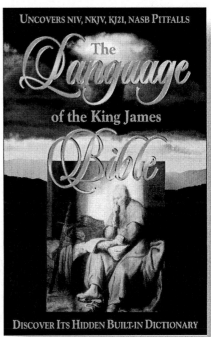

UNCOVERS NIV, NKJV, KJ21, NASB PITFALLS

The Language of the King James Bible

DISCOVER ITS HIDDEN BUILT-IN DICTIONARY

AUDIO CD SET $9.95
Set includes both:
- The Language of the KJV
- Language & Corrupt Lexicons

Tracts

NIV, NASV Verse Comparison   20¢

Compares 78 critical NIV or NASV verses, which clearly shows their substitution of liberal and New Age teachings for the historical Christian doctrines seen in the KJV.

NKJV Death Certificate   33¢

Compares over 200 verses with the KJV. Shows 21 verses in which the NKJV demotes Jesus Christ, several dozen where it follows the Jehovah Witness Version and dozens and dozens where the NKJV supports New Age philosophy. A comparison of 138 words proves the KJV is easier to read than the NKJV. Folds out to 11 x 17 poster.

New Living Translation: A Critique   50¢

Compares over 100 verses with the KJV. This translation says the "number of the beast" should be called the "number of humanity"! Millions of unwary Christians are watching Pat Robertson promote this new corrupt 'bible' which he calls 'The Book'.

Book

NEW AGE BIBLE VERSIONS

by G.A. Riplinger   **$16.95**

- Over 2,500 verses compared
- 1,480 referenced footnotes
- 700 pages, 42 chapters

30% discount off 5 or more ($11.87 ea.)

40% discount off case of 14 ($10.17 ea.;

$160.00 includes shipping)

New!	Word and Name Index to New Age Bible Versions	**$3.00**
New!	Scripture Location Index for New Age Bible Versions	**$2.00**

New Book!
The Only Authorized Picture of Christ:
is the Holy Bible   by Russ & Riplinger
Critiques the movie, 'The Passion.'   **$6.95**

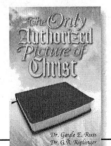

Folios   by Riplinger

New!	Subliminal Embeds Exposed	**$2.50**
New!	Collation of Corruptions in Holman's Christian Standard Bible	**$2.50**
New!	Old Scofield Bible vs New Scofield	**$1.50**

In Awe of Thy Word

Understanding the King James Bible
Its Mystery & History
Letter by Letter
by Gail Riplinger $29.95
1200 Page Hardcover, color-coded

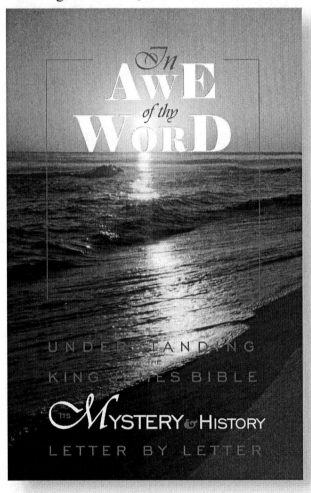

Discounts:
- Buy 3 at the regular price, get one free.
- Buy 5 at the regular price, get 3 free.

*T*HIS BOOK is the first and only *documented* history of *the words* of the Holy Bible.

- It is based on word-for-word and letter-by-letter analysis of a vault of ancient, rare and valuable Bibles. Ten thousand hours of collation rescued echoes from these documents almost dissolved by time.

- See for yourself the unbroken preservation of the pure holy scriptures, from the first century to today's beloved King James Bible. Watch the English language and its Holy Bible unfold before your very eyes.

- Examine the letters and sounds, shown in red, which bind the words of each successive Bible from the Gothic, Anglo-Saxon, pre-Wycliffe, Tyndale, Coverdale, Great, Geneva, and Bishops' to the King James Bible.

- Uncover time-buried eyewitness reports, views and Bible study secrets of history's great translators and martyrs.

- See word-for-word collations, aided by the KJV translators' newly discovered notes, revealing exactly *how* the KJV translators polished the sword of the Spirit.

- Watch in horror as the destroyer, through the NIV, TNIV, HCSB, NKJV, NASB and ESV, teams up with Jehovah Witness and Catholic versions to silence the utterances of the Holy Ghost. History's Bibles and their champions defeat their challengers, as they meet on this book's pages.

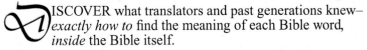

*D*ISCOVER what translators and past generations knew— *exactly how to* find the meaning of each Bible word, *inside* the Bible itself.

- Understand also what translators, such as Erasmus and Coverdale, meant when they spoke of the vernacular Bible's "holy letters" and "syllables."

- See how these God-set alphabet building blocks build a word's meaning and automatically define words for faithful readers of the King James Bible—which alone brings forward the fountainhead of letter meanings discovered by computational linguists from the world's leading universities.

- Learn about the latest research tools from the University of Toronto (EMEDD) and Edinburgh University, which prove the purity of the KJV and the depravity of the new versions.

- Find out how only the King James Bible teaches and comforts through its "miraculous" mathematically ordered sounds.

- Meet the KJV's build-in English teacher, ministering to children and over a billion people around the globe.

- Journey around the world and see that only the KJV matches the pure scriptures preserved "to all generations" including the Greek, Hebrew, Old Italia, Italian, Danish, German, French, Spanish and others.

CD-ROMs

*I*N AWE of THY *W*ORD

The book is also *searchable* on

 3 CD-ROMS

$39.95

These include:

- **The King James Bible** searchable by words, letter groups and phrases.

- **In Awe of Thy Word** by G.A. Riplinger (searchable!). Plus exact photographic facsimiles of three complete documents used in the book's research:

- **The Nuremberg Polyglot** (A.D. 1599) containing the Gospels of the New Testament in 12 languages, as they appeared *before* the King James Bible (approx. 1100 pages). The Greek, Hebrew, Syriac, Latin, French, Spanish, Italian, German, English, Bohemian, Polish and Danish match the KJV precisely and prove the TNIV, NIV, NKJV, NASB, HCSB and ESV in error. This documents verse comparisons in *In Awe of Thy Word*, chapter 28.

- **The Tome of the Paraphrase of Erasmus Upon the New Testament** (1548-1549) Vol. 1 and Vol. 2 Erasmus' commentary on the New Testament (the original English translation), valued at over $30,000 today, has never before been made available to everyone. It is about 1880 pages, accompanied by the English New Testament of the Great Bible of 1540. It provides an addition to chapter 27 of *In Awe of Thy Word*.

- **The Acts and Monuments** by John Foxe This is the rare *entire* 8 volumes of Foxe's *Book of Martyrs*, nearing 6000 pages long. It was originally written in 1563; this is the 1837-49 printing. Reading this is a spiritual experience of a lifetime. It documents quotes in chapters 15 - 28 of *In Awe of Thy Word*. Print a page a day for 16 years of devotionals.

System requirements: PC with Windows 95/98/NT4; 486 processor (Pentium or better recommended), 16 MB RAM (24 MB+ recommended), 10 MB free hard disk space, NT4 should have Service Pack 3 or higher, PC with Windows 2000/Me: Pentium 90 or better, 32 MB RAM (64 MB recommended), 10 MB free hard disk space. Macintosh: Power PC or better processor, OS 9 or better system software, 8 MB RAM, 10 MB free hard disc space. Windows XP and Macintosh OS X computers meet all systems requirements.

Audio Tapes & CDs

In Awe of Thy Word
by Gail Riplinger
$21.95
Four Audio Tapes or 5 CDs / 4 Hours
Discussing the material in the new classic book.

Transparencies

In Awe of Thy Word audio lectures (above) can be presented by
teachers and pastors using these overhead transparencies.
Set 1: $35.95   **Set 2: $35.95**

Tract

In Awe of Thy Word: A Summary   40¢

*Share with others over 100 comparisons from the
book proving why only the King James Bible is the
pure word of God for English speakers. Help them
learn how to understand the words in the Bible.*

Folds into an envelope, then opens into a 16" x 26" poster,
which demonstrates errors in the NIV, TNIV, NKJV, NASB,
ESV, New Living Translation, and Holman Christian
Standard Bible, which often match the Jehovah Witness and
Catholic versions. Demonstrates 12 reasons why 'Only the
King James Bible' is pure.

Answering The Skeptics

Blind Guides $5.95

30% discount off 5 or more ($4.20 ea.)

Riplinger's detailed and scholarly responses—unanswerable by skeptics like James White, Hunt, Cloud, Hanagraaff, House, Morey and Passantino.

Answers Minton I: NIV, NASB, NKJV errors $2.50

*Riplinger answers KJV critic Ron Minton, providing support for the unwisely criticized KJV readings in Titus 2:13, II Peter 1:1 and Psalm 12:6,7. Includes Harvard professor's concurrence regarding B. F. Westcott's denial of the creed. Adds data about the earliest papyri and the NKJV's faulty **Hodges-Farstad** so-called **Majority Text**.*

Answers Minton II: NKJV Errors $2.50

Proves KJV superior to NKJV at every point.

Riplinger's defence of the use of the KJV's words 'God' and 'blood'—omitted numerous times by the NKJV. Proves conclusively that the NKJV ignores the Hebrew text, uses weaker renderings, paraphrase and new age buzz words.

King James: Unjustly Accused

by Stephen Coston $15.00

Conclusively proves false the myriad of lies propagated about King James.

Double Jeopardy

by Laurence M. Vance $9.95

*A complete collation of the various editions of the NASB, documenting the correction, in 1995, of **some** of the errors exposed in **New Age Bible Versions** and the introduction of over 20,000 **new** faulty translations, including gender inclusive vocabulary.*

Bible Problems

by Gerardus Bouw Ph.D. $15.00

Answers every question. A classic! Proves KJV error free!

KING JAMES

The

Introduction by HIS GRACE THE 10TH DUKE OF ATHOLL

Book

New Release!
WHICH BIBLE IS GOD'S WORD? UPDATE

by G.A. Riplinger   **$12.95**

Updated transcript of the series of interviews with G.A. Riplinger by Noah Hutchings of the nationally syndicated program Southwest Radio Church. Answers these and many other common questions concerning bible versions.

- *How do new versions change the gospel?*
- *How do the NIV and NASB support New Age philosophy?*
- *What about the NKJV, KJ[21], and others which say they merely update the KJV?*
- *Where was the bible before the KJV 1611?*
- *What errors are the KJV critics making?*

30% discount off 5 or more ($9.07 ea.)
40% discount off case of 14 ($7.77 ea.;
$124.00 includes shipping)

The Audios 2 CDs Audio transcript of *Which Bible*: **$9.95**

The best audio CDs available on the KJV issue. Thoroughly exposes the corrupt NKJV, as well as the NIV and NASB.

The Book About the Spanish Bible Issue:

The Elephant in the Living Room
editor Mickey Carter   **$8.00**

Chapter by Gail Riplinger includes:
1) Historical precedent for translating foreign Bibles directly from KJV, not using corrupt lexicons to interpret currently printed editions of Textus Receptus
2) Collation from Nuremburg Polyglot (1599).
6 other contributors discuss problems in modern **Spanish** *editions.*

Video, DVD, CD, and Audio Tapes

RESEARCH UPDATE
by G. A. Riplinger

Double Videos (or DVD)   **$24.95**
3 CDs $9.95   Double Audio Cassettes $9.95

INFORMATION OVER-LOAD! Over three hours of lectures are presented on these two videos. They begin with a half hour overview presenting problems in the NKJV, followed by nearly an hour update and overview of errors in the NIV, NASB and other new versions. Listeners will learn that 1) Rupert Murdoch, owner of the Bart Simpson television program, now owns the NIV's printing rights, 2) Roman Catholic Cardinal Carlo Maria Martini, the man Time magazine said is most likely to be the next pope, now edits the Greek text underlying the NIV and NASV, 3) Martin Woudstra, a supporter of the homosexual movement, was the NIV's Old Testament chairman!

TAPE TWO IS A 2 HOUR PUBLIC QUESTION AND ANSWER SESSION. The following are just a few of the many questions answered: What is the origin of the Catholic edition? Why do "good men" unknowingly use corrupt versions? Why is "Easter" the correct rendering in Acts 12:4? How is the KJV's own self-contained dictionary superior to definitions given in Greek and Hebrew lexicons written by unsaved liberals like Thayer and Briggs? Why is "Lucifer" etymologically the correct rendering in Isaiah 14:12? What are the Satanic parallels to NKJV's logo? Why is the KJ[21] more difficult to read than the real KJV? Why are the so-called "literal" translations in Berry's, Green's, and Kohlenburger's Interlinears in error? What are the parallels between the Jehovah Witness version and the NKJV?

Riplinger also discusses many other subjects such as: 1) The KJV's use of cognitive scaffolding which makes it a perfect tool for teaching "little folks" to read, 2) the dangerous Dead Sea Scrolls 3) the recent discovery by the world's pre-eminent mathematicians of names imbedded in the KJV's Hebrew text. (Nothing could be found when they tried their statistical analysis with the texts underlying the NKJV, NIV and NASB) and 4) Lucis Trust (Lucifer Publishing Co.) documents discussing their planned infiltration of the church.

These lectures were televised on Scripps Howard cable network and WPMC-TV. They were taped at Temple Baptist Church.

Video and DVD

Transparent Translations & Translators

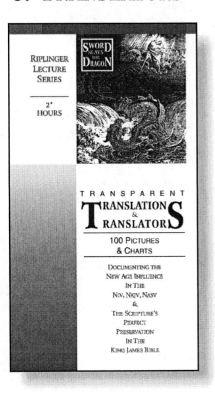

Video or DVD	**$25.00**
Transparencies	**$35.95**
Handout Master	**$14.95**
Summary of Version Issue (12 Xerox pages)	**$1.50**

Thousands of participants in nearly a dozen of the major U.S. cities viewed this presentation filmed at a TV station or heard it aired on radio. Dr. Riplinger lectured 2½ hours, presenting on a huge screen, nearly 100 actual pictures and charts documenting the new age and occult influence in the counterfeit new versions. The audience often gasped in shock, seeing such things as the NKJV's 666 logo—now on the forehead of the latest smart card owners. This "picture show" is one-of-a-kind.

*This is the **best** video to share with friends who need a thorough analysis of the thousands of errors in the NIV, NASB & NKJV.*

NKJV Logo Exposed   Video or DVD $12.95

Participants flew from France, Australia, and Canada and watched this pictorial history of the NKJV logo as Dr. Riplinger traced it from its origin in Baal worship and through its migration to the Druids, the church of Rome, the Masons, and the Satanists.

Video, DVD, Audio CD and Tapes

OVERVIEW by G. A. Riplinger

SingleVideo or DVD $14.95
3 Audio CDs **$9.95** **Double Audio Cassettes** **$9.95**

This single two hour video clearly presents the differences between the corrupt new versions and our beloved King James Bible. It presents the history of the Bible chronologically—its inspiration and perfect preservation by God—as well as attempted corruptions, past, present, and planned.

The material is presented simply and slowly for viewers who would like an overview and introduction to the subject. It is excellent for beginning a discussion with Sunday School classes, youth groups or precious friends who unknowingly use new corrupt versions like the NIV, NKJV, NASV, NRSV, CEV, TEV, REB, KJ²¹, RV, NAB, Good News, New Living, Phillips, New Jerusalem, Message or New Century versions.

These lectures of Dr. Riplinger's were televised over WBFX and aired over WPIP radio from The Berean Baptist Church.

OVERVIEW
2 HOURS

INTERVIEWS

Nationally syndicated Christian programs in which host interviews G. A. Riplinger about the book *New Age Bible Versions*. Discussions thoroughly cover the contents and topics in the book.

VIDEO or DVD

Niteline $19.95

This video has gone all around the world converting many precious souls to the KJV. 90 min.

Action Sixties $24.95

Used successfully in scores of churches as a teaching series to educate members regarding the errors in corrupt new versions. One pastor commented that his most hardened new version fan "melted like a popsicle in a microwave" after viewing these 4 programs. (4 hours)

Audios

New Age Bible Versions Album $35.95

30 interviews with the author by talk show hosts across the nation. Lots of ideas for answering tough questions. 16 CDs

KNIS Radio Interview
with Riplinger/Feltner   **CD $5.95**

(Single Audio Cassette) **$5.95**

Ankerberg's Fiasco $5.95
with Riplinger/Texe Marrs
NASB editor loses his voice (CD)

DETAILED UPDATE

2 Audio CDs $9.95   **Audio Cassette $5.95**

Hundreds of pastors gathered to hear Dr. Riplinger's very detailed and convincing answers to the excuses given by new version users; includes important textual alerts for pastors and students. NKJV is thoroughly discussed. 2 hours

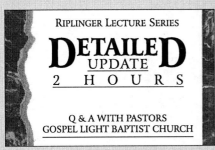

RIPLINGER LECTURE SERIES

DETAILED
UPDATE
2 H O U R S

Q & A WITH PASTORS
GOSPEL LIGHT BAPTIST CHURCH

From NASB to KJV, Dr. S. Franklin Logsdon   **(CD $5.95)**   (Audio Cassette) **$5.95**

NKJV Errors $5.95
with Riplinger/Texe Marrs
The NKJV is not easier to understand (CD)

Testimony: Mrs. Waite Interviews Dr. Riplinger *DVD or 3 Audio CDs*   **$10.00**

Books: The Classics

The Last Twelve Verses of Mark   **$15.00**
Defended by John Burgon (Summary $5.00; CD-ROM $9.95)

The Revision Revised by John Burgon   **$25.00**
*The definitive book on manuscript evidence and translation
techniques.* (Summary $5.00; CD-ROM $9.95)

The Causes of Corruption of the Traditional Text by John Burgon   **$15.00**
(Summary $5.00; CD-ROM $9.95)

The Traditional Text of the Holy Gospels by John Burgon   **$16.00**
(Summary $5.00; CD-ROM $9.95)

Which Bible? edited by D.O. Fuller   **$13.95**
*The classic defense of the KJV which led Dr. S. Franklin Logsdon, who had set forth
the guidelines for the NASB, to renounce his own NASB and all new versions.*

The King James Version Defended by Edward F. Hills   **$18.95**
*The author, a graduate of Yale University and Westminister Theological Seminary,
with a Th.M. from Columbia Seminary and Th.D. from Harvard, presents overwhelming evidence for the historical accuracy of the KJV.*

Recent Scholarship

The Answer Book by Samuel Gipp Th.D.   **$6.95**
*Answers the 62 questions most frequently asked by the cynics. Includes answers to
false arguments about King James, Erasmus, the word "Easter" etc.*

New! **A Testimony Founded Forever: The King James
Bible Defended In Faith and History** by Dr. James Sightler
*Riplinger said this is "the most exhaustively researched book on the KJV
issue in the last 100 years!" Focuses on the sinister beliefs of B. F. Westcott, the chief editor of the corrupt Greek text-type underlying the NIV
and NASB. Other books by Sightler below.*   **$17.95**

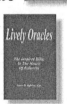

Westcott's New Bibles
$7.00

Silver Words and Pure
Questions & Answers
$5.00

Lively Oracles
Defends KJV Inspiration
$4.00

History of the Debate Over 1 John 5:7-8 $29.95
Powerful release by Michael Maynard M.L.S.

Forever Settled by Jack Moorman $21.00
An excellent history of the Bible and its documents. It answers well the question 'Where was the Bible before the KJV 1611?'

A Closer Look: Early Manuscripts and the A.V.
by Jack Moorman $15.95
Great tool! Examines the papyri, uncials, cursives, as well as the Latin, Syriac, Coptic, Gothic, Armenian, and Ethiopic versions, and the church 'Fathers', in light of their agreement with the KJV.

Missing in Modern Bibles:
An Analysis of the NIV by Jack Moorman $12.95
Contains a collation of important changed passages and a discussion of the poor theories and manuscripts underlying them.

When the KJV Departs From The Majority
by Jack Moorman $15.95
The NKJV footnotes erroneously point to the 'Majority' text, when they are in fact only referring to the faulty Greek Text According to the Majority (1982) by Hodge and Farstad. It falls far short of a full collation of manuscripts since it is based primarily on Von Soden's collation of only 414 of the over 5000 manuscripts.

Early Church Fathers and the A.V. by Jack Moorman $8.95
Documentation proving that the early church 'fathers' were quoting a KJV text type.

Conies, Brass, and Easter by Jack Moorman $4.00
Proves correct many often criticized KJV words.

The Identity of the New Testament Text by Wilbur Pickering $17.00
The best single book (facsimile) documenting that the most recent scholarship and collation of the papyri prove that the KJV readings are earlier than those in modern versions. The author has a Th.M. in Greek Exegesis from Dallas Theological Seminary and M.A. and Ph.D. in Linguistics from the University of Toronto. D.A. Carson admits it is, "The most formidable defense of the priority of the Byzantine text yet published in our day."

Preface to the KJV 1611 by the translators $1.95

KJV1611: Myth of Revision by Reagan *A must!* $2.00

My Plea For The Old Sword (KJV) by Ian Paisley $9.95
Member of the British & European Parliaments

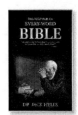

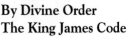

By Divine Order	**$12.95**
The King James Code	**$14.95**

By Michael Hoggard
These two books by Hoggard explore the miraculous ordering and number patterns in the KJV.

The Need For An Every-Word Bible
by Dr. Jack Hyles
Wonderful! **$15.00**

Easy To Read

If the Foundations Be Destroyed by Chick Salliby   **$5.95**
An easy to read and beautifully written comparison of the NIV and KJV text, proving the bankruptcy of the NIV.

Things That are Different by Dr. Mickey Carter   **$6.95**
Helped NKJV editor switch.

Let's Weigh The Evidence by Barry Burton   **$4.95**

Did the Roman Catholic Church Give Us the Bible?   **$8.95**
by David Daniels
Chick publications make learning fun & easy. A classic!

Answers To Your Bible Version Questions by David W. Daniels   **$10.95**

Words in the Word

By Definition by James Knox   **$8.95**
Interesting KJV word studies.

KJV's Own Definition of Over 800 Words
by Barry Goddard   **$12.95**
(80 pages) This British gentleman's findings will spark your enthusiasm for finding the Bible's own definitions for its words. Read Riplinger's latest 1200 page book, In Awe of Thy Word, to find out exactly how the KJV provides its own meanings for words.

KJV Companion by David Daniels **50¢**
500 words defined in carry-along booklet.

American Dictionary
of the English Language edited 1828 by Noah Webster **$69.95**
A must for every home. Defines words as they were used during the writing
of the KJV 1611. Contains scripture references, etymologies from 28 languages
and pronunciations. Modern dictionaries reflect cultural corruptions; consider and
compare definitions for words such as sin, marriage, truth, spirit, and Jesus Christ.

Also available on CD-Rom: Requires MS 3:1 or higher **$29.95**

Electronics

New Testament on CD **$29.95**

Franklin Bookman **$59.95**
Electronic Computer Bible and Concordance (pocket edition)
This is the greatest Bible study tool I have ever found! It was very helpful in researching
*The Language of the King James Bible. If you key in two words, like **always** and*
***always**, it will take you to all of the places they occur anywhere near each other.*

Music

God Hath Done All Things Well **$14.95**
Bryn Riplinger **CD**

This first musical production from the Riplingers and
AV Publications seeks a return to "Speaking to your-
selves in psalms, and hymns, and spiritual songs, sing-
ing and making melody in your heart to the Lord." With
a voice like an angel, Bryn sings and writes songs of
calming comfort, conviction and praise to the Lord.

Music: Scriptures sung on cassette or CD

Zana Reichen		Patti Vaillant	
Pure Words	**$8.00**	**Scripture Songs III**	**$9.95**
This Book of the Law	**$8.00**	**Scripture Songs IV**	**$9.95**
Teach Character	**$8.00**	**Scripture Songs V**	**$9.95**
Psalms	**$8.00**	**(on CD)**	**$12.98**
Herein Is Love	**$8.00**		
(on CD)	**$15.00**	Chris Stansell	
		Scripture Songs	**$9.95**
		(on CD)	**$15.95**

TO ORDER

BY PHONE: **1-800-435-4535** (credit card only)

BY FAX: 1-276-251-1734

(other callers 1-276-251-1734)

BY MAIL: Send check or Money Order or VISA,
MasterCard, American Express, or Discover Card Number
and Expiration Date to: **A.V. Publications**
P.O. Box 280
Ararat, VA 24053 USA

SHIPPING: $1.01-$4.00 add $2.00 $30.01-$40.00 add $7.00
$4.01-$20.00 add $5.00 $40.01-$80.00 add $8.00
$20.01-$30.00 add $6.00 $80.01 and over add 10%

VA RESIDENTS: Add 5% sales tax

FOREIGN ORDERS: Send check payable through a U.S. Bank in U.S. funds
or send a Postal Money Order. Double shipping on orders under $50.00. Add
30% on orders over $50.00.

BOOKSTORES: Call for discounts.

VISIT OUR WEBSITE
www.avpublications.com

- View complete and updated catalogue of KJV Bibles and books, videos, and tracts supporting the KJV.
- Place secure credit card orders
- Download verse comparison tract; see research updates.

"Finally, brethren, pray for us, that the word of the Lord may have free course, and be glorified, even as it is with you:" II Thess. 3:1